THE SHIFT
CONSCIOUSNESS

By Lilli Bendriss and Camillo Løken

GALILEO FORLAG

THE SHIFT IN CONSCIOUSNESS

© 2011 Lilli Bendriss and Camillo Løken
Published by Galileo Forlag
www.galileoforlag.no
ISBN 978-82-998464-3-1

Front page picture: NASA, ESA, R. O'Connell (University of Virginia), F. Paresce (National Institute for Astrophysics, Bologna, Italy), E. Young (Universities Space Research Association/Ames Research Center), the WFC3 Science Oversight Committee and the Hubble Heritage Team (STScI/AURA)

Translation from Norwegian to English by
Trisha Cox
9 School Lane
Longstowe
Cambs CB23 2UU
England

This book is dedicated to you and everyone else searching to find out who they are, so that you can experience yourself as something new in your own way, without anyone telling you what you should do, what you should believe or what you should think.

Contents

Editor's Notes

Ever since the turn of the new millennium, people have been seeking even more for the answers to the questions of our unknown future, as well as our mysterious beginnings. Scriptures, prophecies, even science has determined that humankind is headed into a revolution, as it were, of body, mind and spirit. Never before have so many been so willing to awaken themselves to their origins, as well as take control of their lives as co-creators of their own reality. These surely are exciting and historical times to be alive.

When I was contacted by Mr. Løken to assist with the editorial process of bringing *The Shift in Consciousness* into an English translation, I was thrilled. As I read, I discovered hidden truths rising out of his research. Even though this is information I've known from other sources, somehow bringing it all together in one book make the threads more obvious as to how we are all connected, and that knowledge is an interwoven tapestry, a force field accessible to all. Not only is the collection of information he has obtained intriguing and excellently organized, the range of topics he is able to cover is exceptionally wide and thought-provoking.

What is important to note is that Ms. Bendriss was not apprised of the results of his research. As he asked her questions specific to the topics he was studying, hers was a blind response, as she was unaware of his findings at the time of the sessions. This extraordinary resonance brings even more credibility to the hypotheses put forth and should give readers even more food for thought.

As you read, allow *The Shift In Consciousness* to tap into your imagination and expand your thinking of who you are, why you are here, where you came from, and especially where you are headed as you dive into your own expansion of consciousness. This is a journey, you see, that you don't want to miss.

Barbara With, award-winning author of *Imagining Einstein: Essays on M-Theory, World Peace & The Science of Compassion* and founder of Conflict REVOLUTION®, a process for world peace, one person at a time, starting with you.

www.barbarawith.com

Foreword

Lilli Bendriss

Ever since the end of the 1980s I have had the ability to channel information from various energies, popularly referred to as "the other side." I receive information from other dimensions and frequencies. I have also appeared on the Norwegian TV series, *Sensing Murder* and *The Power of the Spirits.*

Over the years I have channeled information from several energy-beings such as Wounded Eagle, the Council of Elders and Amu Zhar. These energy-beings have provided me with everything from amazingly beautiful poems to advanced messages about anti-gravity propulsion and the Zero-Point Field.

This advanced information has been supported by research carried out in recent years. I hid the notes relating to all these channeling sessions in a drawer, and it was not until now, 2011, that I realized that all along there has been a plan behind these messages. They are now re-surfacing through this book and serve to support our understanding that there is a higher intelligence out there cooperating with mankind in order to help us over the last hurdle.

Camillo Løken

I grew up in a family of physicians, in an atheist, academic, scientific environment. I believed that life on Earth was the result of a cosmic accident and there was no such thing as life after death. For me, when we died we were gone forever. I modified this view during my teens, but it wasn't until I became an adult that I experienced an awakening and became passionately interested in finding answers to who we are, where we come from, what we are doing here and where we go when we die.

Over the years I have devoured many books that provided answers to these four questions. I also acquired much knowledge from meditation, various courses, telephone conferences, webinars and films, and by talking and discussing these topics with like-minded souls.

This book contains material from channeling sessions conducted by Lilli over the course of many years and from my own study material that represent our combined ideas about reality. We obtained further information from the Council of Elders on July 29 and August 11, 2010 when we asked a number of questions relating to this book. They explained that they are an intelligent energy operating on a different frequency on the other side and exist in a future when seen from the perspective of how we perceive linear time. I asked the questions and Lilli went into a trance to channel their answers. Everything was recorded and has been included in this book. As you read, you will become acquainted with the Council of Elders and the answers they gave us.

We believe that we create our own reality here on Earth. We are thinking beings, living in a thinking universe, and we possess tremendous powers of creation within ourselves. We are here to discover that we are the Source that expresses and manifests itself through the uniqueness possessed by each and every one of us. You are unique. Your thoughts are like mental fingerprints. No one can think or feel exactly like you do. When you understand that you really are the Source that expresses itself through your uniqueness, you understand that you also possess the most fantastic powers of creation. You have the ability to think independently of circumstances and you can thus also create everything that your heart desires.

During the last few years increasing numbers of people have been experiencing a spiritual awakening. Who we really are, where we come from, what we are doing here and where we are going—these are all questions with which we are becoming increasingly preoccupied. This awakening is linked to the shift in consciousness that has already started and is also linked to the 2012 phenomenon. No one knows for sure whether or not December 21, 2012 is the date when the world as we know it will cease to exist and a new age will dawn. We believe that 2012 represents a symbolic alarm clock that will wake us up from forgetting who we really are. We will remember who we are and what we came here to do. The time has arrived for mankind to embark on the next step in developing from Homo Sapiens to Homo Luminous—Enlightened Beings, and this requires a shift in consciousness for the whole of humanity.

Our work on this book has provided us with an understanding of who we are, where we come from, what we are doing here and where we are going that resonates with our common sense. For several years we have been reading and studying spiritual and metaphysical material. This has contributed towards our awakening and provided us with hooks on which to hang our understanding. It has given us more pieces of the jigsaw puzzle and influenced our perception of reality. In this book we have included numerous quotations and references taken from this material. These many references have been included to illustrate the huge range of spiritual and metaphysical literature and research that currently exist that can help us obtain a better understanding of what life is all about.

As such, we hope this book and all its references will be of value to you.

Acknowledgements

The Shift in Consciousness is the result of many years of searching to find answers about who we are, what we are doing here, where we come from and where we are going. Over the years we have encountered many people and energy-beings who have provided us with inspiration and enriched our lives with knowledge. We would like to take advantage of this opportunity to express our thanks to you all.

A special thanks to the following people who have been involved in helping this book to see the light of day. Our deepest thanks to Barbara With, our extraordinary editor, for her knowledge, expertise, wisdom, attitude, insight, devotion and dedication to this project. She has been a true pleasure to work with and we highly appreciate her editorial finesse. After reading her award-winning book, *Imagining Einstein: Essays on M-Theory, World Peace & The Science of Compassion*, we realized that her work has much in common with ours. With the knowledge and insight she possesses regarding the secret of life, we could not have asked for a better editor.

A big thank you to Lars Kilevold for all your creative input. Many thanks to Marianne Solberg Behn and Gillian R. Godtfredsen for reading through the manuscript and for your uplifting feedback. Thanks also to T. Nordvik and Anne Marie Beck for their constructive feedback relating to the contents of this book. Many thanks to Samir Bendriss for the picture of your son, Liam, featured on the front page of *The Shift in Consciousness*. Heartfelt thanks to Jan Henrik Hansen for the great illustrations/drawings that appear in the book.

Lilli: I would like to express huge thanks to the energy-beings Wounded Eagle and the Council of Elders for your confidence in me as a presenter of your wisdom.

Camillo: Finally, I would like to express a special thank you to my wife Synnøve, our children and my parents for the support, help and understanding that you have given me after I chose to devote my time, energy and resources to searching for answers to who we are, what we are doing here, where we come from and where we are going. These answers have contributed towards my version of the truth and can also be found in the contents of this book.

Introduction

The Truth

What is the truth? Who has the authority to say that the only version of the truth is their version? No one can honestly say that they know the whole and absolute truth about life and all its secrets. Everything simply is. It is people who decide whether something is right or wrong, true or false. Your experience of the truth might be perceived as being completely wrong when seen from a different perspective.

In this book we will be presenting information obtained from different sources. We ask you to keep an open mind and always consider what resonates best for you.

"Do not believe in anything simply because you have heard it. Do not believe in traditions because they have been handed down for many generations. Do not believe anything because it is spoken and rumoured by many. Do not believe in anything because it is written in your religious books. Do not believe in anything merely on the authority of your teachers and elders. But after observation and analysis, when you find that anything agrees with reason and is conducive to the good and the benefit of one and all, then accept it and live up to it."
- Buddha (563 – 483 BC)

We are all on a journey to discover who we are, to develop ourselves and to experience, but not to trust blindly in everything we hear, regardless of who has said it. Always consult your truth barometer—think about what feels right for you. Use your head and your heart. Use your intellect and your cognitive processes, as well as the wisdom that comes from your intuitive knowledge. The combination of these aspects is a powerful one, and will show you the truth that is right for you.

The truth has many facets, something the Council of Elders explained to us when we asked them a number of questions on July 29, 2010. Lilli was channeling and I, Camillo, recorded the answers. The following is the introductory text they conveyed to us:

"The riddles of life are now in the process of being solved. Through a process of analysis, theories have been turned upside down and postulated. Statements from various quarters are being made in the form of astonishing truths, and other statements containing different truths are in turn, overturning these. But these are also aspects of the multi-faceted nature of creation. Because in fact, there is a common thread running through all these various statements, and this thread is now becoming clearer and stronger through the minds of those who seek the truth—those who seek to understand life's riddles.

"Through the questions being asked here, an understanding is emerging from this plane of consciousness that is part of the truth, because the truth changes face according to which part of the core it springs from.

"In the same way that children in Africa have one truth about life based on their background and the education, children in Norway have a different truth because they have received a different type of education. This also applies when people on Earth contact various planes of existence that have followed a certain line of development and regard it as their truth—because everything can be divided up and pieced together again, like in different mathematical calculations."

- Channeled by Lilli Bendriss, July 29, 2010 - from the energy-beings the Council of Elders

We are living in a time of great change, but there has always been change. We are simply entering a new phase. This phase involves a shift in consciousness where we will progress from the Homo Sapiens stage to the next stage of human evolution: Homo Luminous—enlightened beings.

We are all playing a key part in the changes that are already in motion. The future is nothing but potential. We make our own choices about which future we want for others and ourselves. We are thinking, feeling and sensing beings, living in a sentient universe, with the power to create our own reality.

"I was bold in the pursuit of knowledge, never fearing to follow truth and reason to whatever results they led."
- **Thomas Jefferson (1812)**

Lilli

The Needle
At the end of the 1980s, I reached my mid-life point: I turned 42 years old. During the previous few years, life had started to feel meaningless. On the outside everything appeared to be good; I was a successful businesswoman with three beautiful children and a husband who I had stood by through thick and thin for twenty years. Together we built a business empire within the restaurant and property industry, but in actuality, I had abandoned my own vision; I was a qualified hairdresser. For ten years I worked to succeed in that profession and had even opened my own salon. I was happy and loved the many creative aspects of the job.

However, running restaurants during the evenings with my full-time day work became impossible. A decision was made: my dream would be put on hold. Seventeen years would pass before I managed to pull out of the restaurant trade.

During the latter years, a voice in the back of my head was constantly nagging me. "You're not doing what you're supposed to do in this life." So what was I supposed to do then? Return to being a hairdresser? No, I had missed that opportunity. What about starting up a fashion shop?

I loved clothes and had grown up living above a ready-made clothing factory with my mother and father, who were both qualified tailors. Even though I desperately needed to exercise my creative abilities, none of these ideas sounded appealing. I was so tired—completely and utterly exhausted—and spent my days on the sofa, passively following life via the TV screen. The meaning of life, what was it, actually?

We work, toil, learn and then one day it's all over? Heaven or hell for all eternity? What was the point? There had to be another truth. I was burnt out, and at that point I was diagnosed with abnormal cervical cell changes.

In itself, this was not a surprise, since my father had died two years previously from prostate cancer. Initially described as presenting no danger, he waited almost six months for an operation, by which time the cancer had spread. Here was the hook on which to hang my lack of motivation. I had an excuse for being lazy: it's not my fault, I am just sick. I received a wealth of good advice during the ensuing period, most of which I rejected, but acupuncture was something I thought I could try.

My doctor set an appointment to have a laser operation in three months, so I took advantage of that time to have frequent acupuncture treatments. Needles were inserted with great precision, but there was no noticeable improvement. My fatigue still hung like a soggy shroud over my shoulders. Finally, I decided I was throwing money out of the window and that my next treatment would be the last. This was two days before the operation, and after that I would try something else.

I spoke with my acupuncturist about my decision. There was absolutely nothing wrong with his treatment, I told him, it was probably my body refusing to play ball.

The words were still pouring out of me when he left the room walking determinedly. When he returned, he was carrying a golden needle in his hand.

"This time I'm going to insert a very special needle, Lilli," he said, and without any further explanation he inserted the needle into the area just below my navel. Though he twisted and turned it, it did not hurt like the others, however, nothing extraordinary happened either. I got up, thanked him for the time he had devoted to me and left his office.

Still unaffected when I got into the car, then it hit me. It was like a balloon had burst. Tears were streaming down my face. I sobbed uncontrollably and was grateful that my husband was driving. I simply couldn't stop crying and spent the whole evening in the company of a pile of soggy Kleenex tissues. Early the next morning I rang my acupuncturist and told him about my reaction. "Great, just keep crying for as long as you have any tears left," was the laconic message I received from the other end of the phone.

Though I was feeling slightly calmer, just to be on the safe side, I rang the hospital to check that everything was okay for my operation the following day. Operation? No, there was no one with my name on the hospital's list of patients for the next day. There must have been a mistake. I had not been registered on their computer system. When I asked how long I would have to wait, "Well, probably another three months," was the reply I received.

Fear overcame me: the fear of dying. Was I suffering from a repeat of my father's fate? Right there and then I knew that I had to take control of my own fate. As I had that thought, my gaze fell on a brochure lying next to the telephone. Actually, it had been there for several months without my having thrown it away. Nor had I been tempted to attend the course advertised in it: a course on self-help for people with cancer.

Suddenly that brochure called out to me and without hesitation I grabbed the phone and punched in the number of the Oslo Creativity Center. A friendly voice said that yes, they were still running courses at the center, in fact, a one-week course had started just one hour ago. When I asked if I could jump in at the last minute, I was told, "Just come along."

How often does fate play out its hand on the stage of life so we can enter the stage at just the right moment? This course proved to be of momentous significance because there my body and soul finally learned to play as a team.

Journey Into the Inner Realms
That course was my first so-called self-development course and I had no preconceptions about what I was attending. Meeting the other members of the group was a reassuring experience. Everyone looked quite normal and Kaja, the course leader, sat there like Mother Nature, radiating compassion and security. The various exercises seemed exciting and I slipped into the dynamics of topics like meditation and visualisation without feeling that they were strange or unfamiliar.

Even so, during my first-ever visualisation exercise, I experienced a tremendous sadness. I was unable to conjure up a gift that I was supposed to receive from a being that I met on the top of a mountain. This loss completely floored me emotionally and created further nourishment for the tears that had flowed the previous evening. I thought I had infected the rest of the group like a virus, as everyone was sobbing and crying for the remainder of the day. I was shocked at what I had done but when I apologized, I received a bear-like hug in return. It was probably nothing unusual for Kaja. She had mastered the art of granting acceptance to any soul who wandered into her energy field.

During this remarkable week my ability to reach into an inner world, where one play succeeds another, appeared to flow effortlessly, like a river finding its path through unknown terrain after a flood.

"Are you clairvoyant?" Kaja asked one day.

"No," I replied, "I don't think so."

"Hmm, there's something about you, something about your hands." She wondered whether perhaps I should learn to do massage.

"No," I thought quietly to myself, "I have absolutely no interest in that," although my hands would actually prove to be the key to the power that I had lost. Let's jump forward to the last day of this one-week course.

The Talking Stone

We are sitting in a circle on the last day of the one-week course, saturated by the impressions gained during our time together. Kaja is holding a stone in her hand. It looks like an ordinary grey stone, but she says that it's not quite as ordinary as it looks. It is a sacred stone—a Talking Stone given to her by a North American shaman. The stone was often used at tribal gatherings where everyone was given the opportunity to present their views about the matters discussed. The stone was passed to whomever was going to talk and everyone else remained silent, expect for the person holding the stone. We were about to do the same.

"This is called a Talking Stone," she says. "It is a sacred stone that was used in the circle, with everyone being given the opportunity to say what was on their mind. I want you all to take turns holding it and sharing your thoughts with the rest of the group about how you are feeling now, at the end of this week."

I can hear Kaja's words, but something happens to my body. My heart starts beating madly, my chest constricts and I realize that I don't want to take the stone. What's happening to me? It's because of the golden needle! It started a process inside me that has not yet been completed. That acupuncture needle opened up all my layers of protection and I can almost see it in my mind's eye as it quivers and starts its final task—making a hole in the veil that separates the different worlds.

My Hands Are Burning

I am calm inside, but raw, unfamiliar power is building up inside this calmness. It is a living being, independent of myself, but at the same time I know that I am the one who has to release it. I can feel the fear taking shape.

"Oh my God, don't let me loose control. Pull yourself together Lilli. We've almost finished now. Don't cry. Don't create havoc again like you did on the first day." The stone is passed to me, indicating that it is my turn to speak. I take it in my right hand and hold it.

"Pull yourself together," says the voice inside my head, which is now more panicky. "Just say a few well-chosen words about how great the course has been. It's not necessary to say anything else." But no, my thoughts are flying around like birds in a cage. There is not enough room, not enough air.

I am holding the stone hard while my heart is beating madly and without saying anything I pass the stone on to the next person. Someone takes my hand. Kaja, clever Kaja, grants me permission. "Breathe in deeply, Lilli, don't hold back any more."

Wonderful Kaja. I am finally being given permission to give birth to this power that is tearing me apart. I let go of my control as I breathe in deeply, and my head is thrown back. Suddenly I leave this reality and I am travelling. Travelling and travelling. Through the present, past and future. I don't know, don't want to know.

A panorama opens up to my inner gaze, and I feel a clear presence. I catch a glimpse of an old Indian wearing a worn-out rug over his shoulders. He is sitting down and rocking backwards and forwards. There is a fire burning in front of him and rings of smoke are rising slowly upwards until they disappear into a blue ocean of sunlight. A white eagle is circling majestically up there in the sky. A small boy dressed in white skins is throwing small balls up into the air that disappear into the blue light. I remain standing in front of the old man. He lifts his gaze and without saying a word he slips into my consciousness.

"Come closer, give me your hands." His gaze, full of the wisdom of ages, is all-seeing and I understand everything.

"I have been waiting for you, the time has come."

There is no way back now. I am pulled towards him like a magnet. My will melts away. Everything exists in the now, the old man, the eagle, the boy, Lilli, the blue sky, peace, surrender, acceptance.

He locks his gaze into mine and slowly I stretch out my hands until they are almost touching his. Suddenly, it's as if an intense bolt of lightening hits my head and floods through my body before becoming embedded in the palms of my hands. I experience a sensation of sharp, burning pain so intense that I am hurled back into reality.

"It's burning, it's burning! What have you done?" Kaja's hand has been resting in mine all along, but I now quickly pull my hand back with all my strength. I hold up my hands and study them. They look quite normal.

"It isn't me, Lilli, it's you," Kaja says calmly.

I can hardly think straight. Everything is flowing together and a new consciousness is being born in me. I experience a power that is stronger and rawer than anything I ever experienced before. It is so strong that I am convinced that I will die unless I can get it out of my body and away from me.

My thoughts are racing around inside my head and slowly the pieces start to fall into place. I understand everything, and yet words can't describe what I am understanding. I experience a state of complete unity with everything that exists. Obviously I am not going to die because this is what I have been waiting for. At last I am whole. I also know that this power can help other people, and suddenly I am on my feet.

"Can I put my hands on you?" I ask the women sitting next to me. She nods and I place my hands on her head. I instantly feel power being pumped out through every single pore in my hands and disappearing into the head of the person I am holding. This continues for five minutes, maybe ten, as I am outside time and space.

As quickly as it happened, it's over. My hands are no longer burning and my heartbeat has returned to normal. I calmly return to my place.

Lilli the Shaman

Once, again, I create havoc, but Kaja sits there safe and secure like Mother Nature and explains everything as best she could.

"That's probably not how it usually occurs, but your healing powers were released in quite a spectacular manner. Perhaps that was how it was supposed to happen for you, so that you would notice it in your busy everyday life. I have a message for you, Lilli, and the message is that you will work as a shaman."

"What does a shaman do?" I ask Kaja.

"A shaman is someone who journeys to other realities in order to obtain information from our ancestors. They pass on this information to their tribe, for their highest good. A shaman is also the tribe's healer and teacher. It would appear that these three tasks will be part of your future, but you have to be willing to accept them. That's just how it is."

Every word she says hits home. I do not yet understand how, but I am willing to follow this path and I know that I will not be walking it alone. From now on I will always have someone with me, no matter where I go.

With this thought in my mind, the old man by the fire returns to me. He nods imperceptibly, and a small smile quivers at the corner of his mouth before he continues to suck on his pipe and his eyes appear to gaze into a remote future.

Further Experiences

In my search for knowledge, I once again experience the acquisition of huge amounts of energy. This time it happens on a shamanic course run by Ailo Gaup, a Sami shaman. Instead of the power flowing out of my hands, it converges in my throat and I start speaking with the voice of an old man. This is the beginning of being able to channel directly from the other side, resulting in the most beautiful poetry and other more complicated texts. Some of it comes in English, some in Norwegian. The energy-being that first came to me through the old Indian is called Wounded Eagle.

Since then many other energy-beings have come along, such as the Universal Storyteller, the Source, and the Council of Elders. The following is my story about the first time I came into contact with the energy-beings that call themselves the Council of Elders.

The Council of Elders

Today, when I think back on how my life has changed since the activation of my sixth sense and my ability to transfer energy consciously, it seems like two different people have lived in my body.

Before the activation I was programmed to be a victim. Things happened to me. After receiving teachings from different non-physical teachers I understood that I create my own reality, consciously or unconsciously. The more I experienced that this was actually how things worked, the more I thirsted to understand even more. The universal laws became a map that I could use for maneuvering myself forwards—when the pupil is ready the teacher appears.

The beautiful poems I received touched me deeply. They had a lovely way of showing me how people strive to experience the good within and around themselves. But after that I started receiving messages of a different nature. Sentences came to me, such as anti-gravity propulsion and the Zero Point Field. This was all a bit above my head, so I hid my notes in a drawer. It is only now in retrospect that I can see, all along there had been a plan behind this.

Today the ideas and concepts in this book are supported by research, which in turn supports our understanding of the fact that there is a higher intelligence out there that is cooperating with mankind in order to help us over the last hurdle. It's like standing on the top of a mountain with a wide-angle camera built into your consciousness and seeing the landscape below from that perspective.

In this book we will be including extracts from the words spoken by my teachers. The Council of Elders is particularly relevant with respect to the topics that are being presented. How did I come into contact with them?

In 1992, I was the astonished recipient of lyrical words that arrived in the form of poetry, and it was not hard to relate to them. At the time I felt safe, protected and honored. "Wow," I thought, "what a fantastic gift to be able to pass on to the people around me." At that time I also received information in my sleep—prophetic dreams that I was only able to understand many years later.

In one of those dreams, I am standing alone. The sun is beating down and it is incredibly hot. Where am I? I turn around and take in my surroundings. I see a group of stone benches going round in a semi-circle. An amphitheater— this word comes to me clearly. I am standing in the middle of the semi-circle and can see an elevated stage in front of me with a small mountain range in the background. How strange. What am I doing here? The silence is deafening. There is no sound and no movement, as though the place is holding its breath.

My gaze is directed towards the stage. A long table with a white cloth hanging down and draped across the floor catches my attention. The next moment, initially glimpsed through the corner of my eye, a figure walks slowly in from the right, followed by more figures. They are all dressed in the same way, in long, white robes with white hair flowing down over their shoulders. They are bent over and are carrying thick books under their arms.

One at a time they sit down behind the table. The books are placed in front of each individual and they direct their gaze towards me. Without uttering a single word they transmit thoughts to me, letting me know that I am about to take an exam. If I pass then the books will be opened and I will be able to read the stories written between the beginning and the end of this world cycle.

They are the books of life. I stare intently at the books, but I am unable to see if I passed my exam or whether I have been found worthy, because the next moment I suddenly wake up. The details are still clear as I sit there in my bed and review my dream with a sense of wonderment.

(Ten years would pass before I saw this place again and recognized everything that I had seen in my dream. During a trip to Greece that included a visit to Delphi, I stood in the middle of the arena nodding to myself—The Delphic Oracle. Time, like an arrow, was shot from a bow towards the revelations of the future. Several different entities had visited me during the years that had elapsed between these two events, and the old ones now reappeared in this new setting.)

I could easily go out of my body during meditation. There I experienced boundless revelations where Earth and her denizens were just one tiny aspect of many different life forms found in the huge universe surrounding us. Time had similarly dissolved and I was able to journey into what we call the future.

In a special dream I had about Delphi, I recognize that I am moving slowly outwards, forwards. Floating around in a state of weightlessness in the vast void with stars rushing past me, the scene changes. I find myself in a completely unfamiliar place, wandering along a road. A female being appears next to me and answers my questions without speaking. This is a teaching plane where people come from different places to learn, more or less like we do in our universe.

I see this golden planet from an eagle-eye perspective while simultaneously observing everything close to me. There is an energy dome that enables life, plants and trees to grow in certain areas. The dome is transparent, although simultaneously visible. The lady at my side is beautiful and elf-like, with golden brown skin that contrasts sharply with her snowy white hair that falls in ringlets from beneath a turban. She stretches out her arm and once again, without speaking, she explains that she is absorbing nourishment directly from the air. She says that she can taste nectar from certain plants by placing them beneath her tongue and this gives her a tremendous ecstatic experience. However, the air is her main source of nourishment.

I can see structures that must be houses. They have no straight edges and look like gently curving sculptures. As I sit down with my back resting against the wall it forms itself around my body. The colors are similar to the luminosity and nuances exhibited by pearls. Everything is incredibly harmonious and I experience the energy radiating from the lady as a pleasurable quivering.

"I am a future version of yourself." She looks at me and there and then her words resonate as a truth, as the most natural thing in the world.

While wandering around we have arrived at an open space occupied by a completely different type of building. Towering above us is an enormous obelisk made of pure crystal. I am led into the center of the obelisk and sit down on the only chair there. I close my eyes, and when I open them again the old ones are standing around me in a semi-circle.

There are no books here—only the direct transfer of wisdom. At the back of my head I experience an electric vibration in my head as my telepathic communication center is activated so that it will become easier for me to make contact. I do not protest and feel no fear because by then I'd heard about implants and gaining control of one's own will. This is the contract that my soul entered into before I came to Earth as Lilli, and I am receiving help from one of my many selves as a builder of bridges between the worlds.

The old ones present themselves as the Council of Elders. They and the lady, Amu Zhar, have been with me ever since.

Today when I am channeling for individuals or groups I connect myself to the crystal and feel a blessing from my wisdomkeepers as information starts to flow through me. I always express my gratitude for their confidence in me and say that I will do my best to translate the information received into one of the Earth's languages.

Over the years I have channeled huge amounts of information from Amu Zhar and the Council Elders—sometimes up to several sessions per day. Much of this information is relevant to our current time and is therefore included in this book.

Camillo

How We Met: A Coincidence?

During the autumn of 2009, over the course of a few short weeks I went from having no idea who Lilli Bendriss was to working closely with her, developing training courses, being featured in various magazines, TV and radio appearances, and now the publishing of this book. Was this a coincidence? If you had asked me a few years ago, I would have said yes, definitely. Today I have a completely different opinion: without a doubt this was not a coincidence.

I grew up believing in Darwin's theory of evolution. I thought that life on Earth was a cosmic accident and that when we die we are gone forever. I considered it to be pure luck that our planet has to be just the right distance from the sun to provide the right conditions for life on Earth. If our planet had been even a tiny bit further away, Mother Earth would have been a block of ice; if it had been a bit closer, we would have been burnt like a barbecued sausage.

I imagine that this type of belief is normal for people with a scientific upbringing/background. Growing up in a family with several physicians, obviously my beliefs were rooted in all things scientific. From the day we are born we rely on our five senses to show us what is real. We need to see to believe and we rely on science to verify the so-called truth for us. To believe in something that cannot be explained or verified by science is hard. We are prisoner of the reference frameworks of the time we live in. We have to have proof in order to believe.

Nevertheless there is much between heaven and Earth that cannot be explained by the science of today.

Even though something cannot be proven, this does not constitute proof that it does not exist.

"Absence of evidence is not evidence of absence."
- Carl Sagan

Although I grew up believing that nothing exists beyond that which we can perceive with our five senses, as a teenager I became extremely curious about everything that could not be explained—the so-called unknown. I was drawn into a world of books dealing with near-death experiences, reincarnation, UFOs, ghosts, parapsychology, the power of thought, the Silva Method and other related topics. This enduring interest became so strong that I wanted to dig deeper and study these subjects at university where I could look for the answers to my questions.

At the end of the 1970s these interests were not regarded as being quite "acceptable." Getting an education in such interests was a world away from the "acceptable" subjects being studied by everyone else.

The people in our lives and the times in which we live shape our formative years. So despite my passion, I ended up choosing an entirely different direction in my life—a path that was more common and acceptable.

Today I know that I failed to listen to my inner voice—to my inner feeling. My interest in the unknown, which I experienced as being very exciting, sparked a flame inside me. It was my inner voice and feeling trying to tell me something, but I failed to listen. The flame started to die down when I made my decision to follow a different direction in my life. It was almost extinguished, and it would take almost 30 years before it flared up again.

In the meantime the days, weeks and years raced by at the speed of light. I focused on my education. I gave all my energy into studying hard in order to secure good marks, which again would result in me getting a well-paid job. I was caught up in an existence that failed to take my innermost desires into account. Everything revolved around getting an education, work and a career. What I really wanted to spend my life doing failed to reach the surface. It was buried deep inside me, overshadowed by the outer world that overpowered my inner voice. In the outer world I gradually acquired a well-paying job. But did I have an all-consuming interest in my work? No, I was not passionate about it. There was no spark like the one I experienced during my youth. My interest in the unknown was like a remote dream, but it would subsequently acquire a dominant place in my life.

Then I became acquainted with the teachings of Bob Proctor, an international lecturer and author from Canada who had been studying the secrets of life for almost 50 years. He was a key figure in films like *The Secret*, *Beyond the Secret* and *The YES Movie*. His message really hit home. He talked about the power of thought and how we create our own reality. He was saying that there are universal laws that are as real as the law of gravitation, and that we are all part of a universal consciousness.

I became sucked into this world which captivated me. Completely engrossed, I became intimately acquainted with this material. What he said resonated with me—it seemed to be so right.

Suddenly I found myself awake as if after a long, long sleep and I was starved of information. My thirst to know and understand the link between who we are and what we are doing here resulted in a relentless search for the answers to four key questions:

Who are we, where do we come from, what are we doing here and where are we going?
In a state of excitement and anticipation, I embarked on a journey into the world of books. I devoured everything that could provide me with answers. I consumed a wide range of topics—auras and guides, the meaningful universe, 2012, the Mayan Calendar, consciousness, near-death experiences, the power of thought, channeling, reincarnation, energies—many subjects all found their way

into my mind. You must dig deep to find the answers to the riddles of life, and this was just the first thrust of the spade.

I dug deeper and started meditating. I participated in various courses, webinars and telephone conferences. I watched films and talked with like-minded souls. Over several years I collected a vast quantity of information. This was my passion—something that I lived and breathed for. Such a liberating feeling—to find something that I was really passionate about. It was like coming home!

My search for answers was like searching for the pieces in the jigsaw of life. One piece here, one piece there. Slowly I started to see a connection, a common thread running through all the material that I'd come across that became clearer and stronger as I continued to pursue my studies. The more insight I gained, the more inspiration I acquired in my ongoing search for answers. It was (and still is) extremely exciting to search for these pieces in the jigsaw of life.

One of the obvious pieces that turned up during my search for answers was the 2012 phenomenon, a truly fascinating subject. In my opinion there is a direct link between the 2012 phenomenon and who we are, where we are going and what we are doing here.

My search for answers became all-consuming, and when an opportunity occurred to leave my permanent job in the pharmaceuticals industry, the decision was easy to make. So I left a secure job with good future prospects. But how important was that, when my mind and heart were longing to do something else? The flame that had been lit during my teens had returned and there was no going back. I did not know why I was so attracted to finding answers about the so-called unknown, but my whole body started tingling every time I went "hunting" for information. All I knew was that I wanted to do this for the rest of my life and received support from my wife, Synnøve, to continue with this adventure. Synnøve has always embraced alternative views and had no problem in understanding that I would now be working full-time on finding answers to the riddles of life.

Everything that could provide me with answers was being thoroughly investigated. When the TV station Kanal FEM launched a program entitled, *The Other Side,* Synnøve and I became regular viewers every Thursday evening. This program addressed the very topics that I was so passionately interested in. One autumn evening in 2009, on our regular Thursday night date in front of the TV to watch *The Other Side,* Synnøve and I saw for the first time the guest of the evening that would so change our lives. There sitting on the sofa with the hosts was a Norwegian woman named Lilli Bendriss. Neither of us had heard of her before. During all my searches for answers I had only read English books and had not paid much attention to the spiritual scene here in Norway.

During the program Lilli told the story about how she had become activated as a medium at the age of 42. This had quite an impact—I felt like she was coming out of the TV screen at me. My intuition told me that I had to contact her. She appeared to be clear, pure and strong. I felt that she could provide me with answers—answers about why I was so passionate about the so-called unknown. Why did I suddenly "wake up" with this passion to find answers to the riddles of life? Why had I given up my permanent job to work on this? Would she be able to help me?

A few days later I called Lilli's office to make an appointment. The date I was given was Friday, November 13, 2009. Some regard Friday the 13th as being an unlucky day, but for me it was just the opposite. Later on I also discovered that Lilli's lucky number is actually 13.

Prior to our meeting, I read up about Lilli Bendriss, the medium. I learned that she had appeared on two Norwegian TV series: *The Power of the Spirits* and *Sensing Murder,* that she was a channeler and one of the most well-known mediums in Norway. Channeling was a subject that I had read about and I knew what a medium was. But I had never actually met a real medium or seen a channeling session being conducted. I was really looking forward to this experience.

The day arrives and a mystical, exciting and dark lady receives me politely. She asks, "How can I help you?" so I explain my interest in the unknown, about the flame that was ignited when I was a teenager and how, almost 30 years later, I have experienced an awakening of sorts and acquired a voracious appetite for books, films, courses and like-minded people that can provide me with answers. I ask her:

"I would like to know why I am so drawn towards finding answers about the so-called unknown. Why am I so passionate about this?"

Lilli replies that she will have to perform a channeling session in order to obtain answers. She tells me that if I want to I can record the session on my mobile phone. I begin recording and sit back in anticipation. Lilli makes herself comfortable and that's when it all starts.

She does a few breathing exercises to help her receive the energies from the other side. One minute later she has gone into a trance and I am thinking: "What's going to happen now?" I was not prepared for what occurred. After a moment of silence I suddenly hear a deep voice saying the following in English:

"Moving through cyclical times we have followed you into the darkest corner of the universe where you found a star around which you centered your consciousness, calling it your home. Star traveller—throughout time as it is understood from physical dimensionality—this has been a theme which has occupied you in several lives on planet Earth. Your theories and theses were not understood by the others living in your time, and great frustration and loneliness occurred in your personal identity, yet you could not stop ..."

This continues for around 10 to 12 minutes until Lilli's voice changes and is replaced by a lighter voice which says:

"Now let us move to a different frequency. It is the feminine resonance, which is needed at this time to open your female intuition, and from your own willingness you are taken aboard a vehicle of light and sound where your cellular system is tuned to the higher frequency above physical reality.

"The feminine heart is the teacher aligning itself with your mental capacity which resides within the masculine reality-self, and these two are merging.

"In the next ten years or so humanity will be given the opportunity and task to accumulate and hold the frequency intact so that a quantum leap may be taken—for the few will create gateways for the many. For human resonance will change the visible picture of your planet—the great purification is to empty the junk from your cells and recreate the DNA strands in their actual high potential form and make this a blueprint for the many. And this is science mated with consciousness. And through consciousness science will take its quantum leap as well.

"And then the star travellers from the future will find the depth where they can plant their seed and fertilize it so that it may blossom into the new gracious contribution. To us is said in the Bible: 'and there shall be a new Earth and a new Heaven.'

"You came this time because you knew it is now or never, and you wanted, together with many other soul friends, to do your utmost to ignite the flame, making this a possibility to reckon with."

After 25 minutes it's over and Lilli comes out of her trance. Wow, what an experience. Heavy stuff, really "spaced out" but incredibly exciting. My thoughts are racing through my head: "Star traveller..." "Several life times..." "Change the visible picture of your planet..." "You came this time because you knew it is now or never..."

This was a lot information to take in at once. I subsequently listened to the recording numerous times down in order to obtain an even better understanding of the content. I have never been in any doubt about whether it was something that Lilli had made up or whether it came from the other side. Everything inside me told me that it was something that Lilli had conveyed from a source that was somewhere else. Since Lilli is never quite unconscious during her channeling sessions (unlike some other mediums), she is able to remember what she has conveyed immediately afterwards.

We talked about the information that had been passed on to me. The message was that I should share my knowledge and my passion for the unknown with others. Lilli summed up saying that I was on the right track. This is what I was supposed to do—become involved in providing people with information. That was my task.

She also told me that I would need to start networking with other like-minded people and to spread the knowledge that I possessed. She put me in contact with an organization to which she is also affiliated. A few weeks later we attended a meeting at Lilli's home in Oslo. There were about eight of us gathered around the dining table. Lilli and I were sitting directly opposite each other. After about 10 minutes into the meeting, Lilli points at me and says:

"We are going to conduct courses together about the 2012 phenomenon."

This message came out of the blue, like a bolt of lightening. To put it mildly, it took me completely by surprise. Where was this coming from? Actually I did know a fair bit about the subject of 2012. I had written an eBook in English on the subject, but it was quite incredible that Norway's most well-known medium should point at me and suggest that we would be conducting courses together. Lilli said that she had received a sudden impulse/message from her energies/guides saying that we should conduct courses together and that she had reacted instantly by pointing at me to let me know. Obviously I said yes, and this marked the start of an exciting joint venture that has culminated in this book: *The Shift in Consciousness*.

Lilli and I hope that this book will encourage you to search inside yourself to find out who you are and what you really came here to do in this life. My interest in the unknown has taught me that I actually do not need books, seminars, films or other people to find the answer to who I am.

There are no reference works that can tell me who I am or what I am doing here, but they can help me to pause and think. They can provide me with the nudge I need to take a break in my busy everyday life and actually think about life, about who I really am and what I want. Books, films, seminars, courses and other people can trigger something inside us—something that will compel us to move inwards instead of always seeking answers outside ourselves.

It's not about knowing or understanding the unknown. It's about remembering who we are, and when we do, all the pieces in the puzzle will fall into place and you will then experience inner peace. You will understand that everything is connected and that you are part of the whole and the whole is part of you. You will understand that you are EVERYTHING—that you are a thinking being, living in a thinking universe, with infinite powers of creation.

Part 1 _____

Chapter 1 - Who Are We?

"People you meet on your way: some you want to reach out to and grab, to hold on to. Other shadows of lost souls have no meaning for you.

"Future destiny and long past lives interwoven in webs of connecting vibes. Chords, found and given away, a never-ending chain. A multitude of galaxies, each with its tune to sing, together form a choir reaching down to touch your conscious minds. The echo of each tune, a meld, a blend of sounds, blending to the frequencies your soul can reach through time.

"Why are we born? How come we are to die? Never-ending questions of that greater reunion, we fail to see what a blissful moment it is to be. Walk without fear in the shadow of death. Hold hands with friends and make a bridge of loving thoughts that scream:

YOU ARE JUST PART OF THAT BIGGER WHOLE!

"Fly together like Indians do, smoking their pipes and chanting to their God for clearance through the gate that opens up into that other realm. See the fire spewing smoke that reaches up to kiss the stars. Feel the peace within, knowing that you too may travel with the smoke wherever you may choose. See the world as eagles do.

"Remember the beautiful days, and let them overshadow the pain and experience you had to live to cause your soul to grow. Reach out and welcome life, whatever it may hold for you, secure in the thought that one far wiser laid the path all your tomorrows must tread."

- Channeled by Lilli Bendriss, January 10, 1990 - from the energy-being Wounded Eagle

Who are we? This is a question that people have been asking for as long as there have been people on the planet. In our struggle to find answers we have looked increasingly to science. What can science show us? What has been proven? What do we know today about creation and how we were created? We know that everything is composed of atoms, including human beings.

The Universal Laws
We and everything else in the universe are composed of atoms. Atoms form molecules, including the DNA molecules in our cells. DNA—deoxyribonucleic acid—is a molecule that carries the genetic information contained in our cells in the form of "building blocks" called "bases"— abbreviated as A, T C or G, according to their following chemical designations: adenine, thymine, guanine and cytosine.

A myriad of different cells performing different tasks enables our body to function as it should. Many people regard the body as consisting of permanent structures, but most of our tissue (except the brain) is being constantly renewed in a balance between the constant death of old cells and the constant birth of new cells. The average life of these different cells varies considerably. Skin cells live for approximately two to four weeks, while red blood cells, for example, live for 120 days.

On average the upper limit for most of the body's cells is between seven and ten years. This means that everything from which you are composed will have disappeared over the course of that time. You will have become completely new; your body will be composed of new atoms and new cells.

This is hard to imagine, because we identify ourselves with our bodies and all the cells that make up each and every one of us. We assume that our consciousness lies inside our body, but what if our body actually lies inside our consciousness? What if the body is actually the vessel we use for moving around inside ourselves because we are space, we are the universe, we are all that is, we are consciousness—and this consciousness utilizes a physical body in order to obtain experience? Are we anything more than a unique living being that exists along with many other life forms on this planet, our Mother Earth?

In order for life to exist in the universe a number of criteria need to be fulfilled. Everything must be in the right proportions and in the right relationship to everything else. Everything in the universe is composed of atoms that contain protons, neutrons and electrons. The nucleus of an atom consists of neutrons and protons. Swirling around the nucleus are electrons. Everything is in perfect harmony— in balance, enabling life to flourish.

But what if just one of these criteria becomes slightly out of balance and out of proportion to the others. Cosmologist Paul Davies explains that even slight changes made to the existing laws of nature would have a tremendous impact on all life in the universe. He uses the atom as an example:

If protons—the stuff of nuclear matter—were just a tad heavier, all else being equal, they would decay into neutrons, and atoms would fall apart. If the nuclear force were a few percent different than carbon, the life-giving element, would never have formed in abundance by nuclear reactions inside stars. In each case, life as we know it would be impossible. Taking into account many such "fine-tunings" in physics and cosmology, it looks as if the universe is a fix—a big fix. [1]

For life to exist everything must be in the right proportions to everything else as shown in the example provided by Davies. If the Earth was closer to the sun, it would be too hot for life to exist, and if had been further away it would be too cold. Why does the universe appear to be so finely-tuned with respect to the existence of life, including intelligent life that is capable of asking the question, "Why?"

Believers would say that God created life, while scientists try to invent complicated extra-dimensional multiverse theories in order to explain how lucky we are to live on a planet where everything is so perfect for the existence of life. Do universal laws—laws that are equally valid as the law of gravity, govern our lives? Laws such as vibration, attraction and cause and effect, just to mention a few.

Many people think so. One of these is the successful author Jack Canfield:

"Everything that comes to us is governed by laws. When we understand these laws and apply them consciously, we can create whatever we desire. We can all acquire wealth if we first undertake an assessment and then think in a special way. That is the law."[2]

Many people support the idea that there are such laws in the universe and that someone must have created them. Did a higher intelligence create a universe based on these laws which in turn govern our lives?

According to Dr. Wernher Magnus Maximilian Freiherr von Braun (March 23, 1912 - June 16, 1977), the creator of the space program, the laws must have been created by someone. Von Braun was one of the leading figures in the development of rocket technology in Germany and the USA. He thought that the creation of these laws was no coincidence.

Von Braun says, "These natural laws of the universe are so precise that we have no difficulty building a spaceship to the moon and we can time the flight with the precision of a fraction of a second. These laws must have been created by someone."[3]

Is there a higher intelligence behind creation? The world is divided between those who maintain that everything is a cosmic accident and those who believe that some sort of God is responsible. In his book entitled, *The Symbiotic Universe: Life and Mind in the Cosmos*, astronomer George Greenstein entertains the idea that a Supreme Being might be responsible:

"As we survey all the evidence, the thought insistently arises that some supernatural agency must be involved. Is it possible that suddenly, without intending to, we have stumbled upon scientific proof of the existence of a Supreme Being?"[4]

Everything in the universe moves in cycles. Everything appears to be finely tuned, including our bodies. Is this the result of a cosmic accident or is there an architect behind it all? The Anglo-American physicist and mathematician John Freeman Dyson, who is famous for his work on quantum mechanics, the development of nuclear weapons and politics, and the search for extraterrestrial life, as well as being a winner of the Templeton Prize (2000), has stated the following:

"The more I examine the universe and the details of its architecture, the more evidence I find that the universe in some sense must have known we were coming."[5]

Albert Einstein is said to have been one of the most ingenious scientists ever to live. Despite his scientific background he also expressed the view that there must be some form of higher intelligence behind the universal laws.

"Anyone who becomes seriously involved in the pursuit of science becomes convinced that there is a spirit manifest in the laws of the universe, a spirit vastly superior to that of man."
-Albert Einstein

The renowned scientist Max Planck shared the same views:

"All matter originates and exists only by virtue of a force which brings the particle of an atom to vibration and holds this most minute solar system of the atom together. We must assume behind this force the existence of a conscious and intelligent mind. This mind is the matrix of all matter."[6]

These are just a few selected statements made by famous and respected scientists. They all agree that some sort of energy, a spirit, a being, and an intelligent mind designed the universe and its laws. But what is this mysterious energy that they are all talking about?

Chapter 2 - The Inner World

During the last few years, spirituality has acquired a greater place in our busy lives. Increasing numbers of people have been experiencing spiritual awakenings. More time is being devoted to key questions like who are we, what are we doing and where are we going, but do we believe that there is a creative force behind all life?

More people believe in life after death and a creative force—a higher intelligence behind all creation, than those who do not. Is this creator outside us or we are part of it? Is it inside us? Does the inner world create the outer world that we live in? Many of us would say that it does. This force in the inner world has many different names—

- The One
- The Source
- The Force
- The Absolute
- The Great One
- The Supreme Power
- Higher Intelligence
- Universal Consciousness
- The Supreme Good
- The Father
- The Universal Mother
- God
- The Divine Operation

—and many more.

In 1901 a British judge, Thomas Troward, wrote *The Dore Lectures* in which he described the Divine Operation. He shows that the Source wants to express itself and to keep expanding all the time. It wants to develop—to grow—to become more—to learn more. It does this with and through us.

David Wilcock, an author and lecturer on the subject of 2012, shares this view. "We are part of the Source and the Source is part of us," he says. "We are all one and our free will is part of our design which enables us to express what we want so that the Source can acquire many different experiences." He maintains that there is just one of us here—just one being, but that the greatest gift this being has given us is the opportunity to discover that we are one with it in our own way—without anyone telling us what we should do, what we should believe or what we should think. It just is. It is our path and we can do anything we want. We have free will. He also says that if we use our free will to oppose the free will of others then it will bounce back on us. This is karma and it is how the universe works.[7]

We are like the instruments in a universal orchestra. All the instruments are unique and the Source wants each and every one of us to express ourselves at full capacity in order to create new, beautiful music—music that has never been played before. To play your instrument to the fullest, you need to break through the barrier of fear—discover your passion—and live out your dream.

Having free will also means that you do not have to express yourself to the full, although deep inside we all have a passion that wants to come out. Perhaps you are saying: "No, I don't have a burning desire to do anything. I don't have an inner drive to express myself to the maximum in any particular area in my life. Just trying to live is more than enough for me." Many people think this way until suddenly, one day they discover that inner flame—a flame just waiting to shine with all its force.

From the very day of our birth we are so blinded by the outer world that our inner world is overshadowed. Our inner world contains the desire to express ourselves and to make the best of our lives. It is latent in everyone, in every living thing, but we have allowed the outer world to decide what is important to us.

There is a reason why you are here on Earth. You are unique and no one can think or feel exactly the way you do. The impressions you leave behind are something that this world will never see again. Will you live out your dream and discover your life task, or will you do the same as many others—be content with a nice comfortable life in the fluid zone, which means you will die full—full of ideas, talent, dreams and hopes?

Have you thought about what your current life is like? Are you living your dream? Is your life today like you imagined it would be before you made choices about your education, career, partner, way of life and leisure interests, etc? Are you happy with whatever you spend your valuable time on? Are you living in the now? Are you listening to yourself and do you know who you really are? Or are you too busy with your hectic everyday life to allow your innermost thoughts to reach into your consciousness?

There are many people who have met the infamous "wall" and changed their ideas about what is important in life. One such story is about a professional woman and mother named Anette. Her encounter with the "wall" helped her discover a new world. Keen to share her story, she is a typical example of how life can ensnare you so there is never time to listen to yourself and your innermost thoughts. A major trauma a few years ago resulted in a long-term sick leave that gave her the time to discover her inner world.

Anette

I was right in the middle of a work meeting when something happened inside me. My head was spinning. I collapsed and was taken away in an ambulance. I was diagnosed with a viral infection of the vestibular nerve (vestibular neuritis) and loose crystals were discovered in my auditory canal. I was suffering from exhaustion syndrome and immediately signed off on long-term sick leave.

I was 38 years old, a mother of three children, working full time and active on all fronts—like most mothers. I had never believed in a Higher Power nor been involved in anything of a spiritual nature, but this episode changed all that.

I was living a hectic life with thousands of constant tasks and suddenly I was on sick-leave, drained of energy and lacking motivation, and the world that I knew ground to a halt.

Before my "collapse" our family led a very busy everyday life. Work, leisure activities, hobbies, voluntary work, family visits—everything took time and the clock governed us. There was always something going on. Every weekday was brimming with various tasks—and the same applied to our weekends.

After a typical, hectic day of work and activities, we'd collapse onto the sofa in front of the TV to while away a few hours watching trivial programs before creeping up to bed, tired and exhausted. There was no time to think about anything. I never understood that I needed time for myself, time to do nothing—I needed time just to be, listening to my inner self.

Before I collapsed, such thoughts had never even occurred to me. I was so preoccupied with relating to everything being fed to me by the outer world that there was no time for the Anette inside me.

My husband quickly understood that my new existence no longer included the active life that I had been living. I would have to fill my daily life with something new. Heavy demands are placed on people who are not supposed to do anything.

My husband discovered Morten Eriksen's website and his information about meditation. Together we learned to breathe, relax and meditate. Our evenings in front of the TV were replaced by engaging conversations. During the weekends we went for long walks in the forest and followed Eriksen's meditation program twice a week. This enabled us to view life from a different perspective. Slowly I managed to create a new everyday life for myself, one with meaning.

My first meeting with a local healer also helped to shape my new life. She saw me for what I was—my true self. She provided me with the insight to listen to my inner self. This required practice and a certain degree of acceptance of myself. I discovered peace and quiet and gradually started to enjoy my own company.

So much has changed. Previously, for example, when walking our dog, I was planning the remainder of the day, living in the future. I now enjoy the sounds of nature, the company of our dog and my walks in their own right. My "collapse" provided me with the opportunity to find myself, to allow myself time to engage in reflection and contemplation, to listen to my inner voice. I am learning to live in the now and there have been some surprising results.

One evening I went to bed early, on my own. I was planning to meditate a bit before going to sleep. While lying there I experienced a feeling of tremendous calm. My mind switched off and I was just about to doze off when suddenly I heard a crystal-clear voice saying: "Hey, Anette, could you tell Annie that I'm OK?"

It was as if someone was in the room, but the voice was inside my head. I jumped and I realized that it was Nora, my deceased great-grandmother—it was her voice, speaking in her positive tone. This was not a dream—I could really hear her voice in a conscious state.

This was one of many episodes I have experienced since I started living in the now. I feel more energy around me than before, and I experience strong reactions, both physically and mentally. I can also see into other dimensions. Last summer during a trip to England to explore crop circles, I experienced tremendously strong energies as I stepped into the circles. In one of them I could see all the energy that was constantly surrounding us. The space around us was full of a plasma-like substance containing small bubbles of various sizes that were flashing at me. My hands were literally burning with heat, but when my husband took hold of them, they were cold. In another crop circle I saw my third eye quite clearly. These were fantastic experiences that left me feeling extremely calm and peaceful. Whenever I experience them, I feel safe, with a powerful love inside me, and tears come to my eyes.

What the future holds is uncertain, but how strange that sometimes you have to "crash" in order to stop and listen to yourself in order to recognize your true self—to live in the now.

I have a completely different attitude to spiritual matters now because of my experiences and I feel that life has meaning. I am a better mother and wife—a better person. I now understand the value of the time that we spend here on Earth and I am happy inside myself because of the person I am—I am unique!

~ ~ ~

Many people have met the "wall," just like Anette. They realize that all we have is the now. Time does not return. You are living right now. Bob Proctor uses a great illustration to demonstrate how we can look to the moment and the present.

Visualize a large hourglass with the sand in the upper bulb running through the narrow connecting neck into the bulb below. The upper bulb represents the future. The narrow neck in the middle through which the sand runs represents the present, and the lower bulb represents the past. Visualize that the upper bulb is covered so that you cannot see how much sand is left. All you can see and relate to is the narrow neck through which the sand is trickling— the present. You will never know when the last grain of sand will run out of the upper bulb and it's all over.

No one knows how much time we have left of our lives, but even so we project our dreams to some point in the future. "When I retire…" or "When I earn a bit more money…" or "When I get a bit more free time, then I will…"

We constantly bombard ourselves with excuses for not living the life that we really desire—one that we dream about—saying that we do not have the time to be here in the present. We are so busy that we don't have time to appreciate everything that is living and breathing around us at any moment. If you want to change your life you must do it now. Right now is when you lay the foundations for the future that you have left. It is now that you are living. The motivational guru Les Brown explains this in the following way:

"We must strive to die empty. All our ideas, dreams, talent and hopes must be lived out in this life. That's why we came here." [8]

In our innermost being we have access to the most amazing power. There is huge potential inside each one of us. It is like an electricity socket, where the Source is the current and all we need to do is to insert the plug in order to gain access to this vast, infinite source of power. Power is located inside each and every one of us. Power for creating—for expressing ourselves.

But how do we get our light to shine? How can we find the power inside each of us? By understanding that we are co-creators with the ability to think. We are thinking beings, living in a thinking universe.

"We are here in order to create, not compete. Creating ensures more for all, less for none. That is what the Source desires." [2]

- Bob Proctor

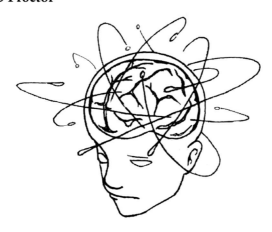

In order to create, we need to move inwards, inside ourselves. All the answers can be found within ourselves— not outside. In 1912, Charles F. Haanel published his book entitled, *The Master Key System*. This is an exciting book about the universe, energy and the world inside us all—the power of our thoughts. Here is an excerpt from his book:

"What is the Source of all power? The source of all power is the world within, the universal fountain of all that exists, the infinite energy that we can all access. As we become conscious of the inexhaustible power in the world within, we start to draw on this power to utilize to develop great possibilities, because whatever we become conscious of will always manifest in the objective world.

"This is because the infinite mind, which is the Source from which everything derives, is one and infinite, and each individual is an outlet for the manifestation of this eternal energy.

"Our ability to think depends on our ability to influence this universal force, and whatever we think is what is created and manifested in the objective world.

"The results of this discovery are nothing less than fantastic, and this means that the mind has quite extraordinary qualities, boundless capacity and contains undreamed-of possibilities."[9]

Even though this was written 100 years ago, many people throughout history have said the same—what we think is what we create. Whatever we give energy to is what manifests itself. Here are a few examples:

"A man is but the product of his thoughts—what he thinks, he becomes."
- Mahatma Gandhi

"We become what we think about."
- Earl Nightingale

"A man's life is what his thoughts make of it."
- Marcus Aurelius

"What you think, you create. What you feel, you attract. What you imagine, you become."
- Adele Basheer

Chapter 3 - The Strangest Secret

Earl Nightingale (1921-1989) was a pioneer in the field of personal development who understood the power of thought. He realized that we become what we think and first shared his ideas about this subject with the whole world more than 40 years ago, when he created his audio recording entitled, *The Strangest Secret*. This is one of the most significant recordings ever made and is full of valuable information for anyone wishing to expand their current level of consciousness. It still changes the lives of everyone who hears it. As Earl says in the recording: "We become what we're thinking about. As you sow so shall you reap." He continues:

"The human mind is far more fertile and mysterious than the land, but it works in the same way. It doesn't care what we plant—success, failure, fear, courage. So why don't we use our minds to grow what we want?

"The mind is free and things that are free are perceived as having no value. Things we pay money for are things that we appreciate.

"The paradox is that the opposite is true. Those things that are important in our lives are free. Our minds, our souls, our bodies, our hopes, our dreams, our ambitions, our intelligence, love of our family and friends—all these valuable assets are free, but the things that cost money are actually very cheap and can easily be replaced at any time. A good person can be completely ruined, but they can build up a fortune again. But the things that are free can never be replaced."[10]

Earl Nightingale is telling us that whatever we focus on becomes manifest.

Few people understand that our lives can be controlled and run by universal laws, but people like Esther and Jerry Hicks (and Abraham), Rhonda Byrne and everyone else involved in the film entitled, *The Secret* have done a good job teaching the world about one of these laws: the law of attraction. Since 1986 Esther and Jerry Hicks have published a number of books, DVDs, videos and articles about the law of attraction. Furthermore, Rhonda Byrne introduced several hundred million people to it through the book and film, *The Secret*, published in 2006 that became an international bestseller. Much of the material in this book was inspired by Wallace D. Wattles' work, *The Science of Getting Rich*, which was written in 1903 and published in 1910. One of the main messages in Wattles' work is the following paragraph:

"There is a thinking stuff from which all things are made, and which, in its original state, permeates, penetrates and fills the interspaces of the universe. A thought, in this substance, produces the thing that is imagined by the thought. Man can form things in this thought, and, by impressing his thought upon formless substance, can cause the thing he thinks about to be created."[11]

By sending our thoughts out to this Source—the formless substance—we can create whatever we want. Our thoughts create things. Everything you see in this world that has been created by man started off as a thought. Someone initially had to think the thought. It is impossible to create anything without first having the thought. Thoughts are consciousness expressing itself. Consciousness was here first. Consciousness creates matter, matter does not create consciousness.

Inventions such as light bulbs, airplanes, telephones and cars were initially thoughts in the minds of Edison, the Wright brothers, Bell and Ford. First they had the thought—and then the thought became reality. We live in a thinking universe in which we, as thinking beings, are co-creators of the universe. This is exactly what Gregg Braden refers to in his book entitled, *The Divine Matrix*:

"A growing body of research suggests that we are more than cosmic latecomers simply passing through a universe that was completed long ago. Experimental evidence is leading to a conclusion that we're actually creating the universe as we go and adding to what already exists! In other words, we appear to be the very energy that's forming the cosmos, as well as the being who experiences what we're creating. That is because we are consciousness, and consciousness appears to be the same stuff from which the universe is made."[12]

If consciousness appears to be the same "stuff" from which the universe is made and we are all consciousness, are we then particles of one mind—a universal mind? Yes, according to A Course in Miracles. This books explains that we are actually part of one universal mind:

"You think with the Mind of God. Therefore you share your thoughts with Him, as He shares His with you. They are the same thoughts, because they are thought by the same Mind. To share is to make alike, or to make one. Nor do the thoughts you think with the Mind of God leave your mind, because thoughts do not leave their source. Therefore, your thoughts are in the Mind of God, as you are."[13]

So is everything thoughts and consciousness? Are we co-creators of our own universe? Yes, we are, according to many researchers and esoteric and spiritual teachers. Those involved in studying and researching quantum physics/ mechanics are primarily researching things that occur at atomic and sub-atomic level. At this level scientists have also discovered tiny "packets" of energy referred to as quanta.

Sceptics maintain that research carried out in the field of quantum physics cannot be proven. Everything is theoretical, although authors such as Gregg Braden and Lynn McTaggert, and scientists like Professor John Hagelin, Dr. Alan Wolf, Dr. William Tiller and Professor Stuart Hamerhoff have all produced experimental evidence that concludes that we are actually all co-creators of the universe. We are thus part of a universal consciousness. The inner world creates the outer world.

Furthermore, in recent years increasing numbers of people have experienced a spiritual awakening and are experiencing things that cannot be explained within the framework of our current knowledge, i.e. from the perspective of our five senses. The things people are experiencing and the results of this new research tend to indicate that there is a higher power—a universal thought behind everything—a force which we are all part of—a force in the inner world.

Making Choices is a Function of Consciousness

Most people do not think independently of the circumstances surrounding them because they are ignorant about the power that allows them to create their world from the inside out. They allow themselves to be governed by the outer world. The more energy and focus you devote to the outer world, the more you will create the same type of results. Our lives may seem to be controlled by luck and coincidence, but it is always the inner world that creates the outer world. Here is a small excerpt on coincidence from the book *Conversations with God,* by Neale Donald Walsch:

"For nothing happens by accident in God's world, and there is no such thing as coincidence. Nor is the world buffeted by random choice, or something you call fate. If a snowflake is utterly perfect in its design, do you not think the same could be said about something as magnificent as your life?"[14]

French philosopher François-Marie Arouet Voltaire said that luck and coincidence are words that were invented to express the known effects of unknown causes. In our world we see people who appear to have been born under a lucky star. Life is just a game for them and everything seems to fall straight into their lap. If we are unable to see why, we turn to words like luck and coincidence. We are unable to see a logical connection and the only explanation we accept is that it has to be luck or coincidence. We do not see that thoughts are actually behind everything. Invisible thoughts collect in a collective field of consciousness and play a key role in how life develops for different people. This inner world governs the outer world.

If we are not aware of what we are creating, we are at the mercy of whatever the outer world feeds into our subconscious. Our subconscious controls what we feel, and this in turn results in our actions which create the results we see in our lives. Therefore things that appear to be coincidences or luck are simply the result of what you have been thinking—what the outer world has fed to you. The only way to change the results, to obtain a better and more fulfilling, meaningful life is to start off by creating it in your inner world—in your thoughts—in your mind. The more focus, feeling and energy we devote to our inner picture, the faster the outer world will shape itself into whatever we desire.

Everything is energy, including our thoughts, and whatever we devote our energy to will become our reality.

Chapter 4 - Energy

Michelle Belanger, author of *The Psychic Energy Codex - Awakening Your Subtle Senses* expresses energy in the following way: "Energy is a non-physical force that contains the potential for activity."

Kinetic energy is the force that can cause objects to move. Energy stored in a piece of wood will be released when the piece of wood is burnt. Sunlight, electromagnetic pulses, sound waves and radio waves are all different types of energy, and most of these can be measured using conventional technology. For example, an electrocardiogram can pick up the heart's energy field. A mobile phone can pick up the energy transmitted by a satellite and convert it into a voice. A voltmeter can measure electrical voltage/frequencies in practically all types of appliances.

Energy is not just restricted to measurable frequencies. Some frequencies cannot be measured or heard. A dog whistle is one such example. We can measure the sound of a dog whistle, but we cannot hear the sound it produces. On the other hand, dogs can pick up such sounds because their hearing operates at higher frequencies.

According to Belanger there is an ocean of energies, and even though we cannot perceive these with our five senses, they do have an effect on us. For example, she talks about life energy known as qi or chi in China and as prana in Sanskrit (one of the world's oldest languages in the Indo-Aryan branch of languages). Life energy exists inside us, through us and around us. Belanger writes:

"The world that you are familiar with, the physical, material world, is not the only one in which you move and interact. Every day when you get up, shower and go to work, each and every step reverberates through two sides of reality at once. Your physical body walks in the world of matter, but a subtler aspect of you, woven within and throughout your physical body, moves and interacts on a level of pure energy."[15]

Burt Goldman shares Belanger's view that we are constantly surrounded by energy. He has devoted much of his life to research in fields like hypnosis, yoga, psychology, remote viewing, healing, NLP, and meditation. For many years he has been talking about parallel or alternative universes that exist side by side:

"There are energies that surround us, just like radio waves surround us, and these energies float around as particles and waves. These energies all have a particular vibration. We all have a particular vibration—our own, special vibration that we radiate out from ourselves."[16]

Many people agree that we are surrounded by energy and that energy permeates the universe. It is everywhere, even in what we call ghosts, as explained by Lilli.

Lilli on Energy and Ghosts

With the help of the spirit world, I would like to explain how I experience and understand the phenomenon of ghosts. Typical ghosts appear as shapes, something that many people have seen with the naked eye. We have all heard about ladies descending staircases in old English castles, or floating across courtyards like luminous clouds. Like a film that keeps being replayed year after year, these ghosts do not say anything and their style does not change. They do not disturb anyone and they do not intervene in the daily lives of the residents of the places in question. Like imprints, or the negatives of photographs, they exist in a frequency that resonates at a slightly higher rate than that of the physical plane. Sometimes they become hooked into the physical plane and this is why they can be observed.

I do not see such shapes with my physical eyes, but activate my sixth sense at a soul level by allowing myself to receive higher frequencies than those recognized on an everyday level by my physical body. During this shift in consciousness I experience physical changes such as palpitations, a slight feeling of dizziness and denseness, or buzzing in my ears, as though the pressure inside my head is changing. This is followed by the emergence of words and images that are not like thoughts, and they often take me completely by surprise. You could thus easily be forgiven for thinking that this is something created by my own imagination. The challenge is to follow these images and allow them to create sequences, rather like watching a film. However, the film jumps around and keeps stopping, but by cooperating with my subconscious I am usually able to tune into the story, picking up moods such as sorrow, irritation and frustration through my emotional field.

The most important thing is to understand the essence of the story—this is what can hold someone captive between two worlds. I have gradually come to understand on a personal level that people go where they are supposed to go when they die in order to continue their development, but that strong emotions, obsessions or the need to exercise control could have been so intense in their lives that these remain as an echo.

If we consider that everything is energy, even thoughts, then any fluctuations in the latter can cause disturbances in a particular field. For example, imagine that someone was passionate about a particular hobby, like making things on a lathe in their cellar. They spend many happy hours creating different objects. This experience of joy and satisfaction can create an imprint that can be felt after their death by any sensitive people who subsequently live in that place. Or the person might actually be seen. Other instances might be less constructive, such as memories of unredeemed jealousy or revenge. Someone who dies suddenly may also have a strong desire to send a message to the people they have left behind. Everything exists within the same energy field, but my experience of such energy varies. I can experience frustration, anger, sorrow.

A fairly typical example is when the memories incorporated in the original structure of an old house are activated when someone starts to convert it. The person who created and became emotionally involved in the original structure will react when it is changed. "Help, someone is invading my home. I don't recognize it. I've got to stop it!" Or perhaps they are saying: "I know it's no longer mine, but they are doing everything wrong. I've got to help and let them know what to do."

Where do TV programs exist before you press the remote control and the picture appears on the screen? Ninety percent of the paranormal cases I've been involved with are actually sensitive people who are unknowingly activating the invisible realms. They alter the wavelength through their own energetic fields, like pressing the "on" button for a TV that you can't turn off. The program constantly keeps being replayed. It also seems clear to me that the more energy one broadcasts to a disturbed energy field, the stronger the impact will be on our sphere of existence.

How then is it possible that others working in the same field and I can clear or cancel out these energy fields? The most important thing to understand is the story behind the disturbances and to simultaneously tune into the frequency at which any such thoughts existed in their own reality. Through this field I have the opportunity to actually explain the situation to the person concerned and at the same time encourage either him or her to switch their focus. This switch in focus is what changes the energy field and thus hopefully also removes the disturbance involved. Sometimes there are cases of total confusion, where the person who has died is locked into a dream state. They do not understand that they have passed over into a new state called death and that they are trying desperately to make contact with the people who have been connected to their life history.

My guides have explained that when the physical, three-dimensional body ceases to exist, the vibrational field that has held the physical atoms together will change its geometrical pattern and continue spinning at a faster rate. This is invisible on the physical plane, which will always resonate with other physical elements. However, it will never cease to exist. The story will be stored in a frequency band that is unique to that person, and can be accessed by someone with the ability to tune into that frequency.

Chapter 5 - Everything is Energy

Everything does not consist of energy—it is energy. You are energy—your thoughts are energy.

"All thoughts are energy."
- Eckhart Tolle

With the help of industrialist Andrew Carnegie, one of the world's richest men of his time, the author Napoleon Hill spent two decades interviewing hundreds of people who were well-known for their wealth and achievements. Their collective wisdom was collated in a book entitled, *Think & Grow Rich,* published in 1937. In his book Hill also writes about how matter began as an intangible form of energy:

"This Earth, every one of the billions of individual cells of your body, and every atom of matter, began as an intangible form of energy. Desire is thought impulse. Thought impulses are forms of energy."[17]

Everything is combinations of energy. This gives an illusion of form, something solid. Our five senses perceive everything around us as being solid and separate because everything is vibrating at such a high speed that it appears to be solid. David Cameron, author of *A Happy Pocket Full of Money,* has the following to say about the subject of energy:

"Science shows us that everything is made up of energy. It is the building block of all matter. The same energy that composes your flesh is the same one that composes the bricks of your house and the trees outside. It is all the same. It is constantly at flow, changing form all the time. This is a very simple explanation of a rather complex thing."[18]

Everything in the universe consists of the same stuff. It is simply present in different shapes and forms.

"There is a place where all things begin, a place of pure energy that simply is."
- **Gregg Braden**

All objects are constantly vibrating at their own frequency— the book that you are reading now, your sofa, your mobile phone, your car, even your whole self. You are broadcasting frequencies all the time. Your thoughts are cosmic waves that penetrate all time and space.

Our entire body is like a giant beacon. According to the book entitled, *Seth Speaks*, by Jane Roberts, we are like transformers. Jane Roberts was an American author, poet and medium. In December 1963 she started receiving consecutive messages from a personality/energy-being who eventually identified itself as Seth. This marked the start of a long period during which she channeled information from this source.

All the information she received was published in books and became known as *The Seth Material*. One of her most popular books, *Seth Speaks*, has sold millions of copies. The book is all about different levels of consciousness. It explains how every feeling and every thought has its own unique electromagnetic reality:

"You do not realize that you create your larger environment and the physical world as you know it by propelling your thoughts and emotions into matter. Each of you acts as transformers, unconsciously, automatically transforming highly sophisticated electromagnetic units into physical objects. You are in the middle of a matter-concentrated system. Each thought and emotion spontaneously exists as a simple or complex electromagnetic unit, unperceived, incidentally, as yet by your scientists."[19]

According to *Seth Speaks*, three-dimensional objects are created in the same way as the images we see on the TV screen, but with one major difference. If you are not tuned into that particular frequency you will not see the physical objects. We are constantly vibrating and broadcasting at different frequencies. Everything is all about frequencies.

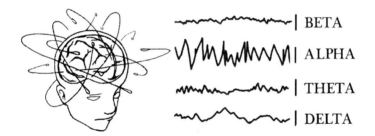

BETA

ALPHA

THETA

DELTA

Everything has its own special frequency, including our brain waves.

José Silva conducted research into mind waves for 40 years. He divided our brain waves into beta, alpha, theta and delta waves—all operating at different frequencies. In our waking state our brain waves are operating at beta level and we are broadcasting at a frequency of between 14 and 21 cycles per second. When we go to bed at night we become sleepy and our brain activity starts to quieten down. We then switch over to the alpha state with a frequency of approximately 7 to 14 cycles/second. At this level José Silva discovered that it was possible to program the subconscious. There is a division between the conscious and the subconscious—between the physical and the spiritual—between the outer world and the inner world.

In *Seth Speaks*, Jane Roberts (Seth) also writes about this state, saying that it is like a threshold between the physically-oriented parts of the personality and the inner self.

"The alpha state is a threshold, a preliminary state between the physically oriented portions of the personality and the inner self."

Seth also says that energy is available to be used as we so wish. It is the fountainhead or pool in which reservoirs of energy are held in reserve, pulled between the inner and outer selves. It is thus ideally sited for manipulating the physical organism. Your intent before you enter the alpha state largely predetermines the kind of experience you will have, by automatically focusing your attention into the areas concerned.

The alpha state is also the state in which we dip in and out of when driving a car. Have you ever driven a long way and allowed your thoughts to wander? You "disappear" into the world of thoughts, but part of you is still focused on the traffic. You suddenly arrive at your destination and are unable to remember how you got there. It is as though you failed to register the route along which you drove. The left half of your brain was keeping an eye on the road and the traffic, while the creative right side of your brain was daydreaming. You were dipping into the alpha state. This state is the one accessed during meditation. If you move even deeper you enter the theta state, oscillating at four to seven cycles/second, and finally the delta state, oscillating at one to four cycles/second.

We all pass through these states every night. When we are awake we are in the beta state. When we go to bed we slowly enter the alpha state, followed by the theta and delta states. All levels oscillate at their own frequency. So does everything else. Everything has its own frequency—just like our brain waves. DNA has its own frequency. Your words have their own frequency. Every particle of energy has its own frequency. Everything in the universe is vibrating, nothing is at rest. We are living in an ocean of energy and movement. When you recognize these vibrations you call them feelings. When you feel unwell you can change your feelings by thinking good thoughts and you will thus alter your vibrations and your frequency. When you pick up bad vibes from someone else you realize that they must be having disturbing thoughts. You must not allow their negative vibrations to affect your way of thinking. Your thoughts are vibrations that you broadcast to the universe. When you concentrate, these vibrations are stronger.

Your thoughts are cosmic waves of energy (vibrations) that penetrate all time and space. Universal laws, such as the law of vibration, govern everything. This is the law that enables the law of attraction to work. The law of attraction is actually secondary to the law of vibration.

Since everything vibrates, including our bodies, our thoughts and our cells, we are more like an electric light being than a being of flesh and blood. German professor and physicist Fritz-Albert Popp demonstrated this in his research on biophotons (small particles of light). These particles of light, which have no mass, convey information within and between the cells. His work shows that the DNA in living cells stores and releases photons that create "biophoton emission." We transmit and receive these particles. We are radiating all the time from our DNA.[20]

We are like beacons, but we cannot see what we are broadcasting. Your frequency is different to the frequency of other things in the universe. That is why you appear to be separate from everything you can see around you— people, animals, plants and trees, etc. But it is possible to switch frequency. This works in exactly the same way as a radio or TV station. If you want to listen to a different radio program or watch a different TV program you have to switch to another channel. By switching channels you set your radio/TV set at a different frequency which receives different signals. In a radio context we are talking about FM channels. FM stands for frequency modulation. We change/modulate the frequency in order to hear a different radio program.

The same applies to people—we transmit and receive signals at different frequencies. Our reality/dimension operates at one type of frequency, but some people are able to switch between different frequencies and are thus able to enter other dimensions, other realities. Some people can talk to and see the dead. Others can communicate with animals. Yet others say that they can see and communicate with extraterrestrial beings that operate at other frequencies and are thus invisible in our three-dimensional world. Most of us are unable to switch frequency and cannot understand that this is possible either. This means that many people who possess such abilities are laughed at or written off as crazy or one step away from the nut house. They are not taken seriously. They are told that they are just imagining things, that their brains are playing tricks on them.

Although something cannot be seen, this does not necessarily mean that it does not exist. You cannot see bacteria with the naked eye, but your skin is crawling with them. Before the invention of the microscope, no one would have believed you if you told them small "creatures" were crawling around on our skin. They would have labeled you totally mad. Today we know that our skin is covered with bacteria. The skin, which is the body's largest organ, is like a gigantic zoo. In a study conducted in 2007 by the NYU School of Medicine, scientists found proof of the existence of 182 different species of bacteria in skin samples. If you had told people this before the invention of the microscope they would have locked you up and branded you as being completely mad.

There is much more to this world than can be seen with the naked eye. It is therefore important to have an open mind. Nothing sensible can enter a closed mind. An old Chinese proverb goes like this: "A closed mind is like a closed book, just a block of wood."

In our world there are many who do not believe there are people who can see or talk to the dead or who can see/experience other dimensions. They deny any such possibilities. Everything must be proved and we should be able to see it with our own eyes. Only then will we believe it, but we do not need to see in order to believe. Believing is seeing. He who believes will see. He who opens his mind will increase his awareness and see the bigger picture behind the nature of reality. Even though something cannot be proved, this does not constitute proof that it does not exist. The absence of evidence is not evidence of absence.

In the film *Contact*, starring Jodie Foster and Matthew McConaughey, Foster plays an astronomer named Dr. Eleanor Arroway who does not believe in a higher power. McConaughey plays a priest, Palmer Joss, who believes in God. Arroway wants proof to show that things exist. She cannot believe in something that she cannot see or verify using scientific instruments. In the film Joss asks Arroway if she loved her father, to which she replies that she did. He then says, "Prove it." Dr. Arroway looks surprised and has trouble finding an answer. Even though something cannot be proved, this does not constitute proof that it does not exist. History has repeatedly shown us that the masses and so-called scholars have been wrong. Established truths have had to yield to new truths.

We used to believe that the Earth was flat. Everyone believed that you would fall off it when you reached the end of the world. We subsequently thought that the Earth was at the center of the universe, but Copernicus and Galileo showed that the world was wrong. Galileo Galilei supported the work of Copernicus who claimed that the Earth was not in the center of the universe. When in 1633 he stated that the sun was at the center and that our Earth orbited the sun and not the other way round, he was put on trial. He was 70 years old and had been accused of heresy. He was convicted, but escaped having to go to prison because of his age, and was instead sentenced to house arrest at his home in Arcetri, Florence for the rest of his life. He died in 1642. He opposed the Roman Catholic Church, scholars and the masses, and was convicted for his views, but today he is hailed as the father of astronomy. Galileo was right and the others were wrong.

Another historical case showing that the masses and the scholars were wrong involves the discovery of radio waves. Guglielmo Marconi was an Italian inventor who showed the world that radio communication was possible. But no one believed him. No one thought that it was possible to transmit signals through the air without wires or cables. His colleagues and other scientists thought that he should be institutionalized.

On June 2, 1896, Marconi applied for a British wireless telegraphy patent. Shortly afterwards he also applied for and was granted a US patent. He knew that is was possible to transmit wireless signals through the air, even though all the experts in the world said that this was impossible.

Marconi was granted the honor of inventing the radio, but we feel it is worth mentioning that Nicola Tesla was the first one to patent the wireless transmission of radio signals. He demanded that Marconi's patent should be invalidated since he claimed that Marconi had used his technology. Several months after his death in 1943, Tesla was finally recognized as the father of radio.

Stories such as these show the advantage to keeping an open mind. A closed mind is a narrow mind and serves no useful purpose. An established truth is only valid until a newer version of the truth is presented and accepted, and it is often those brave souls who dare to oppose the masses who enable the world to progress. They operate outside the accepted frameworks for what is regarded as being the truth. People like Galileo and Marconi were ridiculed, but today they are celebrated for their work. They helped to increase the consciousness of humanity. We have continued to develop because of people like them.

Even though everything around us appears to be separate from us, we are not separate. You are not separate. You live in an ocean of energy. We all do. Everything is moving, everything is vibrating.

"We live in an ocean of motion."
-Bob Proctor

We are all connected at this energy level, the lowest level. A level that Professor John Hagelin calls the unified field.

Chapter 6 - The Unified Field

The nature of reality has been subjected to scientific scrutiny for hundreds of years, with deeper analysis being undertaken during the last 70 to 80 years. Science has delved into the world of the atom and sub-atomic particles and have discovered that the universe is structured in layers of creation, with a basic unit existing at the lowest level.

John Hagelin is a Professor of Physics and the Director of the Institute of Science, Technology and Public Policy at the Maharishi University of Management, as well as the President of the David Lynch Foundation for Consciousness-Based Education and World Peace. He calls this lowest level the unified field:

"Our universe is like a thought wave, an invisible state or quantum wave spread over time and space. Not a wave of matter. But wave in what? In a universal ocean—an ocean of pure potentiality—a unified field—a superstring field of which we are all made." [22]

At this level we are all united. We are all linked together and we are part of the universal consciousness—a universal mind. Everything is one. Everything is the same. Everything is part of the Source.

This is why we should not judge others, because we are all part of the Source—we are connected. To judge others is to judge oneself.

"Observation is power. Judgement is weakness. "
- **Leland Val Vandewall**

At the lowest level quantum physics talks about a universal consciousness—an intelligence. As does Mellen-Thomas Benedict, who died in 1982 after suffering for several months with incurable and inoperable cancer. When he "died" he was "gone" for one and a half hours. This near-death experience changed his life completely. When he was on the other side and talking with the light, he understood the whole of creation. He also refers to the "void" which he experienced. This void was believed by scientists to exist in both space and in each individual atom. However, the empty space between the core of an atom and its electrons is not empty. It is pure energy. Mellen-Thomas Benedict explains:

"It took me many years after I returned from my near-death experience to assimilate any words at all for the void experience. I can tell you this now; the void is less than nothing, yet more than everything that is! The void is absolute zero; chaos forming all possibilities. It is absolute consciousness; much more than even universal intelligence.

"The void is the vacuum or nothingness between all physical manifestations—the space between atoms and their components. Modern science has begun to study this space between everything. They call it *zero-point*. Whenever they try to measure it, their instruments go off the scale, or to infinity, so to speak. They have no way, as of yet, to measure infinity accurately. There is more of the zero space in your own body and the universe than anything else! What mystics call the void is not a void. It is so full of energy, a different kind of energy that has created everything that we are. Everything since the Big Bang is vibration, from the first word, which is the first vibration. The Biblical "I am" really has a question mark after it: "I am? What am I?"

"So creation is God exploring God's Self through every way imaginable, in an ongoing, infinite exploration through every one of us. During my near-death experience I began to see that everything that is, is the Self, literally, your Self, my Self. Everything is the great Self. That is why God knows even when a leaf falls. That is possible because wherever you are is the center of the universe. Wherever any atom is, that is the center of the universe. There is God in that, and God in the void."[21]

Mellen-Thomas Benedict experienced the void in his near-death experience 28 years ago, and several scientists have subsequently discovered that he might actually have been right: the void is not a void. It is energy, everything is energy, and this energy surfs on a wave of consciousness, a sort of information field that Mellen-Thomas Benedict calls the absolute consciousness of which we are all part.

Our analytical brains seek logical explanations when we are presented with information similar to that discussed by Mellen-Thomas Benedict. In our waking state we regard ourselves as being separate from each other; separate from animals, plants and nature. Everything is separate. We look like solid "entities." All five of our senses tell us that we are separate and that "I" am the "I" that is separate from "you." I have my own life and you have yours. We have nothing to do with each other, but what if we have? What if we are all one, linked together on this lowest level—the unified field?

We and the whole universe are all made of the same substance. When we break everything down we see that our bodies are made of pure energy. This energy appears to be "surfing" on an ocean of universal consciousness.

In the film *What the Bleep Do We Know?* scientists like Dr. Hameroff and Dr. Wolf talk about the universe being "an ocean of energy" and that we are all part of this. We are drops in this large universal ocean and we are thus all connected. They talk about a universal consciousness that binds all life together. Our own individual consciousnesses are all part of this universal consciousness. Stuart Hameroff MD, the Director of the Center for Consciousness Studies, explains:

"If we go down the scale in the emptiness, eventually we come to a level, 'the fundamental level' of space-time geometry. Here we find information—a pattern called 'the Planck scale' which has been there since the Big Bang."[22]

Fred Alan Wolf, PhD, a theoretical physicist who has been researching subjects such as quantum physics, consciousness and the relationship between them, talks about this level in the following way:

"There is no empty space. When we go down—down—down—there are vibrations—stuff popping—invisible connections." [22]

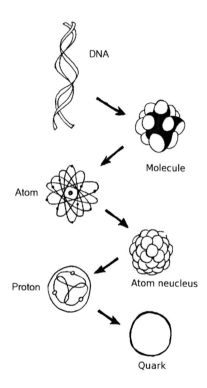

Scientists know that when they move down the scale from cells to molecules to atoms to atomic nuclei and to subatomic particles they will find leptons, bosons and quarks. These vibrate at extremely high speeds and constitute the ocean of energy in which we exist. Our thoughts travel in this ocean of energy, creating waves and they make a difference. Every day when you are thinking, your thoughts create waves in the universal ocean. Your thoughts produce an effect—they mean something.

Your thoughts create waves and affect people on this planet. In *The Master Key System*, published in 1912, Charles F. Haanel discusses this invisible level as follows:

"In the atmosphere we find heat, light and energy. Each realm becomes finer and more spiritual as we pass from the visible to the invisible, from the coarse to the fine, from the low potentiality to high potentiality. When we reach the invisible we find energy in its purest and most volatile state."[9]

Haanel wrote this 100 years ago, and it would appear that he was right. We are discovering that energy exists in incredibly small units. Quantum physics states that these energy units, such as quarks and leptons, "surf" on an ocean of pure potential, an ocean of pure consciousness, a sort of universal consciousness. This field of consciousness—of information—has also been called the *Zero Point Field*, as elaborated on by John Assaraf in his book entitled, *The Answer*. He refers to quantum physicists who are conducting research on staggeringly small scales, scales so infinitesimally small that they are almost beyond our comprehension. Moving from cells to molecules, to atoms, to sub-atomic particles such as electrons and protons and then to quarks, bosons, leptons, etc., they are discovering a power that even seems to be present at a temperature of absolute zero, at which all forms of energy disappear. It has thus been called the Zero Point Field. Beneath this level of energy there is an even more fundamental level. What we find at this level is actually no longer energy or even a vacuum. It can best be described as a field of information. This undifferentiated ocean from which energy arises appears to be an ocean of pure consciousness. Assaraf says: "Everything in the physical world is made out of atoms. Atoms are made out of energy. And energy is made out of consciousness."[23]

The universe is made of consciousness. Matter and energy are just two of the forms adopted by consciousness. This has been confirmed by many who are researching the Zero Point Field, including Lynne McTaggert who wrote *The Field* in 2003.

Her book explains that everything is linked by the Zero Point Field (ZPF), an ocean of energy that unites mind and matter, classical science and quantum physics, science and religion. She describes the Zero Point Field as being like a spider's web of energy-exchange, the exchange of energy between sub-atomic particles. It is like a dance, with energy being sent back and forth. Our electrons and sub-atomic particles dance a tango with the electrons and sub-atomic particles in the Zero Point Field. We transmit and receive waves of information, like a hologram of information containing everything that has ever existed. According to Bob Proctor our consciousness affects our subconscious that in turn affects our feelings. These feelings permeate each and every one of our cells that vibrate out what we are feeling. It could consequently be said that our cells are communicating with an intelligent energy field via vibrations and that this field is trying to provide us with whatever we are vibrating out.

"Consciousness creates reality. Consciousness is real. Consciousness obeys the laws of physics."
- **Candace Pert PhD, brain scientist**

Scientist Nassim Haramein shares the same views, i.e. that the empty space surrounding us is jam-packed with energy, and that all atoms are mini black holes.

Mini Black Holes
In 2009 Nassin Haramein received an award for his work showing that all atoms are mini black holes. Instead of searching for the smallest particles in existence (the building blocks of the universe) he says that we should be looking at the principles governing the division of space.

Nassim Haramein was born in Geneva, Switzerland, in 1962. He developed the basis for a unified hyperdimensional theory about matter and energy which he called the Holofractographic Universe. Haramein has spent most of his life exploring the basic geometry of space. His studies have included a number of different fields, ranging from theoretical physics, cosmology, quantum mechanics, biology and chemistry to anthropology and ancient civilizations. By combining this knowledge with keen observation of the behavior of the natural world, he discovered a special geometric matrix which he believes underlies all creation, and the basis for his unified field theory started to take shape.

Haramein says that we are living in an expanding universe, an infinitely large universe, but that no expansion can take place without contraction. Therefore we must also be living in an infinitely small universe because something must be contracting. He uses a balloon as an example to illustrate his point. When you blow up a balloon the air comes from your lungs. As the balloon gradually expands your lungs contract. The air leaves your lungs and goes into the balloon. When something expands, something has to contract. This also applies to our universe. When the universe expands, something has to contract. He continues by asking the following question: "But how do we fit infinity into a finite space?" The answer, he says, is a fractal.

Haramein has discovered a whole new paradigm in physics based on finding the fundamental principles that apply to the division of space. His theory is based on the vacuum being packed with an energy density—the void in the universe—with matter being created in geometric fractals. [119]

A vacuum packed with energy is exactly what Mellen-Thomas Benedict described after his near-death experience in 1982. After almost 20 years of atomic research, Nassim Haramein has arrived at the same conclusion. He has devoted himself tirelessly to thoroughly researching the unified field. In 2009, 27 years after Mellen-Thomas Benedict explained that the vacuum in atoms consists of pure energy, Nassim Haramein received an award from the University of Liege, Belgium at the 9th International Conference on Computing Anticipatory Systems (CASYS '09) for his research on the Schwarzschild Proton. He won the prestigious Best Paper Award in the fields of Physics, Quantum Mechanics, Relativity Theory, Field Theory, and Gravitation. His research shows that infinite and finite systems are completely complementary. All atomic nuclei are really mini black holes, jam-packed with energy.

What does this all mean? Haramein says that actually all matter has infinity at its center and that the definition of an infinite density is a black hole. This means that every single cell, atom and proton, etc. is a mini black hole. We wondered what the Council of Elders would have to say about Nassim Haramein and mini black holes.

Camillo: The scientist, Nassim Haramein, explains that all cells, atoms and protons are mini black holes. Would the Council say something about whether or not this is correct, and if it is, what does it mean?

The Council of Elders via Lilli: Mini black holes are a transformation from one state to another. You are pulled into a black hole and come out into something new. Cells have an inherent ability to transform themselves into new states.
Channeled by Lilli Bendriss, on July 29, 2010 - from the energy-beings the Council of Elders

This is exactly the type of transformation that Mellen-Thomas Benedict was talking about after his near-death experience in 1982. He says: "Do you know what is on the other side of a black hole? We are; our galaxy, which has been reprocessed from another universe."[21]

Whatever contracts into a black hole comes out on the other side as a new Big Bang. Benedict explains that he was taken on a journey where he was shown infinite number of Big Bangs. Nassim Harmein does not talk about black holes as places where transformation takes place as Benedict does, but he does say that all black holes both contract and radiate. All matter has a radiated side and a contracted side. These two sides of the same coin are connected by what Haramein calls the Event Horizon or rim of the black hole and there is an energy exchange, or a "feedback" loop, between the radiated and contracted sides. Einstein said that gravity is the result of space-time curving. Haramein says that yes, it curves, but that is not the whole story. It also spins—it creates spin. He says that everything is spinning. But what makes everything in the universe spin? Haramein shows that the infinite density at the center of everything is spinning—every atom, every particle, every planet, every galaxy provides the necessary torque to keep everything spinning as it has for billions of years.

All matter is spun into creation in the form of a double torus shape (often called a doughnut) with a black hole or infinite density in the center, creating a feedback loop with the infinite energy field. Torus is a mathematical term for a specific three-dimensional body that looks like a doughnut. When you have massive energy or information in a feedback loop with itself, you have the definition of consciousness—a conscious energy field. Humans are made of the same stuff as everything else in the universe. If we look at the human body and go down the scale we find cells, molecules, atoms, sub-atomic particles and pure energy. The whole universe is made up of energy and at this level, everything is vibrating. Hence we are all made of this energy and these energy packets that are "surfing on this sea of universal consciousness," all connected and living in a "thought universe." The intangible world affects the tangible world. The spiritual world affects the physical world. The power is not outside us, it is inside each and every one of us, but even so we wage war and kill each other in a meaningless battle for more power.

The perception of power as external brings only pain, violence and destruction. This is how we have evolved until now.

"Our deeper understanding leads us to another kind of power, a power that loves and honors life in every form that it appears, a power that does not judge what it encounters, a power that perceives meaningfulness and purpose in the smallest details upon the Earth."
- **Gary Sukav**

Take a look at nature and learn from Mother Earth. In the forest you will find all sorts of trees, plants and flowers, and they are living there in harmony. They are growing and living side by side in peace and harmony. Why don't people do the same?

"Deep within our core we are all united."
- **Professor John Hagelin**

Regardless of the color of our skin, our religion, our cultural background, our personality, our schooling and our upbringing, we are all connected in our inner core through the universal consciousness. We are beautiful, spiritual beings with a physical expression, and we all have access to infinite power via the unified field.

"We have unlimited potential. We are souls."
- **Dr. Michael Beckwith**

Chapter 7 - The Soul

I, Camillo, grew up thinking that all we have is our body. That's it. The body is me and I am the body. Now I believe we are much more than our bodies. So who are we really? Have you ever considered that you are more than just a human being on this planet? That you are soul—that you don't have a soul, but that you are a soul.

"You don't have a soul. You are a Soul. You have a body."
- C.S. Lewis

"You are a soul and the soul is constantly searching for its consciousness about its unity with the Source. The more we become conscious about our unity with the supreme Source, the more this will be reflected in the results we achieve."
- Bob Proctor

John Holland is an internationally-renowned psychic medium, spiritual teacher and author. His books include *Power of the Soul* and he has participated in the film Infinity. "We are souls with infinite potential," he says. In his book he refers to one of his affirmations that will help us to realize that we are souls.

"I am soul. I have unlimited potential. I now step into my power and appreciate all of me. The Divine Source flows in me through me and from me and I can achieve anything I want. I now know myself as I really am. I own my power. I am power."[24]

His affirmations take us to a place where an inherent understanding of who we are and what we are can occur. We are spiritual beings in a physical body, and our strength is the strength of the soul.

Oscar Wilde once said: "Ordinary riches can be stolen, real riches cannot. In your soul are infinitely precious things that cannot be taken from you."

When we die we cannot take money, property or any of our material possessions with us. But if there is something after death, what can we take with us? Can we bring with us all the feelings we have experienced throughout our lives? Is everything that the soul experiences in a human body stored so that we can take it with us on our journey after death? Is this how the Source acquires experience of feelings on the physical plane? What does the Council of Elders have to say on the subject? We asked them:

Camillo: We believe that we are souls that have physical experiences, that we are part of the Creator's consciousness and that we are here in order to develop and grow so that we can continue on our path back to the Source. What does the Council have to say about this?

The Council of Elders via Lilli: This can be summed up as follows: the Creator has a symbiotic relationship with each soul that takes on a physical garb and allows its physical identity to become the overriding experience of I am.

Throughout eternity and through the resonance of physical experience patterns are created that identify people by virtue of their uniqueness. Like a fractal, where each minute part is a perfect image of the whole, new thoughts or deeds can create new patterns which in turn change the whole. People are on Earth to pursue their abilities and incorporate their personal experiences into the Creator's hologram. This occurs, regardless of whether or not the person concerned is consciously aware of it.
Channeled by Lilli Bendriss, on July 29, 2010 - from the energy-beings the Council of Elders

Mellen-Thomas Benedict entertains no doubts about this matter. We are souls that have a physical experience. In his near-death experience he talks about seeing an angel when he cried out for help after having "died." The angel appeared, and he understood it to be his higher self. He was taken to a rainbow-shimmering light through a light beam. Part of the "beam" was going to the light and part of it was going from the light.

As he was ascending towards the light he realized that the ascending "beam" consisted of people who had just died. Their souls were ascending towards the light. On the other side of the same light, in "the beam" descending in the other direction, he saw all the souls that were ready for yet another life and were descending to Earth to be reborn. Benedict was then taken on a journey away from the planet to the stream of all life. He describes this as follows:

"I saw the Earth fly away. The solar system, in all its splendor, whizzed by and disappeared. At faster than light speed, I flew through the center of the galaxy, absorbing more knowledge as I went. I learned that this galaxy, and the entire Universe, is bursting with many different varieties of life. I saw many worlds." [21]

He was taken to creation before the Big Bang and he says that there are an infinite number of Big Bangs. He asked the light questions about all sorts of things and received answers. He acquired a huge amount of knowledge about everything on the other side. The American doctor, author, lecturer and spiritual guru Deepak Chopra has called him, "The dictionary of life after death."

After one and a half hours in the light, he returned miraculously to his body in a state of complete remission from his illness. There were absolutely no signs of cancer in his body.

He became the most-studied near-death case in the world. A prominent investigator of near-death experiences, PMH Atwater, refers to the Mellen-Thomas Benedict case as the only case she has come across (and she has talked to or interviewed over 3,000 near-death survivors) where someone has consciously changed the episode scenario of what is actually happening. His story about life after death is amazing.

Since his near-death experience Benedict has retained direct contact with the universal intelligence and he can return directly to the light just by using the force of his will. He is a bridge between science and the spiritual. He has been involved in research programs on near-death experiences, and he has developed new technology for health and well-being.

"This body that you are in, has been alive forever. It comes from an unending stream of life, going back to the Big Bang and beyond." [21]

Scientists who have been researching multidimensional experiences share Benedict's views. We are souls that have a physical experience. Alice Bryant and Linda Seebachen are a mother/daughter team who have interviewed and investigated many people with multidimensional experiences. They have the following to say about the soul:

"Our physical body is our earth-ship and the vessel in which our Soul visits Earth. Our earth-ship is made up of the same elements as the planet. This ship is biological and all steering and controls are connected to our consciousness via our nervous system.

We must find a way to interface between the vessel (physical body), the pilot (the ego) and the higher dimensional forces that can communicate across all frequencies (the Soul). When this interface has been completed, the Soul can inhabit the earth-vessel and pilot its return home.

In order for this journey to be successful, our Soul must totally embed itself in and integrate with our physical earth-ship. First the pilot (our ego) will have to completely surrender all "control" to our Soul because our limited third-dimensional consciousness is incapable of perceiving the myriad of messages that are necessary to complete our journey.

All reality below the fifth dimension is programmed for separation, limitation and polarity. The only way to consciously pilot our vessel into the fifth dimensions is to allow our Soul to enter into and captain our vessel."[25]

According to Alice Bryant and Linda Seebachen, the soul must take over the ego, but how?

By looking inwards.

By realizing that the answers we are searching for in order to be happy are not outside ourselves, but inside.

When we reach the core of who we are, our ego will relax its hold and we will see that the ego-world in which we live is not the answer to the future evolution of mankind.

We must find our way back to our soul, but it has become completely overshadowed by our ego. The ego has its own function, but when the ego becomes all that is, it has gone too far.

Chapter 8 - The Ego

Where does our ego come from? Why does it stand in the way of the soul? What should we do about it? The ego is a product of our interaction with the external environment— the world outside ourselves. We have no "ego" when we are born, no separate feeling of "me." This is created by our surroundings.

In her book, *Light Emerging*, Barbara Ann Brennan describes how the ego is formed:

"When we are born, we are still very connected to great spiritual wisdom and power through our core. This connection to our core and therefore to spiritual wisdom and power gives the feeling of complete safety and wonder. During the maturation process, this connection slowly fades. It is replaced by parental voices intended to protect us and make us safe. They speak of right and wrong, of good and bad, how to make decisions, and how to act or react in any given situation.

"As the connection to the core fades, our child psyche tries desperately to replace the original innate wisdom with a functioning ego. Unfortunately, the overlay or internalized parental voices can never really do the job. Instead, what is produced is a mask self. With this mask self we attempt to express who we are in a positive way that is also acceptable to a world that we are afraid will reject us."[26]

We do what we can to fit in based on what we think the world believes is right and good. Why? In order to be accepted and feel safe. The ego therefore grows stronger and does everything in its power to hold onto the mask. It takes over control of the vessel, of the physical body, and the soul is relegated to the back seat.

If there is a higher power, a creator, why are we designed to develop an ego that seems to stand in the way of our spiritual development? This seems to be counter-productive. What actually is the function of the ego? A few years ago I, Camillo, came across a very interesting book by George Green entitled, *The Handbook for the New Paradigm*. The book describes the function of the ego. He describes the ego like a mask in a play, very similar to that outlined by Barbara Ann Brennan. Green is a former banker (a Registered Financial Principal with the NASD—the National Association of Securities Dealers), a broker and a property developer. He has also worked for the American military, where according to his own account, he participated in work that involved contact with extraterrestrial beings who instructed him to publish *The Handbook for the New Paradigm*. The content of this book is their work. It was agreed that this information should be published in order to awaken us earthlings.

The book explains that the ego is necessary so that we can be aware of manifested experiences. Talking about the role of the ego in our lives, it says:

"If there is no ego, there will be no awareness of the manifested experience! The ego is your tape recorder. It is the observer of your thoughts, wants, needs and desires. It takes these thoughts in a type of robotic focused format, and this allows them to manifest into circumstances and situations that create your experience. It literally filters your thoughts, feelings and desires and causes them to coalesce into manifested experience.

"It is a process, not an entity, over which you have complete control if you can take charge of thoughts, feelings and desires and actively direct them toward what you want to experience.

"The process of how this works involves the law of attraction. Once an idea is formed with the positive understanding that it is possible, then the ego holds this picture and completes the process through positive/negative polarity energy.

"Since instant manifestation of ideas on this planet at the moment is very difficult, the ego incorporates the process within your supporting idea of time. If you are unable to remain focused on your desire of a certain experience, then often times you deny yourself that desired experience."[27]

These are exciting ideas that we wanted to discuss with the Council of Elders.

Camillo: Is *The Handbook for the New Paradigm* correct when it talks about the function of the ego?

The Council of Elders via Lilli: It has been written eloquently and brilliantly.

Camillo: So it is correct when it explains the ego to be a mask in this life that is being acted out in a play?

The Council of Elders via Lilli: A necessary mask for ensuring that the play can be acted out at all. However, it is not only on Earth that the play can be experienced in this way. These are codes that repeat themselves in an upwardly transforming consciousness system so that, for example, when someone dies they retain their ego during their next stage of development and learning in the astral world. There they become involved in their new existence and are able to continue acting in the play. However, they acquire a greater insight and understanding about the deeper psychological aspects of the play.

Actors on the stage of life are often unaware of being involved in the play. As the soul gradually merges more beneath the mask, people will acquire an increasingly better understanding of their role in the play and will become aware that they are creating the play while simultaneously acting in it, and both themselves and their fellow actors will subject their experiences to psychoanalysis.

The internal actors evaluate their roles, and the difference between the higher and physical planes of consciousness is that the actors on the higher planes evaluate themselves and understand what they have learned, but they also jump into and evaluate the opposing roles through themselves, while those playing the opposing roles are simultaneously doing the same. Let us call this the astral desire plane, where the ego needs more learning and more understanding because the desire to continue acting in the play still exists after one dies. These are souls that, on the higher consciousness potential, can choose to experience themselves infinitely through the ego, until their desire has burnt out their need to experience themselves in this way. Their ability to love will constantly be scaled up and because this love is manifested so strongly through the feeling body they will also start to judge themselves in a different way. They also evaluate, observe and experience through a form of emotion, but far greater clarity is achieved when one understands the play through the resonance of love.

Then comes the point when the soul lets go of the play and understands the intricate aspects of the world of illusion and can be the observer that lovingly allows its fellow players to continue if they so wish. They move on in a world that is more static, based on a recognition of happiness, a sense of belonging, being in an ocean of ecstatic experience where cleansing takes place and the soul becomes increasingly more fluid and finally unites in an awareness and understanding of the fact that everything it has experienced has been valuable and important. The soul will no longer be judgmental or have the need to judge, because it is simply all that is in a unique understanding of the fact that things simply are—I am and you are, everything is. The human brain finds it hard to understand this expression because it has no experience of being able to remember itself in that state and only a few people have been allowed to travel and return with the code which in turn helps to activate more high-frequency empirical models through the essence of love.

Channeled by Lilli Bendriss, on July 29, 2010 - from the energy-beings the Council of Elders

How does this relate to being part of the whole, of the Source and the fact that we are all connected? The ego creates separation and is designed to observe your thoughts, needs and desires—in other words something individual. The explanation could be that the "tape recorder" referred to by Green functions like a sort of instrument to provide the feeling of you as an individual instead of you as the universe. You know what you have done in your life, what you have experienced, because you did it. If the Source wants to express itself in this play, but at the same time allows free will to be part of the game, the Source cannot create "clones" of itself, the self that knows that it is the Source.

You are the Source that experiences yourself. You have an awareness of being a person because you are an expression of the Source's creativity, but you are wearing a mask in the form of your ego. You are unique. The Source has only created one of you with your unique thoughts and feelings, because this is the universe's way of expressing a particular character. The Source expresses itself through the unique you as a conscious being. You have a unique role in the play. No two roles/masks are the same and each and every one of us therefore has a unique role to play in the play of life.

You perceive your life here on Earth in a particular way and you feel that you are the one doing this. But it is the Source that does it. You are the Source that is pretending that you are not. This is the ego's function—creating a feeling of individual expression for the purpose of experiencing as much as possible through its role.

What you experience is unique to you. What your parents, children or siblings experience is unique to them, but it is also just the Source that is expressing itself through them. Thus, through all people, the universe or the Source experience a huge range of unique "entities" which are all the Source.

All people are a "unique you" with their own unique thoughts, feelings and desires—for better or worse. This is how the Source experiences itself and learns about itself. The Source does this through all of us. We are the Source. It is not an external unity that is outside us. You are the Source. I am the Source. We are all the Source.

"We are a way for the Cosmos to know itself."
- **Carl Sagan**

Everything is staged by the Source and is governed by various universal laws that are as real as the law of gravitation. This is like a game for which the omniscient Source has designed the rules and we have the free will to operate within the framework of these rules. This provides the game with an unknown dimension.

Another great book which further enhanced my understanding (Camillo) of the game we all are playing is entitled *Ra - The Law of One*. It explains how this game has been designed to ensure a state of perfect balance between the known and the unknown.

The higher self is like the map in which the destination is known and the roads are very well defined. These roads are designed by intelligent infinity working through intelligent energy. However, the higher self can only program the lessons and certain predisposing limitations, if it wishes. The remainder is completely the free choice of each entity. There is the perfect balance between the known and the unknown. [28]

The Law of One is a five-volume book that was channeled between 1981 and 1984 from an energy being calling itself Ra. The material was channeled and written down by Carla Rueckert, Don Elkins and Jim McCarty.

Ra's description of life on Earth, which is compared to a map on which the destination and paths are well known, provides an interesting angle on the subject. After searching for answers for many years, this angle is one that I, Camillo, have also considered as a model for explaining how life evolves. I was keen to hear what the Council of Elders would have to say about my interpretation of the subject.

Camillo: I have an idea about life here on Earth that I would like the Council to comment on. I believe that life can be compared to a map where the terrain is known before we are born, as also mentioned by Ra in the *Law of One* books. The Source knows every rock, every mountain and every path on this map, and thus we also know them because we are the Source. There is a starting point and a destination on this map. The starting point is our birth. However, before the soul incarnates, it chooses a path leading towards the destination that it wishes to follow, and this is based on unresolved karma and the lessons it wishes to experience and explore in this life. It then incarnates on Earth in a human body.

Due to free will all previous memories are deleted about who we are and what we are supposed to be doing here. We can start to follow the path leading towards our destination. There are an infinite number of paths, all leading towards the same destination. Some of these are harder and involve greater challenges than others. Some of them run through rugged terrain with tall mountains and sinister marshy landscapes, while others are wide paths that are easy to follow with just the odd bump here and there.

All these paths lead towards our destination, which is death. When we die we take with us what we have experienced and explored in the form of all our feelings as they evolve. It is therefore important to live in the now and to be aware of all the feelings being played out. It is the memories of these that we take with us when we die. They enrich the Source. Thus when seen from the point of view of the soul, a life that might to all appearances be tough, involving poverty and misery, could actually result in as much or more gained experience as an affluent life lived out in safe surroundings.

Because we have free will, we can opt to change our path en route as we head towards our destination. There are an infinite number of places on the map where these paths cross and where we can choose a different path to the one we actually started out on. This is free will in action. In addition, we all have the power of thought since we are thinking beings in a thinking world, this world of illusion, and we can therefore influence how the path we have selected will continue running towards our destination. What does the Council have to say about these views concerning life on Earth?

The Council of Elders via Lilli: This is very much like we would have expressed it ourselves.
Channeled by Lilli Bendriss, on August 11, 2010

As mentioned earlier, life can also be compared to a film or a play. Before we come here, the Source has divided itself up and selected various roles on the stage of life. The stage corresponds to the map that is known with its different paths. It is like a partly-prepared script, but the actors (humans) have free will to control the direction of the play. The roles have been allocated, but not the lines and the plot. In this way, and because they have free will, all the actors contribute towards diversity and a colorful performance, for better or worse. They can guide the play in any direction. The play is shaped according to our individual and collective consciousness, according to what we are thinking. Is this how free will works? We were keen to hear what the Council of Elders would have to say about this.

Camillo: What is the function of free will?

The Council of Elders via Lilli: Without free will everything would be mechanical and controlled and the actual plan would have no purpose. Free will is God in process with himself/herself, expressed through whoever takes on the role of being God on Earth, whoever integrates God into themselves for the ultimate purpose of recognizing that his/her will is God's will—it is the same. It is perfection in physical existence—the recognition of oneself—that the ego's will coincides with the will of one's soul and the will of our origins.

Camillo: So is free will only active in our three-dimensional world, or does it also exist in other dimensions/densities?

The Council of Elders via Lilli: It exists everywhere.
Channeled by Lilli Bendriss, on July 29, 2010

According to the Council free will is an essential part of this play. If the Source had just expressed itself in one special way or through just one actor, and that actor knew it was the Source, the performance would be predictable and very boring. There would be nothing to discover/experience/learn/express. It would be like watching a film which you have seen many times, where you remember all the lines, all the scenes and how the film ends. The excitement and element of surprise would be gone. Everything would be known. Free will involves an element of the unknown. Each and every one of us has the free will to choose which direction our lives will take and which roles we will adopt. In 1990 Lilli channeled information about the roles we play:
   "We have been moving in the universe in circles of eternity, like a dance on a film screen, with different partners and different roles. This time we might be a mother with a son who was her father in a previous life—a father who had a passionate lover. Who knows what roles we will be asked to play. We are provided with a helping hand in order to find the right place and the right role."
Channeled by Lilli Bendriss in 1990 - from the energy-being Wounded Eagle

"The tape recorder" referred to by George Green, is the ego that records all experiences. Hence the the ego should not step aside for the soul since it needs to know its role in the play. If there were no egos and masks, there would no longer be a play. Without the ego the play would stop and the Source could no longer experience itself, express itself or develop itself to the fullest.

It is as such important that we know how the ego functions. Such an understanding provides us with a completely different way of looking at each other and all creation. Everyone would understand the concept of unity—that we have all come here together in order to express the universe in a vast, advanced and sophisticated play. Life acquires a completely different meaning when you know that even though everyone is wearing a mask called the ego, the Source of everything is hiding behind the mask.

Authors and scientists like David Icke, Gregg Braden, Michael Talbot, David Bohm and others maintain that the universe is a hologram. David Bohm was a pupil of Einstein, and we look closer at his ideas about the universe as a hologram in Chapter 23. We should not dismiss the idea that the play described by Green has been arranged as a hologram with advanced props and actors, staged by the Creator, for the purpose of expressing, developing and experiencing oneself. The Source wants to experience itself, but the only way it can is by forgetting that it is also the actor acting through all the various "clones" of itself. The Source needs this contrast as this mirror to reflect its actions back to itself.

In *The Law of One*, Ra refers to an exercise that we can do in order to understand that we are all one entity. He refers to us as being one mind/body/spirit complex and says:

"The universe is one being. When a mind/body/spirit complex views another mind/body/spirit complex, see the Creator. This is a helpful exercise."[28]

When you look at another person, see them as the Creator who is wearing a different mask than yours. Understand that you are one. We are all the Source. We are unique actors wearing masks designed to hide the Source from itself.

We allow ourselves to be influenced by the exterior world

that then creates thought patterns in our subconscious. Our subconscious creates feelings and vibrations that help to shape our reality. We are thus co-creators, but this occurs at an unconscious level. We allow our subconscious to be a co-creator subject to the law of vibration. It is all about the vibrations that we send out through our feelings. Our subconscious is the key, and it is programmed by the world outside us from the very day we are born. We are a product of the ideas about life that have been "fed" to us by the exterior world. Very little of this has been filtered because we do not have a filter that questions whatever is presented to us—is it good for us, or not?

From the time we take our first breath here on Earth we should be taught that anything is possible. We are thinking beings with the ability to create whatever we want. However, neither our parents nor the education we receive at school/ university tells us that anything is possible, that the ego has a function, or that we are all individual expressions of the Source that has the potential to create a world that we ourselves want.

Our parents are a product of their time and what they have been taught. They were not provided with knowledge about the fact that anything is possible. They have therefore "fed" us according to the best of their abilities with what they believe is achievable in this world. Unless we are critical about the information we absorb through our five senses, our subconscious thought patterns will keep repeating themselves for generation after generation.

For a long time now there have been people who have been aware of this play and the power of creation, and they have been controlling the play to their advantage. They control the masses, guiding them in whatever direction they see fit. Due to our lack of awareness, the majority of us allow ourselves to be controlled. We are influenced by so many different factors, and one of the most significant and effective of these is the TV.

We register an incredible amount of information quite unconsciously, and marketing people are fully aware of this. They influence us by employing techniques such as subliminal marketing, i.e. communication with the subconscious, aiming to influence the recipient without the recipient being aware of the influence. It is incorporated into films, TV shows, advertisements, and advertising posters—everywhere. Our consciousness and the naked eye do not perceive it, but our subconscious does. Those in power have exploited this to their advantage. The big multinational companies have known about this for many decades. And with the advent of TV they acquired a new outlet for influencing the masses.

In *The Law of One*, Ra explains that television and other "toys" such as mobile devices dampen our vibrations because they promote inactivity in our mind/body/spirit complex. The following is an extract from the book on this topic:

Questioner: What is the general overall effect of television on our society with respect to this catalyst?

Ra: I am Ra. The sum effect of this gadget is that of distraction and sleep.

Technological devices such as televisions, mobile phones and games, etc. cause us to be occupied, distracted and apathetic, incapable of listening to our innermost thoughts, to our intuition. We are guided in the direction dictated by those in power.

This also applies to energy. We think that we are dependent on oil, gas and coal as sources of energy, but for the last 75 years we have had the technology to obtain energy from the air. According to Steven Greer, those in control of oil, gas and coal have exploited our ignorance in order to build up a multi-billion empire. Greer is talking about an industry valued at $5,000 billion.

Steven M. Greer is an American doctor, author, lecturer and UFO investigator, as well as the founder of *The Orion Project* and *The Disclosure Project*.

He says that technology exists which can provide us with free energy. And that this can be traced all the way back to the time of the inventor Nikola Tesla during the last century.[29]

What would free energy mean to the powerful owners of the multinational oil, gas and coal companies? They would lose their power and wealth, and obviously this is something they want to avoid at all costs. They do not want the masses to know about a reality where we could have free energy—energy that can be obtained straight from the air.

This may sound like science fiction, but this is because we have been encouraged by those in power to believe that we do not possess the ability to create something like this. We are "just" people. Energy generators have been created that can utilize what has been called the quantum vacuum, i.e. the electromagnetic potential contained in the empty space around us. It has been estimated that:

Every cubic centimeter of space has enough potential energy to run the world's energy needs for one day. [29]

Many scientists have established the existence of this energy field and a number of inventors have managed to generate such free energy.

We wanted to hear the Council's views about the energy in this empty space.

Camillo: Is it possible to obtain energy direct from the air, from the so-called empty space that exists between the nucleus and electrons of an atom?

The Council of Elders via Lilli: This is the way that energy is obtained on most advanced worlds and levels of existence. Not just for energy as energy. But as a source of food for physical or semi-physical bodies.

Channeled by Lilli Bendriss, on August 11, 2010 - from the energy-beings the Council of Elders

According to the Council, more advanced life forms are using this method for obtaining energy from empty space as a source of food and for other energy requirements. If this is true, what does it say about the human race and its dependence on oil, gas and coal? We are destroying Mother Earth for the sake of energy, while all the time our energy requirements could be obtained from the empty space around us. If this energy became available to everyone on Earth, all our energy crises would be resolved. Hunger, energy pollution and the depletion of resources would be a thing of the past.

"The fact that free energy technology has been kept secret for 75 years shows the greed of those in power," says Greer. "Even when threatened with a global crisis involving famine, the depletion of resources and environmental pollution, they would not budge an inch if this meant that they would lose control."[29]

Those in power feed and control us through the mass media. They know what is happening; they know that we have the power to create our own reality and that we can utilize free energy from the air, but this would mean losing their enormous empire. We allow ourselves to be deceived by the five senses and do not see what is lurking in the wings, what lies behind the world in which we live. We believe that this world is the only reality that exists, but there are many different stages and realities. There are many different plays being acted out in different dimensions. We are ignorant about what is taking place on our own stage, in our three-dimensional world. Our five senses are constantly being bombarded by impressions from the outside world. We have no time to think about who we are. Our consciousness has more than enough to do when coping with all the impressions it is exposed to during our busy, everyday lives.

Films, TV, advertising, the Internet, telephones, mobile phones, music and many other technological gadgets capture our attention. This goes back to our childhood and having dedicated TV channels for children. The television has become a modern babysitter. We absorb everything and do not have time to think. Everything is happening so incredibly fast all the time, from the time we get up until the time we go to bed. Overburdened with impressions that our consciousness is constantly trying to sort out, we do not have time to allow the brain to take a break and quiet down.

However, if we do take a break and move into alpha brainwave states, we can make contact with our inner world and the heart. There we find answers and discover that we are part of something bigger and that we ourselves have chosen this experience, this play. This is what the time we are living in now is all about: waking up and once again becoming aware of who we are, where we come from, what we are doing here and where we are going.

We are currently undergoing a *shift in consciousness,* but we ourselves must take the initiative to make this quantum leap in our evolution. We have to understand who we really are by increasing our awareness, vibrations and frequencies in order to experience other realities. We can then see that this world is actually a constructed stage and we are actors wearing masks—masks that appear to be permanent fixtures. For a long time we have been acting in this play with egos that believe that they are the master and not the servant. While the ego has a function, it must work in harmony and balance with the whole.

The ego operates from the left side of the brain, the logical, analytical side. It ensures that we can exist in our three-dimensional world of time and space. It is the one who says, "I am" thus creating the illusion of separation. The right side of the brain is our link to the cosmos. If the left side is put out of play, the right side takes control and we would feel as if we were one with everything and everyone. The ego would disappear. However, without the logical, left side of the brain, we would not be able to function in our three-dimensional world where we perceive ourselves as being separate and are able to express our individuality.

Neural networks

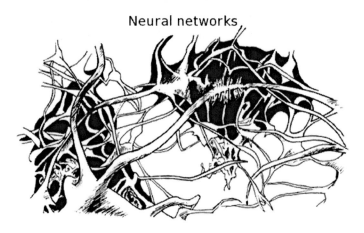

When the ego believes that it constitutes our totality, then we are on the wrong track. On the other hand, if we do not have a feeling of personal identity, our experiences of this three-dimensional world of time and space would be severely compromised. Consequently there has to be a balance. The ego has its function, but it has currently gone too far—we mistakenly believe that it is everything that we are.

We need to lift up our mask (the ego) and experience who we truly are. Only then will we escape from being controlled by this system based on materialism, where the ego is worshipped as the centerpiece. Periodic breaks between the various acts of the play provide the actors with the opportunity to remember who they are if things become too far removed from the original plan.

The last time this happened was during the age of Atlantis, but humanity elected to ignore that window of opportunity meant to move us on to our next stage of evolution. Instead people started believing that they were all that was—that they could control everything by themselves and that they were independent—instead of realizing that they were a part of a greater cosmic plan. This created a setback in our evolution of consciousness.

These periodic breaks are symbols of cosmic cycles

that occur at regular intervals——cosmic energy waves that affect us and our DNA, and change our development. These waves are referred to by Dr. Carl Johan Calleman and David Wilcock as the Energetic Engine of Evolution.

Dr. Calleman, a former cancer researcher who has studied the Mayan Calendar for more than 20 years, is one of the world's foremost researchers on the subject and has written several books about the calendar that he maintains is a cosmic timetable.

"People are affected by cosmic energy waves that come in cycles," he says. According to Dr. Calleman we are now in the last wave in the cosmic calendar.

The question is whether or not humanity will now take advantage of this window of opportunity that is reappearing—an opportunity to embark on the next stage of development for the entire human species. We simply must if we want to move on to the next phase. Earth is increasing its frequency and preparing for this shift. If we do not do this now, we will once again become caught up in a long karmic cycle, one in which we will have to reincarnate into life after life until another window of opportunity opens up some time in a distant future.

Chapter 9 - Reincarnation

"You have trodden the Earth, your path has been of different destinies as swordsmen, kings and slaves. You know the humbleness, you know the power. Integrated in yourselves is the knowledge of your different existences."
Channeled by Lilli Bendriss, July 11, 1993 – from the energy-beings the Council of Elders.

"Consciousness does not start at birth—it goes across lifetimes."
- Stephen Schwartz

Reincarnation literally means to come again in the flesh. Carne means meat in Latin. Reincarnation also means transmigration of the soul or rebirth and is the belief that the soul is reborn several times, returning to this planet or other planes of existence in order to develop. This cycle will continue until the soul has reached such a positive level that all negative karma has been worked off. Only then can the soul continue on its journey to become one with the Source of all creation.

In *Conversations with God*, Neale Donald Walsh explains that the soul wants to remember who it is. Our task is to remember who we are in order to experience and create everything that our heart desires. The soul is constantly seeking to become one with the Source, but in our earthly lives the soul has to contend with the dominant ego.

For a long time Indigenous people throughout the world have been saying that we have forgotten who we are and why we came here. This memory loss is so strong that we don't remember that we are spiritual beings having a physical experience. In a state of excitement and eagerness as spiritual beings, we voluntarily agreed to live yet another life here on Earth in order to experience the huge range of feelings that a physical being can embody.

Dr. Michael Newton has been investigating the transmigration of souls for many years. A certified hypnotherapist, a member of the American Counselling Association and a founder of the Newton Institute, he has authored some exciting books about regression and past lives. Dr. Newton has been involved in clinical research and practice for more than 30 years and is one of the few researchers who has employed a scientific approach to discover and explain soul experiences.

In his book, *Journey of Souls*, published in 1994, he shares his comprehensive research on the subject of reincarnation. According to his patients, we make our own decisions about returning to Earth. His book provides documentary evidence of the results of his regression studies conducted over a period of 35 years. When he began his study, Dr. Newton did not believe in life after death or the phenomenon of reincarnation. However, while engaged in this work, he discovered something that conflicted with his own beliefs.

Using hypnosis, he gradually took his clients back in time in order to gain access to their memories. Dr. Newton's clients were able to tell him what their souls had been doing between their lives on Earth or on other planets in the universe. This was incredible to him, since he was not personally a believer.

Yet all his clients expressed the same thing: at the moment of death, their souls left their bodies and they were able to observe their own dead bodies as they floated above them. They were then met by their guides and loved ones who had previously passed on. They could remember every single second of the life they just left, and were now one with everything and everyone. Everything was thought consciousness—and they experienced a review of their lives. Key features of these reviews, for which they were personally responsible, involved understanding the way in which they had experienced their lives and the impact that they had on other people. The overall picture became clear and they could now determine if they needed to develop further. Dr. Newton's research showed that many souls choose to reincarnate on Earth as people, while others chose to return as other life forms and on other planets.

It is all about returning to the Source in order to become one with the Source. *The Law of One* states that there are two main ways of returning to the Source—either by serving oneself or by serving others. Serving oneself may seem egotistical and thus not a viable way back to the Source. However, the book explains that creation is a single entity and if only a single entity exists, then the only concept of service is to self. On the other hand, if this single entity subdivides, then the concept of one part serving another part is created. Thus serving oneself and serving others are of equal value.

Serving only oneself could appear to be illogical as a way back to the Source. Are we not supposed to show consideration towards others? Our curiosity led us to ask the Council of Elders what they had to say about this.

Camillo: In *The Law of One*, Ra says that there are two ways to return to the Source, one which is negative and involves devoting 95% or more of service to oneself because the self is also the Creator, and one which is positive and involves devoting more than 50% service to other people. What does the Council have to say about this?

The Council of Elders via Lilli: An interesting interpretation that contains the wind of truth, and as the wind, is part of how the wind experiences itself. But in understanding the separate polarities of positive and negative, it is possible to also create a new matrix that is both a positive and negative energy structure.

In its infinite wisdom and eagerness to experience itself, the Creator constructs a matrix—an energy structure— to see how souls function when they bind themselves to the matrix. This matrix provides a model through which the soul expresses itself, and a structure for the possible unfolding of a plan that has been put into effect to manifest opportunities for the Creator to learn about itself. Humans either consciously or unconsciously start to experience the existence of the model through thoughts that recognize and describe the model.

The humanoid principle is also a blueprint for a conceived model of Earth, including space-time and everything contained in it at any given moment. In this way, at the very moment the blueprint is thought, it acquires an expression and becomes the physical world as we know it.

This particular model contains an identity that is recognizable through the human ego. This identity is like a code that begins to apply itself from the very first years of a child's life. Children then develop by using one or the other of these role models: they learn through serving others, and also when they serve themselves.

People on Earth are very attracted to experiencing these role models and will try both during the course of many incarnations. But this is just one of many empirical models that are sent from the Creator for finding their way back to the Source.

When you consider that the universe has billions of life forms, know there are many ways back to the Source— other blueprints of thoughts that have been conceived by the Creator that will allow them to experience the way back via a different model.

Channeled by Lilli Bendriss, on July 29, 2010 - from the energy-beings the Council of Elders

This concept might be difficult to comprehend for people who do not believe in reincarnation, life on other planets, or a way back to the Source. The world's largest religion, Christianity, does not believe in reincarnation, although reincarnation is a key concept in both Buddhism and Hinduism. A survey conducted in 2005 by Walter and Waterhouse showed that 20-25% of Europeans believe in reincarnation, and a similar result was obtained in the USA.[30]

Another survey conducted in 2005 by David Moore shows that three out of four Americans believe in paranormal activities. The same survey also showed that around 20% of Americans believe in reincarnation.[31]

A third survey conducted in December 2009 by The Harris Poll entitled, *What People Do and Do Not Believe In* also shows that around 20% of Americans believe in reincarnation. The same survey shows that 71% of those polled believe that the soul survives after death.[32]

In other words, people who believe in reincarnation are in the minority. In my home country, Norway, there are not many people willing to accept that reincarnation is a reality. In an article entitled, *Have We Lived Before?* featured in the Norwegian magazine *Ildsjelen*, the author Kamuara expressed her views about reincarnation. She was no more than seven or eight years old the first time she experienced a glimpse into her own previous life:

"Reincarnation has been a familiar concept in India and other Eastern countries for hundreds of years, but here in the West it has only started to become accepted during the last few years, and then only in certain circles.

"The church and science will still not accept that reincarnation is a reality, and have written it off as just being in our imagination." [120]

Increasing numbers of people are starting to come forward to tell their stories about reincarnation, but these can neither be proved nor disproved. Nevertheless, it is interesting to consider that everything in this universe occurs in cycles. So why shouldn't the soul do the same?

Great discoveries have been made in quantum physics during the last decades. Scientists are saying that everything is energy, including our bodies, our minds and our thoughts. So is the soul also pure energy? Is it an energy that never dies? Does it continue in another form and dimension when the physical body dies? Many people believe that it does. In fact, most people believe that the soul continues, although the majority do not believe that it returns in a different body or life form. In 1990 Lilli received this message from the enery-being Wounded Eagle:

"When you drifted along through life's encounters did you ask: how come you had to die one day? You see my child, there is a reunion on the other side of life. All the joy—all the songs that your heart sings on Earth are the shadows of the feelings that are experienced beyond."
Channeled by Lilli Bendriss, 1990 – from the energy-being Wounded Eagle

In *Journey of the Souls*, one of Dr. Newton's clients explains that dying is like peeling a banana. The banana skin is the body that is left after we die. The soul slips out of the "skin" and floats above the dead body lying below. So what is the soul? Is it a thought or is it energy that can be measured?

This concept of the soul is rather difficult to grasp. And this is exactly what Duncan MacDougal, an American doctor nicknamed Soul Man, wanted to do. He wanted to prove that the weight of the soul could be measured.

In 1907 he published a study entitled, *The Soul Hypothesis Concerning Soul Substance Together with Experimental Evidence on the Existence of Such Substance.* He wanted to conduct tests to see if the soul consisted of matter and thus had a measurable mass. The proof of his theory would be a weight reduction at the moment of death, when the soul leaves the body. He designed a special bed that was placed on finely balanced scales, and six dying people were laid on it one by one. He eliminated as many physiological explanations as possible in order to see if a weight reduction would occur at the moment of death, when the soul allegedly left the body and passed on. In his published research material, MacDougall showed that the six people who died on the special bed lost exactly 21.3 grams when they died.

His research has been regarded as having little merit, and from a scientific point of view his study does not contain enough material to determine that the soul can be measured and that it weighs 21.3 grams.

Although The Soul Man contained no strong scientific evidence, there are nevertheless increasing numbers of people who believe in eternal life and that the soul continues on its journey after death. On the other hand, there are perhaps just as many people who don't.

Tom Shroder, a journalist with the Washington Post, was one such person. He had strong doubts about the validity of reincarnation so he started investigating the subject by interviewing different people who claimed that they could prove that reincarnation was real. None of the people he interviewed were able to prove to him that this was the case. Their contributions were far too vague and provided no strong evidence to show that we come back to live several lives.

It was not until he met the Canadian psychiatrist Ian Stevenson that his opinion changed. In 1967 Dr. Stevenson set up a research unit—The Division of Perceptual Studies (DOPS)—at the University of Virginia in Charlottesville, USA. This became a research unit under the Department of Psychiatric Medicine at the same university.[33]

Stevenson, who died in 2007, devoted 40 years of his life to investigating reincarnation. He travelled to India, Lebanon and South America in order to study thousands of cases of children claiming that they were reincarnated souls. Tom Schroder was sceptical when he accompanied Stevenson on his trips to interview these children, but he was able to hear their stories first-hand and subsequently verify whether or not they were true.

Shroder writes about his travels with Stevenson in his book entitled, *Old Souls* that was published in 2001. He had the opportunity to interview the children himself, to check the facts and to draw his own conclusions. In his own words he says: "When you have witnessed dozens of these cases there will obviously be natural explanations for some of them. But," he says, "in many cases you have to search far and wide in order to find a natural explanation, and sometimes this is simply not possible. What is quite clear," he says, "is that the people involved in these cases are not liars. They have nothing to gain by lying about a previous life. These are real phenomena. We're talking about children who have barely learned to talk and who are completely obsessed with the life of an apparent stranger who is dead."[34]

The children say these lives were their own previous lives, but they were not glamorous lives. Contrary, they were quite ordinary. One example cited by Shroder is a case which occurred in Lebanon where a small child claimed to have been a 25-year-old car mechanic who died in a car accident. There are no obvious explanations as to why a small child should be completely obsessed with the life of a dead stranger as shown in this example.

There are young children in many parts of the world, usually between the ages of two and five, who claim to have lived previous lives. Some of these children have birthmarks and birth defects corresponding to wounds or other marks on the body of the dead person they are remembering. These connections have been confirmed in many cases by reports on the causes of death. Older children are also able to retain such apparent memories about previous lives, although generally speaking, these seem to disappear around the age of seven.[35]

Most of us do not remember having lived before. We have absolutely no recollection, evidence or even feelings about our past lives. Both Lilli and myself have been told by the Council of Elders that we have lived many lives and have been jointly involved in information work in several of them. Can we remember anything about working together in these lives? No. Do we believe this? Yes, because it resonates with our intuition and our common sense.

"Do not believe in anything simply because you have heard it. Do not believe in traditions because they have been handed down for many generations. Do not believe anything because it is spoken and rumoured by many. Do not believe in anything because it is written in your religious books. Do not believe in anything merely on the authority of your teachers and elders. But after observation and analysis, when you find that anything agrees with reason and is conducive to the good and the benefit of one and all, then accept it and live up to it."
- **Buddha**

If reincarnation is real, why do we have to forget? Why, when we are born, do we lose our memories about the lives we have lived, who we were and what we did? If we have lived before, why is practically everyone on Earth completely ignorant about this subject? If we all return with a life task to be fulfilled, why is this removed from our memories the very minute we are born? In *The Law of One*, Ra responds to this very question.

Questioner: Why do we have no memory of what we want to do?

Ra: I am Ra. Let us give the example of the man who sees all the poker hands. He then knows the game. It is but child's play to gamble, for it is no risk. The other hands are known. The possibilities are known and the hand will be played correctly, but with no interest.

In time/space and in the true color green density, the hands of all are open to the eye. The thoughts, the feelings, the troubles, all these may be seen. There is no deception and no desire for deception. Thus much may be accomplished in harmony, but the mind/body/spirit gains little polarity from this interaction. Let us re-examine this metaphor and multiply it into the longest poker game you can imagine, a lifetime.

The cards are love, dislike, limitation, unhappiness, pleasure, etc. They are dealt and re-dealt continuously. During this incarnation you may begin—and we stress begin—to know your own cards. You may begin to find the love within you. You may begin to balance your pleasure, your limitations, etc.

However, your only indication of other-selves' cards is to look into the eyes. You cannot remember your hand, their hands, perhaps even the rules of this game. This game can only be won by those who lose their cards in the melting influence of love, can only be won by those who lay their pleasures, their limitations, their all upon the table face up and say inwardly: "All, all of you players, each other-self, whatever your hand, I love you."

This is the game: to know, to accept, to forgive, to balance, and to open the self in love. This cannot be done without the forgetting, for it would carry no weight in the life of the mind/body/spirit being-ness totality.[36]

To put it briefly, Ra is saying that if we are to live our lives to the fullest, as we have elected to do, we cannot know about everything that lies behind the play. If we had such knowledge we would derive no benefits from playing our roles. If we remember all of our lives, everything we have experienced and everything that we and everyone else will experience in this life, then we are no longer talking about a play where free will can provide the optimum conditions for development and experience. By removing everyone's memories, the Source also hides from itself, thus allowing optimum conditions for experience. The aim of this play in which we are all involved is to obtain the maximum from it, based on all our individual forms of expression.

Whether or not you believe in reincarnation, there are many stories about people who claim to have lived before. Just like the children's stories in *Old Souls*, many people can describe where they lived, what they did and who they were in a previous life. In several cases of regression, patients have told stories that coincide with the lives of people who lived many years ago—people about whom these patients had no knowledge whatsoever.

Whether you dismiss this as nonsense with no scientific basis, or believe that these stories prove that reincarnation is real, one thing is certain. Many who have had a near-death or other similar experience no longer doubt the reality of reincarnation. They "come back" with an entirely different view about life and death, talking about other dimensions and the illusion of time. Some people make a complete break with their former lives in order to spend time helping other people. They see the totality—how we are all part of one entity—and can now grasp the meaning behind being one with everything.

Because we live in a three-dimensional world, many people think that this is all there is. But according to the research of Michael Newton and people who have had near-death experiences, our reality is that this dimension is just one of many dimensions.

This view is also shared by Ashayana Deane. In her books and lectures she talks about realities that have different energy densities operating in different dimensions.

Energy Structures, Density Levels and Dimensions
Ashayana Deane calls herself a Speaker and says that she was born with an eidetic memory about reincarnation, meaning she can recall her past lives in vivid detail. She is also a medium, author of the *Voyager* books and lecturer on the teachings of the Melchizedek Cloister Emerald Order—the MCEO Teachings—which are said to contain templates for information about the history of the universe. Deane says that she receives information from extraterrestrial beings by an advanced form of telepathy that is different from traditional channeling. She also says that the planet Earth exists in one of the many energy structures residing in a time matrix consisting of 15 dimensions. These structures are created by the Source so that it can experience everything that it conceives:

"Everything in creation is the energy of the Source which has been scaled down into smaller units of conscious energy. The process that causes the Source to scale down its energy is called The Stair Step Creation Process." [37, 38]

Deane says that the total energy of the Source is so great that it has to scale down its energy in order to enter into any form or personality that it conceives. The Source has created a process to do this, and we and Earth exist on one of these levels. The same principle is found in connection with the electricity generated by a power station. Before electricity can be used in a wall socket, it must be scaled down. There are many different stages between a power station and the wall socket. When electricity leaves the power station it enters the grid. Once in the grid it travels along high-tension cables to a substation where it is converted to lower-voltage electricity, after which it is transmitted to regional networks, e.g. residential areas. The voltage is once again converted at a smaller substation and transmitted to a local network that sends it to our homes:

"The Source therefore creates energetic structures inside itself that will enable the establishment of systems in which the thoughts of the Source can manifest themselves. The Source does this in order to experience manifested holograms. These energy systems are called time matrices," says Deane. [37, 38]

According to Deane, a time matrix structure has 15 dimensions that range from higher oscillation rates resulting in lower density manifestation, to lower oscillation rates that produce slower frequencies that have a greater capacity to hold energy, and thus produce more compact matter. Since the Source is so incredibly powerful that it cannot enter directly into the level of density at which we operate, it is scaled down gradually through various levels of density. It is not until it reaches our lower dimensions that the Source is able to manifest itself as compact matter.

In *The Law of One*, Ra also describes multiple levels of density and an infinite number of sub-levels within each level of density. Regardless of the number of levels between our world and the Source, both Ra and Ashayana Deane agree that the Source has to scale down its energy in order to be able to express itself in our three-dimensional world. We wondered what the Council of Elders could tell us about this.

Camillo: I am wondering if the Source has to scale itself down because its energy is so strong that it has to descend to lower levels in order to express itself on our current level?

The Council of Elders via Lilli: That is quite right. It is the actual plan. The creative force is like a diluted homoeopathic remedy. Each homoeopathic drop that has been diluted is as strong as the flower from which it was extracted. The actual flower can be used as a remedy, but the strange thing is that the more the remedy is diluted, the stronger its effect. So here arises a question that might be controversial: Are humans manifest in physical bodies on Earth more powerful than the Creator?

How could this be possible? Because the opposite end of the scale is like a laser beam that is more powerful at its point of impact that at its source.

The Creator is the potential. Humans experience this potential uniquely through individual understanding, emotions, and experiences, and in their downwardly-transformed form. Each drop is unique and therefore essentially almost more important than the whole, for the whole cannot be whole without the individual pieces that create the whole. Humans are like a black hole, towards which everything is attracted and through which everything flows.

This process creates a reference point for the Creator who sees humans as itself and who uses them as a role model for creating planets, solar systems, gas clouds and those whirling masses that can be seen with the naked eye. Humans are the model for creation of the universe. And it is only through their eyes that the universe is able to be perceived in three dimensional form.

Humans and God are thus the same, and the universe is being created by God through the human experience. This is the opposite of what you have been taught, that humanity is being created by God through the birth of the universe. Humans come first and provide the signal for the emergence of the official version of creation.

Channeled by Lilli Bendriss, on July 29, 2010 - from the energy-beings the Council of Elders

Chapter 10 - Lilli on Reincarnation

"I hear you child as you resonate, striking a chord in my being.

"I hear your question. How to explain the coming and going of souls? How to follow them from one state of being into another?

"The clouds in your sky are formed by the rising morning mist. The vapors of the sea, travelling over the vast space of heaven until a moment of joy makes them laugh so hard that tears sprout forth and fall down as liquid gold nourishing the Earth, blessing it by its presence.

"So is it that the soul releases fragments—tear drops—from itself that have in them the memories from many morning mists and rainfalls."
Channeled by Lilli Bendriss, on July 11, 1993 - from the energy-beings the Council of Elders

The ideas and teachings of the Council of Elders, who say that they exist in a future when perceived from outside the concept of time, are not always easy to understand. They are infinitely patient with me. They have explained that I exist on many different planes at the same time, that time is an illusion and that I can communicate across time with my many different selves. They say that I actually contain an infinite amount of information and that in order to release this information all I have to do is adjust my frequency slightly, thereby allowing access to the software that has to be downloaded through many levels of consciousness before it can be understood by my earthly self. In simplified terms I will outline the teachings that I received in response to my questions about reincarnation.

How is it possible that many people remember themselves as being Cleopatra or that I have seen Queen Elizabeth in the aura of several people who have come to me for readings over the years? Did they have inflated egos and wanted to include being a famous person on their resumes? Was this an example of Jung's collective unconsciousness where everything is connected to everything else, or was it something else that I was unable to comprehend?

All lives derive from the One, which in turns creates and downwardly transforms itself into an ordered system. This system can be seen as having coordinates that create each other.

For the sake of simplicity, let us say that one coordinate consists of twelve parts plus a thirteenth which is like a black hole that converts the twelve parts into twelve new coordinates.

This process keeps repeating, creating what we call soul groups. Soul groups are mental systems which evolve by experiencing themselves through the resonance of emotions. They exist on many levels all the way down to the level of the Higher Self which is the level above the human level in the three dimensional world.

Each souls' group is made up of many soul particles. For example, let's say a soul group consists of 20 billion soul particles that exist as a potential. Each particle contains a code, a pattern. At the very moment an impulse from the whole is created through the desire to create, a unique code of, say, 10 million particles will be formed through the dynamics of attraction and repulsion. This subset of souls' particles will be separated from the remaining billions.

Let us imagine this process from a three-dimensional point of view and let us also assume that this specific soul group is completely new and unused. The whole has been thinking and deliberating, and wants to create an illustrious story by sending it out into the ocean of experience. All the particles that resonate with the story will pull together magnetically. An individual will be created, although it will still exist as a thought form. This thought form, which contains the raw materials of the first thought impulse, will then be ready to be diluted, like a homoeopathic remedy.

Now the downward transformation through the dimensional layers takes place slowly. Each dimension is an imprint, like when a candle is made by repeatedly dipping the wick into hot wax. The prepared light is now seen as an object. The process that it was subjected to in order to emerge as this object is not shown. A child is born, an individual, separate from the soul group from which it emerged, but since everything is an exact pattern, recreated from the One, each particle will contain the code of the whole—just like in a hologram.

This child grows up. Let us say that the child becomes Cleopatra. It leads a dramatic life, forming a story that creates impressions and is remembered for thousands of years. Everything Cleopatra feels and experiences is recorded and stored in the soul particles that constitute Cleopatra.

Films are made that reinforce the resonance in the collective unconsciousness. A form of an archetype is created. I, Lilli, recognize myself as Cleopatra. This archetype can also create a reflection in the aura which can be picked up by a medium.

Let us move forwards in time while still locked into the experience of the three dimensions. Cleopatra dies from a self-inflicted snake bite. Her death is as dramatic as her life. Cleopatra's physical body ceases to exist in the three dimensions. The atoms that held her physical cells together in a cycle of physical existence move on to the next frequency. At this level the soul particles brought with them Cleopatra's recorded feelings and experiences.

The memories of Cleopatra's life are now vibrating on a plane that is just above the physical plane, having been stored there like a software program in a computer. This life will thus be available for someone living a thousand years later who tunes into it by causing their brain to resonate with the vibration in question. They will be able to pick up the memories of Cleopatra.

Soul Particles Have Memory

Everyone has a unique set of fingerprints. In the same way every soul has a unique soul print. Every soul is composed of a certain number of soul particles that resonate harmoniously with the plan that has been set up for the journey to Earth of the individual concerned. When we die these particles are released and pulled back towards the soul group from which they originally emerged. They take with them the memories of their physical lives. Whatever the individual on Earth experienced or felt during his or her lifetime has been recorded and stored in the soul particles. The memories which the soul particles bring with them are now merged into the soul group. Here they are recirculated into new physical bodies.

As mentioned above, a soul group can for instance contain 20 billion soul particles that are constantly being merged and recycled after each new experience. Every single person could thus be composed of a subset of these 20 billion soul particles (e.g. 10 million). As such one single person will contain soul particles from many different memories (lives lived). These are not evenly distributed. A person could have more particles from memories of one life lived than another.

These do not come together by chance, but in response to a perfect recipe composed on the basis of the laws of magnetism, geometry and mathematics. For soul particles with similar experiences, for example, those of someone who had a difficult life and committed suicide, these memories will be attracted to the soul particles of other individuals who have come to the soul group with similar experiences.

Though the particles go back to the soul group to merge and recycle into a new life, the memories that constituted the life on Earth continue to play out in the astral world. Hence one's personal history continues to spin, similar to throwing a rock into a pond. The ripples created by the rock keep going and expanding much like the life in the astral world does, but the particles that made up the rock can be reused for another rock (life).

The astral body exists in eternity. Each thought, each deed, exists in the astral world where the development and understanding of one's personal history continues to spin. In the same way that we are currently unable to comprehend our astral existence, the astral body is not able to understand its higher or deeper existence. Height and depth are linear concepts of this process. Man also exists as a causal identity cut off from total enlightenment. Causal identity describes the plane above the astral plane where the individual merges with others to become a group from which the soul particles emerge.

However, there are people on Earth today who are enlightened and have been charged specifically with helping others to wake up to a greater understanding of who they are and consequently raise their own frequency levels.

Jesus told his disciples: "In my father's house are many mansions, and one of these has been reserved for you." I understand this statement to mean that there are an infinite number of realities locked into their own frequency bands and we go to whichever one we resonate harmoniously with.

Soul Particles and DNA

This understanding of soul particles and soul groups that has been passed to Lilli by the Council shows that soul particles store everything that we experience in our lives. We take the memories of our physical lives with us when we die. These soul particles store our thoughts, deeds and feelings in our cells.

Are these "archives" stored in our DNA then? Is DNA the key that tells us who we are and who we have been in previous lives?

Yes, many people believe that DNA is the key.

Chapter 11 - Increased Consciousness with 12 DNA Strands

DNA is arranged in two complementary strands that are twined around each other in a double helix. This phenomenal mechanism has been the subject of considerable research, most notably in The Human Genome Project (HGP), which was coordinated by the US Department of Energy and the National Institute of Health, and was completed in 2003 after 14 years of research. During the early years of the HGP, the Wellcome Trust (UK) became a major partner in the project. Contributions have also been made by Japan, France, Germany, China and Russia, et al. The aims of the project included the following:

- To identify all the genes of the human genome
- To determine sequences of three billion chemical-base pairs that make up human DNA
- To store this information in databases[39]

The Genome Project decoded approximately 2% of our total physical DNA. The remaining 98% was determined to have no purpose. In genetics DNA that has no known function is often called junk DNA, meaning that the components of an organism's DNA sequences do not code for protein sequences and has no known biological function.[40]

In his book, *Supernatural*, Graham Hancock explains that 3% of our DNA codes for protein although some authorities on the subject operate with percentages of up to 10%. Regardless of the percentage, scientists agree that junk DNA constitutes the greatest percentage of the human genome.[117]

This means that most of our DNA is either unusable, as assumed by scientists, or that it has a function that scientists have not yet discovered. If 90-98% of our DNA has a largely unknown function in the human body, why do we have it? Some scientists claim that it is superfluous residue resulting from our evolution. But if our evolution occurred by natural selection and survival of the fittest, why wasn't this surplus DNA material disposed of? Hancock writes: "Why would natural selection preserve such a huge volume of useless gibberish and go to all the trouble of reproducing it in every living cell?" This would seem to be counter-productive. Perhaps the explanation lies in the fact that most of our DNA is not quite as redundant as many would have us believe.

Esoteric and spiritual teachers claim that the so-called junk DNA actually contains your full history, right back to the first time you incarnated on this planet many lives ago. They speculate that it is an archive for the soul and serves as a living library due to the quantity of information stored within it, but that scientists have only succeeded in seeing a tiny fraction of the full story. Author and spiritual teacher Richard Rudd supports this in his book *Gene Keys – unlocking the higher purpose hidden in your DNA*. "It is the junk DNA that holds the entire collective memory pattern of your past," he says.[149]

Is this right? Is there anything to indicate that junk DNA contains stored information? Today's scientists are discovering more about our junk DNA that might indicate that it is definitely not junk.

While Western scientists working on The Genome Project were focusing on 2% of the coding DNA sequences, Russian HGP scientists under the leadership of Dr. Peter Gariaev (Pjotr Garijajev) were researching the other 98%. Dr. Gariaev's team consisted of biophysicists, molecular biologists, embryologists and language experts. Their research shows that junk DNA is not redundant evolutionary residue as previously claimed. Linguistic studies have shown that the coding sequence of non-coding DNA adheres to basic rules of syntax. There is a definite structure and logic in its sequence, just as there is with a biological language. The research revealed that the codons actually formed words and sentences in the same way that our human languages conform to grammatical rules. The language of the genes is far older than any human language and could serve as a sort of blueprint for the development of human speech.

Dr. Gariaev also discovered that the codons of the DNA strands can be rearranged in different sequences. In other words our DNA molecules can be reprogrammed.[41]

In *Supernatural* Hancock writes that the same conclusions were arrived at by Professor Eugene Stanley and his team at Boston University and Harvard Medical School in the 1990s. They say: "The non-coding DNA sequences contain a structured language fundamentally unlike the coding in genes. Even though it doesn't code for proteins, we therefore need to consider the possibility that the 'junk' DNA may carry some kind of message."[118]

When Hancock met Professor Stanley later in 2005, he asked him if he still stood by the discoveries he had made about DNA in 1994. Professor Stanley replied: "You bet I stand by them. Nothing has been refuted."

Does the key to remembering who we are lie in this junk DNA which constitutes 90-98% of our total DNA? Many believe that we are now living in a time when more of our DNA strands will become activated, allowing us to remember who we are and also communicate on a greater number of frequencies. Then junk DNA is not junk, but merely lying dormant, just waiting to be activated.

One person who shares these views is Barbara Marciniak, internationally renowned trance channeller, lecturer and author of the best-selling books *Bringers of the Dawn, Earth, Family of Light, The Pleiadian Book* and *Path of Empowerment. Bringers of the Dawn* is based on more than four hundred hours of material channeled by Marciniak. She presents wisdom from the "Pleiadians," a group of enlightened beings who has come to Earth to help us discover how we reach the next stage in our evolution. They advise us to become media-free, to work in teams and eliminate the words "should" and "try" from our vocabularies. They also concur that the original human was a magnificent being with 12 strands of DNA and 12 chakra centers.

Marciniak explains that our DNA was split into only two strands with very little data and memory. "Science has yet to discover these ten deactivated strands," she says. In *The Pleiadian Book* she refers to our DNA as a fantastic library before it was deactivated.

She says, "Imagine going into a library and pulling all of the books off of the shelf and heaping them into the center of the room and then destroying the card catalogue so there is no way to find information.

"That information exists, but if it is not stumbled upon it is lost. It is not cross-referenced. That is what happened with your genetic structure." She continues by saying: "The time has now come to reconnect our original 12 strands of DNA."[42]

This means that we must continue our spiritual evolution by encouraging DNA transformation in the human body. With the transformation of the 2-stranded DNA to the 12, humans will awaken to our own innate power and recognize the divinity within us. We will become conscious of the fact that we live in many dimensions at once. We will communicate on many more frequencies and thus understand that we are part of the whole and an expression of the universal consciousness. We will understand that our reality is just one of many realities and see the whole picture of how everything is connected. This shift will effect our connection to every area of our lives—the Source/Power, the inner vision, the spiritual guidance, how we communicate (both physical and spiritual) and our relationship to love (both human and divine).

Sheldan Nidle, the author of *You Are Becoming a Galactic Human*, also says that we will develop 12 strands of DNA. DNA is far more complex than we have been taught: "The so-called 'junk DNA' is finally beginning to reveal its mysteries. RNA and DNA are starting to activate a 3rd strand," Nidle says. "The 12-strand is the end product of planned jumps from two to three to six to twelve."[148]

But what would trigger these planned DNA jumps? We believe one trigger could be the special language that Lilli started to channel after a trip to Sedona in 2009. The language is called the *Language of Light*. It is also being referred to as the *Star Language* and the *Language of the atoms*. The language activates DNA in people listening to it. Here is Lilli's own story on how she downloaded this special language.

Lilli Downloads the Language of Light

It's like a dream, thinking back: me standing in front of Bell Rock, with David Singing Bear, shaman and teacher, right behind me with his hand lightly touching my back. The sensation begins—strong currents of energy soaring through my trembling body. I can hardly stand up by the sheer weight of it.

And then the words start flowing from my mouth. They are fire in my throat, strange words and yet so very familiar.

I know this language from time primordial, from the very essence of my being. It is a homecoming; tears are flowing down my cheeks. Time does not exist through the birth of the Language of Light and yet, time brings me back to my conscious self. Slowly, entering my normal state of being, I hear David Singing Bear saying, "Lilli, you downloaded from the Star Nation. This is a sacred language from the beginning of our history, and is spoken and understood by the cells of the body. It is the codes for activation of our DNA."

Brilliantly, the pieces of the puzzle start to fit together, beginning with my urge to go to Sedona. I had been there once almost 20 years back and received profound information regarding my personal path. I knew already I would return one day. Then, in 2009 my co-workers at the time came up with the idea to bring a group of people on a spiritual journey to Sedona. I knew the time had come, but for what?

The group enjoyed the teaching of the local Shaman David Singing Bear. We arrived and all was well, but I felt as if I was still waiting for something. Then came the day where the group was taken to Bell Rock.

Colleague and soul sister Silja told me a few months back about a dream, in which she saw me standing strong and erect between the Red Mountains. As she watched, I got older and older, so wrinkled that I was not recognizable.

"It was like you were transformed to represent the wisdom of the ages," she said. "Something profound is going to happen to you." Yes, in the aftermath of that day, I have come to believe that the The Language of Light is truly what I downloaded, a transformative experience for people who hear it.

Since Sedona 2009, Lilli has been channeling this language on and off. At first, it came through intermittently. However, for the past year it has been coming through each time Lilli channels. We believe this is because it is time to wake up. The time to remember who we are is *now*. We have seen how the Language of Light affects certain people who listen to it. They are being awakened.

Channeling the Language of Light for Hundreds of People

For the past six months, Lilli and I have been attending expos and events in Norway where we speak about *The Shift in Consciousness* for hundreds of people. After my presentation, Lilli goes into trance and starts channeling the *Language of Light*. It lasts for 5 to 10 minutes and we are told by the Council of Elders that it activates DNA.

We have seen strong reactions in the audience after they have been exposed to the *Language of Light*. As Lilli says, "Each time I channel the *Language of Light*, many people approach me, some are crying, saying it felt like lightening was hitting them, pouring love through their hearts. Several people have started talking the words of the stars themselves."

Some people say they can't control their emotions and are puzzled as to what is going on in their body. Something in them has changed. We believe their DNA was ready for activation and the Language of Light was the trigger that activated certain parts of their "junk" DNA.

The Structure of The Language of Light
None of the people affected by this language understood what was being said. Neither do Lilli or I for that matter. However at an expo in Trondheim, Norway in April, 2011 a woman came up to us after the channeling and claimed she understood what was being said. The message of the language was all about building bridges between the different worlds existing in different dimensions.

Then, just a week later, a friend of ours, Tove Stavem Reite, called with some startling information. She is a psychic and had attended our talk on *The Shift in Consciousness* a few weeks earlier where Lilli also channeled the Language of Light. She said she knew what this special Language of Light was all about.

Tove received a channeling herself that same day. It gave her detailed information about the Language of Light. The information came from an energy source calling itself *The Brotherhood*. Tove did not inform us of this channeling until after she had read a passage in the Norwegian version of *The Shift in Consciousness* talking about how everything exists in the so-called empty space. Here is a small excerpt of her channeling.

"This "language" (language is in quotes because it cannot be compared with the way we perceive earthly languages) is of a different order than the phonological language found on Mother Earth. Frequencies not known to the human sphere exist in the intergalactic dimensions. The variables as well as the different variations form a complex system that contains both opportunities and existentialism that will never be known in the earthly dimension. This is an impossibility when the vibrations, features, scope and physics between us can be considered as oil and water.

"Nevertheless, we communicate in the same wave oscillations and we have passage between dimensions, in a somewhat covert way. So the Language of Light will thus work as an intermediate part—albeit a handicap in relation to our language's potential. It is only the language's sound vibrations, in the earthly term, which are perceived by the human senses. The impact is on a more subtle level, but is just as effective as the physical laws. Our explanation for the scope and communication area of this language will appear unreal, unbelievable and incomprehensible (based on earthly terms). But, with the linguistic terms that our channel (Tove) can produce, we will explain.

"The sound waves produced by our sister Lilli are only one layer in the 'language' production index, like one instrument in the large philharmonic orchestra. It is only on this earthly sound level we can reach you. The sound you hear is not necessarily what our senses are hearing. However, it must be like this in the transfer (to Earth) and it sounds like music to our ears when our sister speaks.

"In between the audible sound (when Lilli speaks) gaps exist. These gaps have different length, width and height— in all variables! In addition, the spaces can be influenced in their own space, i.e. they are plastic and elastic. All space components may be affected in 3-D format, but also in shape. The possibilities are uncountable. If one imagines a cable or a pipe, and the Language of Light is collected in this form, one can imagine the possibility of being able to cut off pieces from this 'cable/pipe' of language. In addition to length measurements, these cross-plates will also possess both individual and custom information in a separate dimension/area.

"Within the dimensions contained in the spaces, we find the intention, consciousness, thought, communication, selection, transfer; yes, all the multifaceted variables in the existential mind, and in this case, our being.

"The sound vibrations of our language sister Lilli

speaks will be used for human development/upgrading."
**Channeled by Tove Stavem Reite, February 14, 2011
from the energy-being The Brotherhood**

The Brotherhood is talking about using the language Lilli
speaks for human development/upgrading; hence, we
believe that this language is an important part of DNA
activation for people on Earth in their process towards
becoming an enlightened being with 12 active DNA
strings. Just like Sheldan Nidle says, "The 12-strand is the
end product of planned jumps from two to three to six to
twelve."

The Origin of The Language of Light
A few days later, Lilli did a channeling of the Council of
Elders and received information about the origin of the
Language of Light, confirming what was channeled by
Tove: the Language of Light is a trigger for DNA activation
helping us to remember who we are. Here is what Lilli
received:
     "Around 20 million years ago, a Star Nation was
formed. They came from the farthest corner of your
universe, the beings that held the best intention at heart.
They came to create and associate with several leagues to
promote a great experiment: to create a common sound
resonance that would keep particles rotating through a
vacuum of nothingness, so that structures of beingness
would spiral out into all directions, building reason and
promoting intelligence through a blueprint of love.
     "Through the holographic structure of the universe,
it would be held together through memories and spin
eternally to words, each soul borne under its command.
This is the true story of the Tower of Babel. It was part of
the experiment that the sounds, as well as the void between
the sounds, would be forgotten through the mists of time
and replaced by various offspring derived from the first
creation. Galactic wars broke out, further breaking asunder

the sounds of the ethers with their holotronic weapons. Brother stood up against brother and they could not any longer communicate through the voice of the sacred sounds of love. They fell like shooting stars into oblivion and fell asleep, dreaming about separation.

"Lo and Behold, they are awakening now as star seeds walking the shores of the eternal lands of love. They vibrate and move the strings of your holy blueprint; the tuning fork finding the exact tune for you to sing. The rhythm which once made them fall asleep has awakened them again because this is the time, so that you will sing your way back to resonance of becoming connected to all there is, was and ever will be. Free!"

Channeled by Lilli Bendriss on April 13, 2011 - from the energy-being The Council of Elders

On April 26, 2011 Lilli and I did three channeling session talking to the Council of Elders about the Language of Light. We received some incredible information involving the language, as well as information about the important role of the pyramids in this awakening process. After receiving all this information about the Language of Light, we strongly believe that it is one of many tools for the great awakening prophecied by so many indigenous people. This is why we have chosen to share it with you in this book. If this information resonates with you and you would like to listen to the Language of Light, please visit our website www.TheShiftInConsciousness.com and download a free mp3 file of the language as well as a pdf file containing the messages we received from The Council on April 26.

It seems like the language is a trigger for DNA activation and it is being given to us now because the time has come for the great awakening. Previously, (the summer of 2010) Lilli and I had gathered information from the energy-being The Council of Elders on DNA and activation. We asked them what they could tell us about DNA, and if there is currently anyone on the planet who has more than two active strands of DNA.

Camillo: Does anyone currently have more than two active strands of DNA?

The Council of Elders via Lilli: There are already biological human beings living in the third dimension who have been activated. These people are carriers of a downwardly transformed energy from the future. In your understanding of linear time they will fix or anchor this energy through resonance that is creating opportunities for others to adopt. These people are like an infectious virus, and if someone's body has a transport system that is compatible with the virus then activation will occur automatically. The few will create the wave that will carry the many across the ocean towards a new land. Like Marco Polo who travelled across the mountains and obtained information, at first no one believed him until others began to think that what he said was true. Then others did the same. And this caused his story to grow in their minds and become a story that subsequent generations adopted as a truth. The human race expanded its horizons by following in his footsteps.

The same also applies to DNA, and the few carriers who have chosen to be explorers. In their code has been born the longing for something more. It refuses to let go. They are thus active pioneers, spreading this potential. Many have incarnated in the Western world because the freedom of thought and access to research there.

Indigenous peoples have retained their understanding without always being able to explain why they understand. They simply are, and exist in the All, interacting strongly with all forms of life, be it animals, stones, wind or people. They are part of an active empirical model although they do not have the scientific language for it. The Western world needs scientific expressions and words because people's brains have gradually become more adapted to obtaining information in that way. Humans are able to adapt to their surroundings and change themselves in response to their surroundings.

Channeled by Lilli Bendriss, on July 29, 2010 - from the energy-beings the Council of Elders

During another channeling session I had with Lilli on November 13, 2009, we were told that our DNA would change and that its original form would be activated:

"The human resonance will change the visible picture of your planet. This will be a major cleansing process involving emptying the junk from your cells and your DNA, re-establishing the strands in their original high potential form and making them a blueprint for the many."

Channeled by Lilli Bendriss, on September 13, 2009 - from the energy-beings the Council of Elders

Our DNA strands are in the process of regenerating to their original high potential. This ties in with Marciniak's message as well as Professor Stanley and Dr. Gariaev in their research. The inactive part of our DNA can now be activated.

There are people who claim to see, feel, sense and hear dead people. One of these is Lisa Williams, an internationally-known psychic who has become famous as a result of her TV show, *Life Among The Dead.* In Norway we are familiar with mediums like Gro Helen Tørum, Lena Ranehag and Lilli, and their well-known ability to "tune in" through watching the TV show, *The Power of the Spirits.* People who possess such abilities say they can switch over to another frequency, in the same way that we switch over to another station on the radio. Anyone who can channel information like this has the ability to tune into other frequencies and thus access other dimensions and realities. Marciniak says that everyone will be able to do this when we have 12 active strands of DNA.

But what would it actually mean if we all acquired the ability to tune into other frequencies? We asked the Council of Elders.

Camillo: Will human DNA strands be activated as suggested by Barbara Marciniak? If so, what will this mean for the human race?

The Council of Elders via Lilli: A quantum leap. Complete redistribution, perhaps even an uneven distribution of roles. This quantum leap would open up potential that has previously only been dreamed of, the sort that you see in science fiction films. Such activation would enable humans to make a leap in time. Normally it would take the human race 500,000 years to evolve naturally to a point 500,000 years into your future. But activation of your DNA strands would shrink this time process and thus possibly enable man to make the leap in just 1,000 years.

Interplanetary travel would be possible. For example, let's say that you decide to travel to a planet that does not have oxygen. You would then be able to adjust your system so that your oxygen levels would adapt to the prevailing conditions wherever you happen to visit, without the need for equipment. It would be possible to encode your system in order to take advantage of other forms of existence.

This understanding lies in the future for the human race, although there are already signs that advanced and secret scientific research is starting to discover how this could actually occur.

Camillo: Thank you. So are humans starting to get 12 active strands of DNA as suggested in the work of Barbara Marciniak?

The Council of Elders via Lilli: You are heading that way. No one can say that this will happen on a particular date or in a particular year because it is like a wave, rolling back and forth. This wave lies in the understanding of the mass subconscious. Like an ocean wave breaking on the shore, it rolls forwards and then retreats, following a certain rhythm. This rhythm is different when a storm is raging. Then the waves are stronger, breaking against a high wall that has been erected and stands firm. However, there comes a time when the wave has gathered so much momentum that it actually breaks down the wall or surges over it and crashes down on the other side. This is what is starting to happen now—waves of power and resonance are in motion. They do not stand still. Like everything else they have a rhythm, moving backwards and forwards.

A major disaster is occurring—a tsunami. A massive wave is coming. People are becoming activated through their hearts. They are starting to recognize themselves. They are saying: "My brother was there, I recognize myself." Your hearts are opening up on a major scale, and powerful love is flowing towards those souls who have devoted their lives to ensuring that the wave would awaken consciousness on a much larger scale.

At the same time, when large-scale deaths occur, human DNA strands are activated at the point of intersection between life and continuation. So the strands of most of these souls are activated during their transition. The wave and all the lives together create a pattern so strong that it becomes a code available to the many through an emotional opening of the heart.

Channeled by Lilli Bendriss, on July 29, 2010 - from the energy-beings the Council of Elders

Chapter 12 - DNA Wave Transformation

Dr. Gariaev and his team discovered that DNA absorbs light photons in its surrounding area and causes the photons to spiral through the molecule itself. In an experiment with frog and salamander eggs, Gariaev shone a gentle laser beam through a developing salamander embryo and redirected it into a developing frog embryo. This wave picked up information from the salamander eggs and redirected it into the frog spawn, causing the frog embryo's DNA to completely re-code itself with the instructions to build a healthy adult salamander. They succeeded in transforming a frog embryo into a salamander by transferring the DNA information, resulting in a complete metamorphosis, even though the two embryos were in hermetically sealed containers and only the light was allowed to pass through. The genetic material in the frog spawn became "cannibalized" by the wave of information from the salamander eggs, and salamanders, not frogs, were hatched out from the frog spawn. [46]

Can the cosmic rays mentioned by David Wilcock change the DNA of all life on Earth as in the experiment conducted by Dr. Gariaev? Can such cosmic waves power our evolution? Apparently that is exactly what they do, according to Dr. Calleman, whose book entitled, *The Purposeful Universe,* shows that waves of cosmic energy coming from the center of our galaxy affect us and our lives through our consciousness. They are evolutionary waves of creation.

We received the same answer during a channeling session with the Council of Elders on July 29, 2010. We asked them if our DNA is affected by cosmic waves radiating from the center of the galaxy as suggested by

Wilcock and Calleman and if these power evolution, and the Council responded in the affirmative. They said that this was how everything was connected.

Changes in our DNA will change our consciousness. If these waves of energy change our DNA, would this change our life form and thus our consciousness? Such a shift in our consciousness would take us further along our evolutionary path. Who we are would acquire an entirely different meaning.

Would a greater awareness of how everything is connected enable us to engage in intergalactic communication in our capacity as galactic beings? Would we see into other dimensions and realities that are currently hidden from us?

During a channeling session conducted by Lilli in 1993, the Council of Elders said that our DNA molecules and memory would be activated during the time in which we are now living.

"Now the new energies that we talked about are also creating infrastructures—we can use the word because it's an understandable word—in the grid pattern of Earth to strengthen the weak points, to stabilize, to have influxes of energy that can directly go in and access the human organism, the human energy field, to activate the DNA molecules, to activate the memory banks and the chakras which are not yet in full working condition."

Channeled by Lilli Bendriss on July 11, 1993 - from the energy-beings the Council of Elders

Part 2

Chapter 13 - What Are We Doing Here?

"To be in justice, to be in pureness is what you are seeking—it is what your soul is asking for. For you to reveal yourself in purity, to reveal yourself the attainable wisdom which you are part of. Within the universe exist the fractions of you. These fractions are assisting you in this mission, as a whisper sometimes, as an intuition, as a knowing where to go. This is the Source that is always within you. This is the source that is also called "The Light" within the different galaxies and the different realities to which they are attuned. You are different persons, different entities—that is the way it works on Earth. Each fraction has a different mission with a different goal you hope to attain. The common Source inspires you to reach out your hands to your fellow man and want to make unity. You want your fellow man to also understand your path."

Channeled by Lilli Bendriss on July 11, 1993 - from the energy-beings the Council of Elders

What is the meaning of being here on Earth? Many scientists, authors, course lecturers, film creators, mediums and other people in spiritual circles say that we are spiritual beings having a physical experience. What are we supposed to do with our physical experience? Do we have any tasks that we are supposed to complete? What is the meaning of this life?

According to *Conversations with God* by Neale Donald Walsch, "There is only one purpose for all of life, and that is for you and all that lives to experience fullest glory. Everything else you say, think, or do is attendant to that function. There is nothing else for your soul to do, and nothing else your soul wants to do."[47]

Walsch goes on to say that we are not here to discover ourselves, but to recreate ourselves. Therefore we are not supposed to be searching to find out who we are, but searching to find out what we want to be. We only need to remember who we are and then recreate ourselves again. We are souls in possession of all knowledge since we are part of the Source which divided itself in order to experience itself. Life is an opportunity for us to experience our conceptual understanding in our capacity as souls. "We only need to remember what we already know and act accordingly," he says.

Thus it is all about our state of consciousness. Are we conscious of who we are? What we are doing here? Where do we come from? And where we are going? What are we conscious of? Are we conscious of the fact that we are immortal souls having a physical experience, or do we believe we live only one life that has been created by chance?

Our state of consciousness is crucial, and in his book entitled, *A New Earth,* Eckhart Tolle says that the meaning of life is actually about our state of consciousness:

"As soon as you arise above mere survival, the question of meaning and purpose becomes of paramount importance in your life. Many people feel caught up in the routines of daily living that seem to deprive their lives of significance. Some believe life is passing them by or has passed them by already. Others feel severely restricted by the demands of their job and supporting a family or by their financial or living situation.

"Some are consumed by acute stress, others by acute boredom. Some are lost in frantic doing; others are lost in stagnation. Many people long for the freedom and expansion that prosperity promises. Others already enjoy the relative freedom that comes with prosperity and discover that even that is not enough to endow their lives with meaning.

There is no substitute for finding true purpose. But the true or primary purpose of your life cannot be found on the outer level. It does not concern what you do, but what you are—that is to say, your state of consciousness."[48]

He continues by saying that we have an inner and an outer purpose and that the inner purpose concerns being and is primary. It concerns waking up and realizing the true nature of our consciousness. This is the inner purpose for all humanity.

We wake up to realize that we are all an expression of consciousness. This is the shift: we shift from believing that we are separate individuals ruled by our egos to realizing that we are many different expressions of the same entity, and that physical matter only exists in the present—in the now.

Michael Beckwith, a spiritual teacher and lecturer and one of several high-profile people involved in the film, *The Secret* says that we are here to express ourselves with all our power:

"You are here to grow, develop and unfold. To create and express greater and greater versions of yourself. You are here to advance—to let your light shine. You are here to grow, develop and unfold beyond concern about what others might think about you, how they are thinking about you. You are not here to impress other people—you are here to impress the universe with your thoughts of growth so that you can be an advancing individual."[2]

The Source is consciousness and expresses itself through human beings with physical bodies. Consciousness needs the physical body to experience form and matter, and is why we reincarnate. But if we, as expressions of the Source, do in fact reincarnate, why? Is it so that we can experience awakening as described by Tolle? So that we can wake up to our part of creating our personal as well as global community that is becoming ever more saturated with suffering, pain and fear?

Affluent parts of culture measure worth and power against how much money people have. Afraid of not being or looking good enough, not having the best things or a well-paying job, we strive to be seen, noticed and accepted. In that culture, we do everything in our power to satisfy the ego, which experiences the world as being separate. We become governed by this outer world of culture and things that are supposed to make us feel happy only feed our ego and reinforce our illusion of being separate, disconnecting us from everything and everyone. Western medicine promotes gobbling pills for our ailments so we won't realize that we feel inadequate, while in poor countries people suffer from war, torture, famine, and fear. The contrasts between the affluent and impoverished nations are huge, and yet, everyone is suffering in their own way.

If there is a higher intelligence behind all creation and we are part of it, why do we suffer from evil, pain, cruelty and things that make us feel empty inside? What causes children to starve in certain parts of the world? Life in the physical body is regarded by both Buddhists and Hindus as the source of all suffering. It all seems so meaningless. Why would a creator want a world like that?

An age-old question, one that's been asked many times. In his book, *The Art of Happiness*, Howard C. Cutler converses with the Dalai Lama. One of the chapters addresses why we experience pain and suffering. Cutler writes:

"Viktor Frankl, a Jewish psychiatrist and Holocaust survivor once said, 'Man's main concern is not to gain pleasure or to avoid pain but rather to see a meaning in his life.'

"Frankl used the brutal and inhuman experiences he had in the concentration camp to obtain an insight into how prisoners manage to survive such cruelty. By carefully observing those who survived and those who did not, he discovered that survival was not dependent on age or physical strength, but rather on the targeting of one's strength and an understanding of the fact that there is a meaning behind life and all experience."

Cutler also refers to a statement made by the Dalai Lama:

"Awareness of your pain and suffering helps you develop your capacity for empathy, the capacity that allows you to relate to others' feelings and suffering. This enhances your capacity for compassion towards others. So, as an aid in helping us connect with others, it can be seen as having value." [121]

So we experience suffering so that we can find meaning in our lives and develop the capacity for empathy. So how do we transform pain and suffering into empathy? How do we overcome the illusions of separation and use our pain to find meaning in our lives, and unify and connect with others? What, indeed, are we doing here?

First, we must be willing to consider that at the root of everything is a mystery. Science says that everything originates from a Zero Point Field. Mathematically, zero equals nothing, as a void. But where does this void come from? We may never know, but that should not stop us from asking.

If life on Earth is not a coincidence and Darwin was wrong, and behind creation there is actually a higher form of universal consciousness of which we are all part, what does science have to say on this subject?

Science says that everything is energy and that the smallest particles of this energy surf on a wave of information—a unified field—a universal, intelligent consciousness expressing itself through separation. We are like unique instruments in a universal orchestra and the Source wants to create beautiful music using all the different instruments that exist in this universe.

Though we are part of the whole, we have been gifted with free will to make independent choices about our own lives. Free will is therefore involved in creating the world as it is today, including pain, joy and everything in between.

When we asked the Council of Elders to explain how everything is connected, they replied as follows:

"Blessed be the heart that watches over the child through the night. This is the cosmic heart that watches over its children who have emerged from the core in order to divide the heart into tiny pieces so that there is enough for everyone.

"And hearts are recreated from these tiny pieces again and again until finally you can see all the tiny pieces, pulsating and creating synergistic effects between all living things, finally beating with one rhythm. And through this special rhythm and the tone which runs through it—the hearts, like pieces of a jigsaw puzzle that were thrown out to experience all the various opportunities, will be pulled back to the source again. This is happening all the time, wherever there is an outflowing and withdrawal, an outflowing and another withdrawal."

Channeled by Lilli Bendriss on July 29, 2010 - from the energy-beings the Council of Elders

We are not separate—we are all connected like the tiny pieces in this heart. The Source creates separation—an illusion—so it can express itself via the human race. The pain and suffering come into being when our ego convinces us that the separation is real and illusion is all there is.

The trouble is, in order for physical form to exist outside the Source, the illusion of separation must be present. It is precisely what makes the outer world so "real." Otherwise, we would not be able to perceive anything other than the whole. Even though separation is an illusion, it is quite a necessary one in order for the Source to create experience to express itself through. So both the separateness and the unity exist simultaneously. We are both one with the Source, and separate in the illusion of the physical world.

Another principle for transforming suffering and pain into empathy and evolution is understanding that our energy does not die—that everyone is an eternal soul. You do not have a soul—you are a soul, one that returns to the illusion, life after life, either here on Earth or elsewhere in the universe, as various life forms. Believing reincarnation is real reconnects us to the bigger picture.

Humans are subject to universal laws that are as real as the law of gravitation is in the physical experience. The law of karma and the law of cause and effect state that whatever we send out is what will return to us. We reap as we sow. If you have committed bad deeds during a life, these will be reviewed after death. The best lesson you can learn is to experience first hand what you have done to others.

"You can only learn after you have worn the sandals of another."
- Renate Dollinger

Time exists as a dimension only found here on Earth. Energy is eternal and everything is now. A life of pain and suffering on Earth will seem like no more than a second in the light of eternity, even though it may have dragged on while in the body. As souls, we know this and we are willing to experience the pain for the sake of experience and to work off our karma.

To change our suffering into empathy, we must admit that we create our own reality—consciously or unconsciously. Whatever we see in the outer world is a perfect reflection of our inner world. We could put an end to pain and suffering tomorrow if we all sought to find peace within first, since we ourselves are creating whatever we condemn in the outer world.

We are immortal souls that have lived many lives filled with pain and pleasure. Through our physical experiences on Earth we learn to live to the fullest for the good of the whole. Here in linear space-time—past, present and future, and three dimensions—we are allowed to make decisions, to learn and to develop ourselves in a unique way. This in turn allows us to experience and appreciate the whole process of manifestation. We can absorb all the feelings we experience in our physical lives.

Like trees that live, breath, grow and reach up towards the sky, so too does the soul want to live, breathe and grow.

The soul does this by developing and expressing itself in all possible ways, for better or worse.

Everyone wants more, and it is the Source in us that wants to express itself to the fullest.

"Through you the universe is becoming aware of itself."
- Eckhart Tolle [49]

This expression of the Source is described by Thomas Troward in his work entitled, *The Dore Lectures on Mental Science*, written more than 100 years ago.

Troward was a judge in British-administered India during the period 1869-1896.[50]

After he retired in 1896, Troward started studying cases involving cause and effect. He became interested in metaphysics, esoteric studies and mental science.

In the opening of *The Secret,* his teachings were acknowledged as a source of inspiration for the film and its production. One extract from *The Dore Lectures on Mental Science* is called *Divine Operation* and is featured prominently in a book entitled, *Your Invisible Power*, written by Troward's only student, Genevieve Behrend, and published in 1929.

Divine Operation:
"My mind is a center of Divine operation. The Divine operation is always for expansion and fuller expression, and this means the production of something beyond what has gone before, something entirely new, not included in past experience, though proceeding out of it by orderly sequence of growth.

Therefore, since the Divine cannot change its inherent nature, it must operate in the same manner in me; consequently in my own special world, in which I am the center, it will move forward to produce new conditions, always in advance of any that have gone before." [51]
- Thomas Troward 1909.

Troward writes, "My mind is a center." He does not say "the center," indicating that there is more than one mind at the center of the Divine—we are all in the center of the universe. Each and every one of us is in the center of everything that is happening to us. Your mind is the center of your reference frame—my mind is the center of mine. This makes us all part of this amazing field of knowledge/information—the universal consciousness.

"...Because wherever you are is the center of the universe. Wherever any atom is, that is the center of the universe. There is God in that, and God in the void." [21]
- Thomas Mellen-Benedict

This is exactly how Troward expressed it when he wrote *Divine Operation* in 1909: "The Divine always seeks expansion and fuller expression. It cannot change its inherent nature—it must operate in the same manner in me in my world of which I am the center."

Wallace D. Wattles wrote the same thing in 1910 in his book entitled, *The Science of Getting Rich*. He says, "God, the One Substance, is trying to live and do and enjoy things through humanity.

"The Source says, 'I want hands to build wonderful structures, to play divine harmonies, to paint glorious pictures; I want feet to run my errands, eyes to see my beauties, tongues to tell mighty truths and to sing marvellous songs.'

"All that there is of possibility is seeking expression through men. God wants those who can play music to have pianos and every other instrument, and to have the means to cultivate their talents to the fullest extent; He wants those who can appreciate beauty to be able to surround themselves with beautiful things; He wants those who can discern truth to have every opportunity to travel and observe; He wants those who can appreciate dress to be beautifully clothed, and those who can appreciate good food to be luxuriously fed. He wants all these things because it is Himself that enjoys and appreciates them; it is God who wants to play, and sing, and enjoy beauty, and proclaim truth and wear fine clothes, and eat good foods. It is God that worketh in you to will and to do. The desire you feel for riches is the infinite, seeking to express Himself in you." [122]

In the film *The Peaceful Warrior,* based on a true story about Dan Millman, Nick Nolte plays a mentor and humble expert on the secret of life. The message is about being in the present moment, rather than living life in the past or the future. It is about noticing the teeming life that exists in our natural environment, about seeing the twinkle in the eyes of someone passing by, about hearing the wind talk and feeling the caress of the sun's warmth. The teeming life which is the Source is constantly expressing itself through every single atom in the cosmos.

In the film, Nolte makes a great comment when he sees how busy Dan Millman is, running into the future, never stopping for a moment to notice the fantastic life happening all around him. Nolte says: "There is never nothing going on."

There is something going on all the time. It is life, displaying itself in all its splendor.

Life is a force constantly seeking an outlet to live more, be more and experience more, and we are the participating instruments being used for this purpose. That is why anything and everything is possible.

That is why we hear stories about people who have made the impossible possible, like Bill Bartmann who, at the age of 17 and during a recession, went from being a gang member, an alcoholic and broke to becoming a highly successful businessman and billionaire. Or the story about Neale Donald Walsch who went from down-and-out to becoming a best-selling author with his *Conversations with God* trilogy, which has sold millions of copies and has been translated into 30 different languages. Or the story about Legson Kayira, who went from being illiterate and living in poverty in a small village in Africa to studying political science, and becoming a professor at the University of Cambridge in England and a recognized author. Despite being unable to either read or write and having no money, he nevertheless did something that everyone said was impossible for someone in his position—he followed his inner voice, his dream, his flame.

"You are not the victim of your circumstances, but the Master of them."
- **Legson Kayira**

It is the Source's directive that we rise above our circumstances. In his book entitled, *As A Man Thinketh*, James Allan says that people cannot directly choose their own circumstances, but they can choose their thoughts and thus indirectly shape their relationship to their circumstances. Our dreams, talent, hopes and ideas are expressions from the Source which seeks more experience, more life. Anyone who persistently follows their dreams and breaks through their fear will succeed. What is inside us wants to get out. We are part of the whole and the whole is constantly seeking expression through us. It is seeking to create more and better life.

In *The Science of Getting Rich*, Wallace D. Wattles explains how we are part of a whole:

"We assert that there is one original formless stuff, or substance, from which all things are made. All the seemingly many elements are but different presentations of one element; all the many forms found in organic and inorganic nature are but different shapes, made from the same stuff. And this stuff is thinking stuff; a thought held in it produces the form of the thought. Thought, in thinking substance, produces shapes. Man is a thinking center, capable of original thought; if man can communicate his thought to original thinking substance, he can cause the creation, or formation, of the thing he thinks about."[123]

"We become what we're thinking about."
- Earl Nightingale

Anyone who has been successful has realized that dreams also contain the power to be converted into reality. Successful people have a burning desire to turn their dreams into reality, and persevere—that desire inspires them to keep going. They never give up. It is the Source within them longing to express itself. Henry Ford was one such persistent person.

In his book entitled, *Think & Grow Rich*, Napoleon Hill writes about the perseverance and faith displayed by Henry Ford when he decided to develop the world's first V8 engine. His engineers told him that it was impossible to make such an engine. Henry Ford told them to go back to the drawing board and solve the problem.

"Come back when you have succeeded, no matter how long it takes," he said. Six months later they had still not managed to find a solution. A further six months passed without a solution. They tried everything they thought possible, but to no avail.

"It is impossible," they said.

But Henry Ford stood his ground and asked them to keep going until they had found a solution. "Just keep going, because I want a V8 engine, and I'm going to have it."

They continued their work until finally, as though someone had waved a magic wand, they found a solution and Ford got his V8 engine, because he persevered, refusing to give up until his dream became a reality. Henry Ford understood that if you have an inner vision it will become a reality in the outer world. The only thing that would have stopped him is if he stopped himself. He understood the secret of life.

We live in an age where electricity is an essential commodity. Our homes are equipped with power sockets from cellar to loft, and we have a whole host of electrical appliances to help us in our everyday lives. All we need to do is plug them in and we gain instant access to lighting, heat, hair driers, kitchen equipment, vacuum cleaners, shavers, computers, printers, photocopiers, washing machines, tumble driers, TVs, audio equipment, radios, fridges, freezers, mobile phone chargers and electronic photo frames, etc. The list of electrical appliances is never-ending. Electricity and power sockets make everything possible.

Imagine that electricity is the Source, the power inside humans, and that it wants to express itself through us all the time. We are the house where we can access this power through our sockets. The problem is that many of us cannot see the sockets because we have forgotten who we are and what we are supposed to be doing here. It is like living in a high-tech house, full of advanced electrical equipment that we cannot use because we are unable to find the sockets.

All we need to do is to look inside, use our thoughts and imagination, and create whatever reality we want. We do this by using the power within, whose only job is experiencing itself through us.

So why is there so much injustice in the world? Why are there some people who are so rich that they are wealthier than some countries? Why are some people hurt, frightened and abused, while others live a life of luxury? We asked the Council of Elders what they could tell us about pain and suffering:

Camillo: Many people do not understand how a Creator can exist when there is so much pain and suffering here. It all seems to be so meaningless.

Is it right that this pain is linked to karma and that we make our own choices about the lives and roles we adopt in order to release karma?

The Council of Elders via Lilli: Know that a visit to Earth is equivalent to just a brief moment in your greater reality. It is like having a small operation without any anaesthetic— you know that it will be extremely painful for just a short while, but because of it, you will have a chance to grow and evolve. If, for example, you had a splinter in your finger, you would need to decide if you should remove it and suffer the pain for a short while, because if you don't it could become much worse. So you decide to experience the pain in order to heal.

The soul understands that incarnating can feel like lancing a boil. You accept the task, grit your teeth and do the best you can. You are equipped with the resources and the physical helpers to deal with the tasks. Not just to endure them but understand that you have actually created them yourself— you created the boil in the first place.

Scientifically, a boil may occur because you get a splinter in your finger. This is cause and effect. But what caused the splinter? A decision you made to, for example, handle a piece of wood in a particular way. You did not directly "decide" to get a splinter in order to create a boil, but some decision you made facilitated the boil to be created. Now that it is real, you must find a way to "heal" it and that path may be painful, until the boil is drained and gone.

The same applies in a karmic perspective. From the Source, you plan your journey to Earth from a state of love, but once you no longer remember who your truly are, you experience only brief glimpses of your true power of creation. Forgetting that you are creating everything makes you feel like a victim to the circumstances of your life. The challenge is to be able to cope with situations without descending into total bitterness and becoming caught up in the role of a victim.

Many souls that are living their last lives on Earth also take on the karma of others. They take on this mass karma as an act of love. Because of their selfless act, they will remember the contract they made and will thus resolve the karma of many others at the same time. It is an act of love. The crucifixion of Jesus is one such story of a selfless act of love.

When you return to the other side you take with you the plays and dramas that you created while on Earth. But the other side is divided into different layers of understanding, and individual souls gravitate towards the soul group that will assist in its future understanding. If someone deliberately committed evil deeds while living on Earth, they have to face themselves on the other side. There they congregate with others who have committed similar evil deeds. The semi-physical body remains in the soul group until there is nothing more to learn from that state, and then moves on to be given a purifying bath in which it will experience the energy of love.

A life review is again carried out and they come to understand why they were drawn to a lower astral plane, which many masters refer to as hell. There they experience their own deeds, done to them over and over again, i.e. they are repeatedly stabbed by the souls of the people they stabbed. This purification process goes through several stages, and after completion of their reviews, these souls once again receive love, process their roles, the causes and effects, and consider how they could have developed in such a way.

There may be many different reasons as to why they committed the deeds in question, but during the review it will always be appropriate to draw in souls with similar experiences in order to create a new collective body—a new substance—that will either retain the desire to commit fewer evil deeds, or may choose a life of renunciation. Based on this learning, a plan for their next incarnation is then drawn up in consultation with their guides and teachers.

Let's say that one field of such souls contains one thousand souls who have committed malicious deeds. They all spend varying amounts of time on understanding their decisions in life—let's call them sequences—in order to complete their experience. However, once they have completed this learning, they rise up, rather like dew evaporating from the grass in the morning sunshine to ascend and merge with the Source.

Those who have performed good deeds during their lives also congregate with similar souls who hold the same thought patterns and identities. They recognize each other and won't sit there boasting about being the best or claiming to have lived a perfect life. They are surrounded by the energy of love that they were working with during their lives on Earth—the connection to the divine that made it possible for them to perform their good deeds in the first place.

These good deeds are like seeds being sown. For example, a beggar who no one pays any attention to gets beaten. Someone comes along and takes care of him— gives him food, talks to him and helps him. This kindness sows a seed in the beggar, showing him that he is worth something. He still might not believe he could change his fate in that life, but he would have an experience of the divine and realize that he was worth something.

Someone like this meets other like-minded individuals on the soul plane and once again find opportunities for ascending to higher or deeper levels of returning to God, or they can once again decide to reincarnate. Souls that have done many good things can also join forces to create an avatar, a being with incredibly strong, divine light.

All these soul particles merge together and create a field of consciousness on the plane of souls that is responsible for an increase in the ability of people to love on Earth. The avatar might then go to newly created worlds as a global teacher, or they could actually decide to incarnate as Buddha, or as someone who creates tremendous evolutionary upheavals, or play a role that causes overwhelming changes in the love gestalt's experiences on Earth.

Channeled by Lilli Bendriss on July 11, August 2010 - from the energy-beings the Council of Elders

According to the Council, pain on Earth is associated with unredeemed karma that is created through the law of cause and effect: we reap as we sow.

"I am not interested, my friend, about your religion or if you are religious or not. What really is important to me is your behavior in front of your peers, family, work, community, and in front of the world. Remember, the universe is the echo of our actions and our thoughts. The law of action and reaction is not exclusively for physics. It is also of human relations. If I act with goodness, I will receive goodness. If I act with evil, I will get evil."
- **Dalai Lama** [124]

Chapter 14 - Karma

We live in a universe of free will, making our own decisions about what we do with our lives. But what happens if we deliberately injure, destroy and hurt other people? Are there any systems of justice which ensure that we learn our lesson? According to David Wilcock, there are. If we act against other people and hurt, destroy or injure them, the universe is designed to ensure that whatever we do to others will rebound on us. This is karma. It is like a boomerang—whatever you send forth comes back to you. Wilcock continues:

"You can practice the negative route if you want to—you can oppose the free will of others, you can manipulate them, you can lie to them, you can control them, you can steal their money, but you are the one who will be stolen from, lied to, manipulated, controlled, abused and beaten." This is karma. [7]

Morten Eriksen is well known in spiritual circles in Norway. He has shared his views on karma in an interview with Merete Eversen on Krystallkulen (*The Crystal Ball*, an alternative Norwegian website).

"Most of the things people do originate from the emotional patterns that are created when they are young, while others are inherited from their parents and ancestors. When your life starts you are already carrying baggage that is linked to previous incarnations. This is your karma. Karma is unresolved emotions and experiences.

"Before we incarnate we choose our parents in accordance with our karma. The emotions and 'unresolved issues' that your parents struggle with correspond with the things that you need in order to resolve your karma." [52]

This corresponds with the description contained in Michael Newton's book entitled, *Journey of Souls*. The patients in his regression studies explained that they decided in advance what sort of life they would like on Earth. Before reincarnating into each new life, they reviewed the tests they would be challenged by, what they would learn and how they would develop. They made their own decisions about whether or not they would experience pain, deceit, forgiveness, anger or many other human feelings.

They chose parents who could provide them with the framework they needed in order to resolve the karma that they had created in their previous lives. If such choices involved pain, then that was the right thing when seen from the soul's point of view, no matter how hard it is for our human minds to comprehend this. Eckhart Tolle says that suffering has a noble purpose: "The evolution of consciousness and the burning up of the ego."

In his book entitled, *Our Ultimate Reality*, Adrian Cooper explains that karma is part of the law of cause and effect. Each bad or negative action will result in a corresponding bad or negative reaction. Each good or positive action will result in a corresponding good or positive reaction. Like a boomerang, whatever you send out comes back to you.

Cooper goes on to say, "In order to progress along the path of perfection through the Astral and great Spiritual planes on the journey back to our Creator, it is vital that all bad attributes and deeds are balanced, transmuted and completely cancelled. Due to a general lack of understanding of the principle of karma, most people continue through life causing bad effects or bad karma without ever realizing it, often ascribing their experiences to such things as luck, fortune or chance. There is simply no escape from karma—sooner or later, karma has to be balanced within each and every person."[53]

The events we created in previous lives are meant to teach us to balance out our karma in this life. We have chosen the life we are living now and every step we take is designed to lead us out of the prison of this karma. In this life, we are all being challenged to escape our own personal karmic cycle. This is difficult to understand when we are suffering. The question often arises during discussions about karma:

why would anyone want to create such a harsh reality? No one wants to experience dreadful suffering—it simply doesn't add up.

So why would the Creator create a system involving free will, with good and evil, and then allow humans to experience evil? Why would the Creator allow itself to experience evil? Here, we must listen with our soul rather than our human ears.

If we succeed in remembering who we are, we instinctively know that we have the power to create both the good and bad, and in order to escape the prison of suffering, we must learn to choose the good, for our own health and well-being, and also for the good of the whole. But we are unable to see the deeper meaning when looking at it from a human perspective.

The persecution of the Jews and the horrific deeds committed against millions of innocent people by Hitler and the Nazis during the Second World War are historical examples of this. No one would wish for the horrors experienced by many Jews before they died in the concentration camps. We do not wish for pain, fear, suffering and injustice, but this is exactly what millions of Jews suffered. So did they choose this themselves when seen from a soul perspective?

The film entitled, *Infinity* (2009) by Jay Weidner, addresses this question. Infinity's message is the same as Morten Eriksen—our lives here on Earth concern working off our karma.

In this film, Weidner interviews Renate Dollinger, a German woman born in 1924 who lived through the Holocaust. She speaks of the horror of the Nazis shooting her father and her mother being sent to the concentration camp at Auschwitz. Dollinger was saved when she was put on a children's transport train heading for England, which became her new home. At the age of 17, she started having psychic experiences. On VE (Victory in Europe) Day, May 8, 1945, she took the train to London to celebrate the end of the war. In a small restaurant with no customers she sat down at one of the six tables. Shortly after her arrival, a tall, pale man wearing an RAF uniform entered the restaurant, walked directly to her and said: "Hello Renate."

"Hello," she said, "How do you know my name?"

"I know everything about you and I have come with a message for you," he replied.

"Your whole family is dead. They are all dead, except for your sister and you."

"How did they die?" she asked.

"The Nazis killed them."

She thought it was strange that this man knew everything about her and her family and the fact that they had been killed. She asks:

"Who are you and how do you know all this?"

"I am a heavenly social worker."

"Is that like a guardian angel?"

"Yes."

"But why did the Nazis kill everyone in my family?"

"They killed all the Jews."

In the film, she says she didn't hear anything about the Holocaust when she arrived in England. It was never reported or talked about—it was a secret.

"I am going to spend some time with you," said the tall, pale man. He spent three days with Renate and called himself John. Renate asked John many questions.

"Is there a God?" she asked.

"Yes," he replied.

"Why does he allow so much killing?"

"People themselves allow it to happen. Everything is free will and free choices."

"So, my people wanted to die?"

"Yes, probably, because that is how a lot of karma was released and resolved."

"What about evil people like Hitler?"

"They are incomplete people. They just have to grow and learn."

"How do they learn?"

"They will learn by becoming those they hated," he replies.

Renate concludes the story by saying: "You can only learn by walking in the same sandals as another." [108]

Here was a woman who lost her whole family and who was told that we create our own reality—that on a soul level, we seek those experiences that can resolve our karma. If this is true then the law of karma is just as real as the law of gravitation. By being aware of this law and making conscious decisions, we can break out of the karmic cycle and continue with the evolution of our souls.

How Can We Change Karma?

The most effective way for a soul to develop is to choose to forgive, self and the other.

In forgiving another, we change the deeply embedded thought of karma, "You are my perpetrator and I am your victim." We no longer believe in that illusion, therefore we will no longer manifest it. When we can't forgive someone else, we are the ones holding the emotion of resentment, and resentful thoughts, and focusing them on the other. Forgiveness allows us to think new thoughts. For it is these very thoughts that begin to form the reality within, that then must play out in the physical world. This is the quantum level on which we are learning to make conscious decisions.

When you can say, "I forgive you, because I know we are not victims, we are both creating our own lives, with our own decisions," we become the change we are looking for in others. We are not being fooled by the illusion of separation, instead we are using it to evolve ourselves forward by changing our own thoughts.

When you forgive yourself for your mistakes, it means you must stop saying to yourself, "I hate myself for being so wrong," or "I will never amount to anything." These messages are not regenerative, nor are they helping the rest of the planet. And if we are trying to evolve into a unified being, why would we allow ourselves to "act against" our own self in our thoughts that way? It, too, is bad karma.

This is the new frontier, this intricate, intimate level of human awareness: you decide what thoughts you will attach to. Forgiveness allows us to be human, take a breath, move emotion through us, and reformulate a new thought, one that takes in the whole picture, not just the judgment.

"When you hold resentment toward another, you are bound to that person or condition by an emotional link that is stronger than steel. Forgiveness is the only way to dissolve that link and get free."
- Cathrine Ponder

The Source is about creation. As creative beings we are here to learn to create for the good of the whole. We simply must remember who we really are in order to save our suffering planet, as well as break the cycles of karma. Space-time allows us a matrix to play out these lessons of the creation, from concept to manifestation. Like sowing a seed and then caring for it—watering it, ensuring it receives enough sun and nourishment—and then watching the seed start to germinate, grow and burst into full bloom. This is creation. It takes a seed, but it also takes our participation. If we left the tiny seed alone in the pot without water, the potential of the plant would not come to fruition. The seed would have shrivelled and died if we neglected our part. We are creators and we simply must learn our power.

So is there someone/something that judges us for our actions when we pass over to the other side? No, there is no God who sends us to heaven or hell. We are our own judge, jury, defense counsel, prosecutor, as well as the defendant, in such a "court case." What we sent out in our life—every decision we made—was recorded in our cells and have become a part of our consciousness. The law of karma dictates that these mathematics—if we chose to kill someone, we will eventually experience being killed in another life—manifest perfectly. So it is now up to us to realize how powerful every decision we make is. We decide: choose to do good, reap good; choose to do evil, reap evil.

We simply cannot escape this law of karma without thorough knowledge of our true selves: to remember everything, including that we are the creators of everything we experience in life. A seemingly impossible task, and yet it is the next step in the evolution of consciousness. Our job is to pay attention and take care of our own domain, our unique expression of God.

If God is almighty and nothing can harm God, why would God bother about whether or not, say, someone believes in Jesus? Why would God be a judgemental God who generates fear—if you do not obey the laws of God you will end up in hell? Many people say that God is all that is—including people. We are all created in the image of God. If we are God and God is us, why do we send ourselves to hell if we do not believe in ourselves? But if there is a God who is outside us, an external entity who is also almighty, why doesn't he intervene when terrible things happen here on Earth?

In *Conversations with God*, Neale Donald Walsh explains why God does not intervene:

"If you believe that God is the creator and decider of all things in your life, you are mistaken. God is the observer, not the creator. And God stands ready to assist you in living your life, but not in the way you might expect. It is not God's function to create, or uncreate, the circumstances and conditions of your life. God created you, in the image and likeness of God. You have created the rest, through the power God has given you. God created the process of life and life itself as you know it. Yet God gave you free choice, to do with life as you will."[58]

Chapter 15 - Creating Our Own Reality

There is no doubt that as thinking beings, we play a huge role in how we experience our physical world. We have to think in order to create. Thoughts are energy and energy becomes matter.

So how do we create our own reality with our actions? How is this connected to the choices we make while on Earth?

"We all have the power we need to create the changes we choose."
- Gregg Braden

Our Ultimate Reality is a book containing almost 600 pages written by Adrian Cooper. It is a huge reference work for anyone who is seeking answers to spiritual questions. He has written about every conceivable spiritual topic and the fact that we create our own reality:

"Only one factor at this stage, at the time of writing (2007) can be considered as an absolute certainty. Whatever the collective consciousness of humanity and of all life on Earth expects to happen over the next few years and beyond, will happen. We are facing the ultimate proof that we really do create our own reality at all levels." [125]

So if the Source is within us, what actually is this "inner world" of the non-physical? Is whatever we create in our minds something that actually manifests in the outer world? Morten Eriksen and several others support Adrian Cooper's views on this subject:

"You have to realize that life is a self-fulfilling prophecy. What you expect to happen, will happen! The whole world is the result of what we believe about ourselves. We do not see that we are the ones who create that which exists.

We will continue experiencing nightmares on Earth until we understand that our experiences come from within ourselves. We cannot save the world by ourselves, because we would then just be transferring the problems involved. Each and every one of us has to resolve the conflict within us. The world's problems have to be resolved on the inner planes."[52]

- Morten Eriksen

In *Conversations with God*, we are told that we create our own reality through our collective consciousness:

"The world's natural calamities and disasters—its tornadoes and hurricanes, volcanoes, floods and physical turmoil—are not created by you specifically. These events are created by the combined consciousness of man. What each of you do, individually, is move through them, deciding what, if anything, they mean to you, and who and what you are in relationship to them. Thus, you create collectively, and individually, the life and times you are experiencing, for the soul purpose of evolving." [88]

Is there any evidence to show that we can actually influence events with our thoughts—with our consciousness? Professor William A. Tiller, at the Department of Material Science and Engineering, Stanford University, has spent 34 years in scientific circles. He has published over 250 scientific articles, three books and several patents. He claims to have discovered a new class of natural phenomena generated via what he calls "subtle energies," which also manifest themselves in the practices of healers and other practitioners of the paranormal. He defines the term *psychoenergetics* as: the study of these energies in relation to the application of human consciousness.

He sees a connection between both physical and non-physical consciousness and natural phenomena. He says that these findings are not presently accepted by the mainstream scientific community. "Traditional scientists are unable to understand these results since they are looking at this from the framework of present day technology and science. Psychoenergetic science involves the expansion of traditional science to include human consciousness and human intention," he says.

Intention is the key. "People have tremendous power to create if they have the intention to do so," he continues. He believes that human consciousness and human intention are capable of significantly affecting both the properties of materials (non-living and living) and what we call "physical reality." He says:

"For the last four hundred years, an unstated assumption of science is that such a thing is impossible. However, our experimental research of the past decade shows that, for today's world and under the right conditions, this assumption is no longer correct.

"We have discovered that it is possible to make a significant change in the properties of a material substance by consciously holding a clear intention to do so. For example, we have repeatedly been able to change the acid/alkaline balance (pH) in a vessel of water either up or down, without adding chemicals to the water, merely by creating an intention to do so." [59]

Tiller and his team have successfully used a simple electronic device to "store" a specific intention within its electric circuit. This "intention-programmed" device can be placed next to a vessel of water at any physical location to obtain the same results they have achieved in their lab. So the device which contains an intention can affect the pH balance of water simply by being placed next to the vessel containing the water. "Others have replicated this experiment and achieved the same results at multiple locations around the world," he says. According to traditional science this should be impossible in our physical reality. He explains that there are actually two levels of physical reality and not just one. It is this "new" level of physical reality that can be significantly influenced by human intention. Tiller explains as follows:

"There are two basic kinds of unique substances found in these two levels of physical reality. They appear to interpenetrate each other but, normally, they do not interact with each other. We call this the uncoupled state of physical reality. In the uncoupled state we are able to detect our normal physical environment with our five physical senses. But the substance in this normal state of physical reality is not influenced by human intention. The substance in the "new" level of physical reality appears to function in the empty space between the fundamental electric particles that make up our normal electric atoms and molecules." [59]

The empty space that he refers to has also been referred to by several others already mentioned in this book. Haramein, Braden, Belanger and Benedict, etc. say that this is the space in which energy is located. We are in this empty space when we are on the other side. It is the empty space that inter-penetrates everything. However, in our physical world it cannot be measured using today's instruments and technology. Hence this space is invisible to us

Tiller believes that the use of intention-programmed devices affects both realities in such way that meaningful coupling begins to occur between these two very different kinds of substances, and therefore, between these two levels of physical reality. "Then, the 'new' level of physical reality becomes partially visible to our traditional measurement instruments. We call this condition the coupled state of physical reality. In the coupled state, we can measurably influence physical reality via intention," he says. [59]

Tiller's research supports what many others have been saying about the power of thought and the potential for influencing the material world.

Lynne McTaggart has also been successful in this respect with her research. She is the author of *The Field* and *The Intention Experiment* and is also the force behind a global experiment with the same name. She states:

"Human consciousness is a substance outside the confines of the body—a highly ordered energy capable of changing the physical world."

- Lynne McTaggart

The Intention Experiment supports the claims of Professor Tiller—that our intention is capable of changing the physical world. McTaggart's experiment consists of a series of scientifically controlled, web-based research that tests how the power of human intention can affect the physical world. Many volunteers from 30 different countries around the world have participated in the Intention Experiment.

McTaggert is collaborating with a team of internationally recognized scientists consisting of leading physicists and psychologists from the University of Arizona, Princeton University, the International Institute of Biophysics, Cambridge University and the Institute of Noetic Sciences. They are testing the effects of what happens when a group of people focus on the same intention and how this affects physical reality. Using scientific measuring instruments they have obtained sensational results showing that consciousness affects the physical world in exactly the same way as that referred to by Professor Tiller.

One example is the Germination Intention Experiments where psychologist Dr. Gary Schwartz and his laboratory team at the University of Arizona carried out tests to see if intention can affect the growth of plants. They obtained statistically significant results showing that human intention does actually affect the growth of plants.[60]

In 1990 Lilli conducted many channeling sessions, several of which were channeled from the energy-being Wounded Eagle. One of these sessions contained the following message:

"Nothing is new, though it may appear so. It is the old too often renewed and though the pattern changes, the base must stay the same. You are the painter of yourself. You are the artist to whom befell creative mind. You and only you hold the brush that shapes the land you wander through and gives all things one value."

Channeled by Lilli Bendriss, 1990 – from the energy-being called Wounded Eagle

This channeled message resonates with what research has been proving about how we create our own reality. We are the painters of ourselves and we shape the world through which we wander.

We are all born with the amazing power to use our imagination to paint pictures in our heads. Many well-known philosophers remind us that we become what we are thinking about:

"If you can hold it in your head; you can hold it in your hand."
 - Catherine Ponder

"If you can dream it, you can do it."
- Walt Disney

"A man is but the product of his thoughts - what he thinks, he becomes."
- Mahatma Gandhi

"Whatever your mind can conceive and believe, you can achieve."
- W. Clement Stone

You have the ability to think, regardless of what your circumstances show you. This is the secret of life. It is what the Source inside you wants.—to seek more life, more expression, more growth, regardless of what the outer world shows or tells you.

"You are not the victim of your circumstances, but the Master of them."
 - Legson Kayira

When you are thinking, you can use your imagination to conjure up images of the life that you want to live. If you listen to your inner voice you will allow the Source inside you to play along. Use your imagination to create a reality that you want to live in and which will also benefit others.

"Imagination is everything. It is the preview of life's coming attractions."
- **Albert Einstein**

"The power of imagination makes us infinite."
- **John Muir**

"Imagination is the most marvellous, miraculous, inconceivably powerful force the world has ever known."
- **Napoleon Hill**

Within us is the most powerful tool that has ever been created: the ability to think and act regardless of our circumstances. Thinking about success and taking action to achieve it when you are surrounded by a depressed global economy is hard work. Thinking about health and vitality and taking action to create them when you are ill is also hard work. But you have the natural, inherent power to choose what you think and how you act. On the other hand, far more effort is required to do this than to think thoughts that derive from your circumstances and act in accordance to what everyone else tells you.

Thinking and acting in accordance with your circumstances is easy. Thinking and acting about truth regardless of your circumstances is labor-intensive and is some of the most difficult work you might ever undertake.

"There is no labor from which most people shrink as they do from that of sustained and consecutive thought; it is the hardest work in the world."
- **Wallace D Wattles**

So how do we harness this magnificent power of our imagination and take responsibility for every thought and every decision that we make? For if we do not understand the power of our own thoughts and decisions, life quickly becomes accidental and without meaning. Everything just happens to us; people, episodes, situations just seem to come into our lives quite by chance, and we become victims of circumstance.

Where do we begin? Once again, at the Source, that is within us. Know thyself and you will know God.

Chapter 16 - Puppets

So what happens if we do not understand the power we possess? What if we deny that we create our own reality? We then become like puppets controlled by strings in a puppet theater, victims of the ever-changing circumstances happening around us.

The "strings" that control us are thoughts that arise from our subconscious, thinking patterns that have been programmed into our consciousness ever since the day we were born. Our five senses absorb everything that the outer world shows and tells us and our inner voices define that outer world. This string defines what is important, what is possible, what is right, what is wrong, and what is true.

These descriptions create a blueprint that becomes the thought patterns you use when assessing what you think about everything in your life. This blueprint is a dominant influence in our decision-making process and can unknowingly control much of what we do.

According to professor Bruce Lipton, the subconscious mind runs the show. He says, "Over 95% of our life is controlled by the invisible (i.e., generally not observed) programs stored in the subconscious mind. So while we may exercise wonderful positive healing thoughts with our conscious mind, our unconscious mind's programs and beliefs are actually shaping our lives. The problem lies in the fact that the behaviors programmed into the subconscious mind, before age six, were directly downloaded by observing others such as our parents, family and community" [126]

Maxwell Maltz, an American author and cosmetic surgeon, published a book called *Psycho Cybernetics* in 1960. Maltz's techniques have been used by many experts on personal development, such as Zig Ziglar, Tony Robbins and Brian Tracy. The book explains how entrenched our thought patterns are, and how our subconscious controls what we think about ourselves and the world around us.

Maltz explains how we can have a better life by improving our self-image. In his capacity as a cosmetic surgeon Maltz noticed a dramatic change in the personalities of people who had undergone cosmetic surgery in order to correct facial disfigurements. After surgery they experience marked improvements in their social lives. They were willing to meet new people, were more open, more communicative and more self-assured, which served to alter their self-images.

However, Maltz discovered that this did not apply to all his patients. The self-images of some patients did not change, even when major changes had been made to their outer appearance. Maltz was fascinated by the unexpected reactions that he observed in some of his patients, and Psycho Cybernetics was written as a result of his curious observations. He wanted to help these patients. He therefore wrote *Psycho Cybernetics* to show us how we are controlled by our self-image and how our self-image is created by our thought patterns.[61]

Successful author and lecturer Anthony Robbins says that what your blueprint tells you decides your potential and this in turn results in your actions. These actions produce results that reinforce your potential. If you want to change your potential and thus also the results you achieve, you need to change what you think you can do and make new decisions that result in different actions.

"Our self-image, strongly held, essentially determines what we become."
- Maxwell Maltz

So what we think and feel about ourselves decides what we become. Our conscious mind feeds our subconscious mind, which in turn controls our feelings, which lead to actions and subsequently results. If we have bad conscious thoughts about ourselves we get bad results. If we allow ourselves to become emotionally involved in the information presented to us without asking whether or not such information is true for us, then it will control the actions we perform. These actions will in turn produce the results we achieve. We then allow the outside world to control us and to feed even more information into thought patterns that have already been programmed by the outer world since birth.

One example is the global economy. During the last few years we have been bombarded by news reports about the poor state of the economy. However, some people have not been effected by the recession. When you watch news reports about the poor state of the economy, it enters your subconscious mind and has a negative effect on you. You would be allowing the outside world to control you.

It is possible to shut out such information. You can make a conscious decision to focus on seeing your own financial situation flourish. You have the ability to think independently of the circumstances surrounding you.

We need to learn to pause and reflect rather than simply believe all the information that is presented to us. We all have the ability to consider whether or not we want to accept something. Inspirational speaker Anthony Robbins says: "You must guard the entrance to your mind." Whatever you allow into your conscious mind will ultimately end up in your subconscious thoughts, and the more feeling you devote to such thoughts, the greater the impact on your subconscious mind.

We live in a thinking universe, all part of a universal consciousness. We create our own world on the basis of our thoughts, therefore it is important to be aware of what we allow into our minds. In his book *Think & Grow Rich* Napoleon Hill talks about the subconscious mind and control:

"Nature has so built man that he has ABSOLUTE CONTROL over the material which reaches his subconscious mind, through his five senses, although this is not meant to be construed as a statement that man always EXERCISES this control. In the great majority of instances, he does NOT exercise it, which explains why so many people go through life in poverty." [127]

If your mind has been exposed to a vast amount of negative information, then guarding the door to your mind will be imperative. To stop further negative information from entering into our subconscious minds we must realize the negative impact it has. Too many people let negative news, discussions, images, videos, films etc. slip into their minds without realizing the impact it has. Such an uncritical attitude about what the outer world feeds us can quickly result in negativity and fear sneaking into our minds. Then you allow the outside world to dictate your reality.

There is a direct link between this and what we are doing here on Earth. Each of us has something unique inside us, something that we dream about or have a passion for that we would pursue if we didn't allow our fears to prevent us from doing it. Our talents, dreams and ideas are expressions of the Source that want to express itself through us, but we allow fear and negative thought patterns to stop us. We believe that we are not good enough and are afraid what our friends, neighbors or colleagues will say if we pursue our dreams—if we dare to think outside the box and break out of our "normal existence." This fear inside us is strong.

"The enemy is fear. We think it is hate; but it is fear."
- **Mahatma Gandhi**

Most people allow the outer world to dictate what they can achieve. We see inhibiting limitations everywhere, which creates fear and prevents us from truly understanding our great power and potential.

John Assaraf is one of the teachers featured in *The Secret*. He subsequently wrote a book of his own to delve deeper into explaining the secret of life and how we can be successful. In his book, *The Answer,* he explains that by the time you are 17 years old, you have heard the phrase "no, you can't" about 150,000 times. But you will have only heard "yes, you can" about 5,000 times. This is 30 no's for each yes, which creates a strong belief in "I can't." When we fail to guard our minds, we surrender to what culture "feeds" us. [128]

How often do you see a negative front page of a tabloid newspaper compared to a positive one? How often does the TV news feature positive news stories?

We allow ourselves to be controlled like puppets in a puppet theater. But we can cut the strings and come to life like Pinocchio. In order to do this we have to change our thought patterns. We must be aware of what we want and how we want our lives to be.

Bill Gove was a well-known lecturer and speaker with a clear message: if we want to be free we have to be ourselves:

"If I want to be free, I've got to be me. Not the me I think you think I should be, not the me I think my parents think I should be, not the me I think my wife thinks I should be, ... if I want to be free, I've got to be me."

In order to be free we must find out who we really are, and to do this we must not allow distractions from the outer world get in the way. Everything that is fed into our subconscious is simply specific neural patterns in the brain. These thought patterns are so in-grown that they have become automatic. They are not "truth" but have been handed down from generation to generation, put there by your parents, siblings, friends, school, neighbours and the media. We are thus at the mercy of the way in which our subconscious has been programmed, but you can change your thought patterns—your blueprint—at any time.

We often hear about people suddenly undergoing a complete change in their lives, who break away and do something completely different. Something ignites the flame within and they are no longer dominated by their old thought patterns. Something brings alive feelings that they did not realize they had.

Feelings control our lives through the decisions we make, and if we change our feelings about something then we change the direction our lives are taking. This has happened to both Lilli and myself—we experienced a wake-up call—the Source inside us emerged, wanting to break through and guide us to do what we came here to do.

In *Conversations with God,* Neale Donald Walsch is writing about the way God talks to us:

"I talk to everyone. All the time. The question is not to whom do I talk, but who listens? Intrigued, I asked God to expand on this subject. Here's what God said: First, let's exchange the word *talk* with the word *communicate*. It's a much better word, a much fuller, more accurate one. When we try to speak to each other—me to you, you to me—we are immediately constricted by the unbelievable limitation of words. For this reason, I do not communicate by words alone. In fact, rarely do I do so. My most common form of communication is through feeling. Feeling is the language of the soul." [129]

Bob Proctor says, "When people pray they are talking to God and God talks to us through our intuition."

What is often referred to as our sixth sense, our intuition, can be defined as the ability to immediately and inexplicably understand or know something. We often refer to our intuition as a gut feeling. "Trust your gut feeling," is a common expression. When we first experience or encounter something we get a feeling about it. It's that first impression we gain when meeting someone. Our intuition is an opportunity to draw on all our accumulated unconscious experiences. We therefore "know" more than we think we know.

Gut feelings are a physical response to the subconscious mind weighing up all known factors and then making a decision. So are our gut feelings the Source speaking to us? Is this how communication with God takes places, as suggested by Neale Donald Walsch? Or is it just our subconscious mind helping us to make a better decision based on everything stored inside it? Many spiritual philosophies describe the subconscious as a gateway to the spiritual world, one that takes us into our dream world every night.

In order to visit the spiritual world we have to leave our everyday world of bodily sensations and move inwards towards a different state of consciousness. Every night we leave our conscious state of beta waves and enter a calmer state of alpha waves. Slowly but surely our brain becomes even less active as we enter the theta and delta states where the world of the unconscious takes us into the astral plane.

Many famous people throughout history have been inspired after entering deeper levels of their consciousness— Leonardo da Vinci, Albert Einstein, Thomas Edison, Nikola Tesla, Napoleon Bonaparte and Winston Churchill all took power naps in order to gain access to the creative levels of their minds.

In 2009, the founder of Google, Larry Page, gave a speech for graduate students at the University of Michigan, in which he said that the idea of Google came to him in a dream:

"You know what it's like to wake up in the middle of the night with a vivid dream? And you know how, if you don't have a pencil and pad by the bed to write it down, it will be completely gone the next morning?

"Well, I had one of those dreams when I was 23. When I suddenly woke up, I was thinking: what if we could download the whole web, and just keep the links and…I grabbed a pen and started writing!" [130]

This is how the giant search engine Google came into being and made Larry Page a billionaire.

In Jane Roberts book, *Seth Speaks*, Seth states there are multiple levels of consciousness and that we often visit these various levels in our dream state and then wake up the next morning remembering that we had a fantastic dream. Just like the body, consciousness has to use all its levels and activities. When we sleep, our consciousness spreads out in many different directions.

We wanted to hear what the Council of Elders would have to say about the various levels of consciousness referred to by Seth.

Camillo: In the book *Seth Speaks*, Seth talks about several other states of consciousness in addition to our normal waking state of consciousness. Would the Council please explain these different levels of consciousness?

The Council of Elders via Lilli: It is true that the state of consciousness classified as your everyday consciousness is the most relevant and well-known state. The dream states that are described as alpha states, etc. are states where you link into parallel realities from which they can be experienced. For example, the alpha state might be your everyday consciousness in another world from which your physical everyday consciousness will be inaccessible, but you can resonate your way towards it.

In the alpha level, the particles are moving chaotically, but simultaneously creating order in a system that retains and transports information along nerve paths in both the physical and cosmic bodies. This is often expressed as a mass that was previously considered to be empty, but which is a transport system for waves.

In simple terms, thoughts meet each other and communicate independently of time and space. In one way they are outside but moving through the concept of time and space and like a broom they sweep up any available information that might be relevant or useful. This is like a master brain—a cosmic computer that is linked to other cosmic computers, creating a system of networks in everything created on the wave.

Alpha and ancillary providers of alpha are found in the shift in consciousness where everything is possible. This is what people are now reaching for as they start to think the thought that everything is possible. By repeatedly thinking a thought it will culminate in a ball of information that is thrown out like a boomerang that returns with whatever has been thrown out. This occurs on a frequency or wavelength that is activated by the repetitive pattern. It has already been created—everything has been created—but here it activates. You think a thought—this is possible, this is possible, I can, I have already done it, I will—and it creates a resonance.

The law of attraction is correct. The law of adjustment is also correct. When we train our minds by thinking determined and repetitive thoughts, we enter the Source where everything is possible. We then start to attract the manifestation that has been heralded by our thoughts.

We will then experience that in our capacity as three-dimensional beings. We coexist in an alpha state that is as real as our everyday consciousness. When we succeed in maintaining the alpha state, such manifestations will then occur much faster. They can even occur immediately. The catchphrase "instant karma" is currently a popular one. "I did it and it came back immediately. I didn't wait for a year, I didn't wait until my next life." This is an example of someone who already coexists with their alpha state—with their higher consciousness.

When you become aware that you exist in a higher state of consciousness, you start to connect increasingly with the potential for communicating with other worlds and galaxies. By using your thoughts you can actually locate precisely where and who you wish to communicate with if such lies within the framework of the thought you have had.

When a certain number of people are comfortable and familiar with the fact that they coexist with other parts of themselves in other planetary systems or galaxies, it will also be easy to understand phenomena like the UFO phenomenon. "Yes, I am visiting myself from a remote past. I am activating the field that enables me to see this glimpse of light or actually absorb and understand the information."

Two people can stand next to each other, one being on the network of their alpha state in their everyday consciousness, and one who is not. One of them sees a light ship, while the other does not. The first one who sees it has activated the frequency on which it exists.

Camillo: Thank you. Seth also refers to an "A4" state of consciousness, a level involving ideas and concepts from which much of our deepest inspiration arises. How can people stop on this level and obtain all the fantastic innovations, discoveries and ideas that are available there?

The Council of Elders via Lilli: This is, in other words, the same level as the alpha and theta levels. In order to train oneself to stop on this level in the waking state, meditation and exercises in consciousness provide the key. Eastern philosophers have known this for thousands of years. You need to go into the silence—to resonate with the ocean of tranquillity in which all information resonates in the form of sound. The silence contains a sound and a pattern.

Through meditation and being in an alert state of sleep, you will gradually start to obtain information until you arrive at a point where it is simply like pressing a switch and you are able to swim in this world. You can then obtain information from this world.

Channeled by Lilli Bendriss on August 11, 2010 - from the energy-beings the Council of Elders

These levels of deeper consciousness enable us to connect with the Source. Each night when we dream we are moving through these levels, waking in the next morning remembering only fragments of dreams that we are unable to understand. Or we wake up and do not remember anything about our nightly wanderings in dreamland.

We spend our days in a waking state, occupied by all our tasks, and relating to the information provided by our five senses. We are brought up to believe that what we see is true. Seeing is believing. However, a magician can manipulate us to see things that we know are not true. Or we can stand on a railway line and it will look as though the rails cross each other in the distance, although we know that they do not. Or we can sit on a beach looking out across the sea towards the horizon where the sea and sky appear to merge, but we know that the sea continues even though our eyes tell us something else.

We allow ourselves to be fooled, but perhaps we also allow ourselves to be fooled on a much greater scale. Perhaps our whole world is one gigantic illusion. Perhaps we are living in a super-advanced film created by a higher intelligence and our five senses have been designed to perceive everything as being real.

Many people believe that we see with our eyes, but this is not the case. We see with the brain. When you look at something, your eyes send information to the brain about colors, shapes, movement, depth and distance. The brain processes all this information so that you are able to identify the whole object: what it is and where it is. Your eyes are just like windows. The function of the eye is like the mechanism used to operate a camera. The iris—the colored part of the eye—functions like the aperture regulating the amount of light coming into the eye. If the light is strong, the iris will ensure that the pupil contracts. On the other hand, if there is not much light, the iris will dilate so that more light is able to enter. Behind the pupil, the cornea and lens ensure that the rays of light are focused on the retina at the back of the eye. The retina sends the image along nerves to the sight center in the brain so that we can "see" it. Everything is done through electrical impulses.

This also applies to our other senses. All five of our senses send electrical impulses to the brain and even though we feel that everything is real, it is quite possible that our reality is an illusion based on electrical impulses. Perhaps it is a hologram as claimed by Michael Talbot, David Bohm and others.

David Icke certainly believes we live in a hologram. He is a former professional football player, BBC sports journalist, author and lecturer who believes that we are all part of a gigantic, advanced super hologram. He says that this super hologram consists of vibrations that have been decoded to form an illusory world that we think we are experiencing as reality. A computer reads and decodes software and decodes the wireless Internet on your computer. Icke says that in the same way the information (vibrations) we decode from the super hologram is a ready-made world. The hologram sends this information to the body's DNA as frequencies and this is decoded by our five senses as a solid reality in three dimensions, but it is actually a hologram:

"The Prime state of everything is vibrational so that is where the game is played."
- David Icke

Everything is vibrating at the primary level—everything is energy. Brain researcher Dr. Jill Bolte Taylor experienced this when she had a stroke in 1996 that affected certain areas of the left side of her brain. Because she was a brain researcher Dr. Taylor understood what was happening, and was subsequently able to describe what she experienced when these areas in her brain became disabled.

The left side of the brain is the logical, analytical and rational side. Skills such as language, science and mathematics are typical functions of the left side of the brain, while creative, musical and holistic skills are typical of the right side. Dr. Taylor explains this as follows:

"Our left hemisphere thinks linearly and methodically. It's all about the past and about the future. It's designed to take that collage of the present moment, and pick out details after details, categorize them, associate them with all of what we have learned in the past, and project into our future possibilities.

"It thinks in languages. It's the internal chatter that connects us to the external world. It's the calculating intelligence that reminds me when I have to do my laundry. And most important it's the voice that tells me "I am." It is what makes us individually separate from everything around us in our world." [131]

We wondered what the Council would have to say about this topic and so I asked them the following question:

Camillo: What can the Council tell us about the right and left sides of the brain? Is the left side the one that makes it possible for us to function in this illusion—in this holographic universe?

The Council of Elders via Lilli: Yes, the left side of the brain is essential for your existence. In order to just be active in the right, everything would just float around without being able to create whatever is contained in physical matter.

Thoughts create. Resonance changes what has been created. So form is created through the left side of the brain. The cubical form that people are locked into has been created through the left side of the brain. The right side of the brain is sacred geometry in the process of development.

Channeled by Lilli Bendriss on July 29, 2010 - from the energy-beings the Council of Elders

The left side of the brain creates form and the functions controlled by this part of the brain were what Dr. Taylor lost when she had her stroke. One by one she lost these functions that resulted in, among other things, the cessation of internal chatter. Dr. Taylor says that she experienced total silence. She was able to see the energy surrounding her in the empty space that scientists now know is full of energy.

"I felt enormous and expansive. I experienced myself as an energy being connected to all the energy around me, through the consciousness in the right side of my brain," she says. Because she lost the left brain functions that create form, she saw the world as it really is—as an ocean of energy. "We are all energy beings connected to one another through the consciousness of our right hemispheres as one human family," she says. "However we don't see this because inside us we have that little voice that says 'I am. I am.' It ensures that we experience ourselves as being separate from everything around us—from the energy that we are all part of."[131]

Dr. Taylor goes on to say that she saw pixels in the energy. A pixel is one of the many tiny points that together constitute the representation of an image. They are the smallest elements of an image. In other words Dr. Taylor saw the smallest elements in an image—a hologram as described by David Icke.[62]

According to Icke, this hologram operates like a voice telling us what to believe and that what we believe is real. It is similar to how a queen ant communicates with the other ants in the colony. She transmits frequencies that the other ants pick up and respond to. Many ants are able to work as a cohesive unit in what appears to be a chaotic and complex situation because they pick up signals from the queen in a vibrational blueprint.

This is similar to what Dr. Carl Johan Calleman writes about in his book entitled, *The Purposeful Universe*. He says that we are governed by cosmic waves of energy that have been influencing us ever since the Big Bang and that each one lasts for specific periods of time. He explains how the Mayan pyramids are symbolic of this and that each step of a pyramid represents one of these waves of energy. These pyramids have a total of nine steps.

Dr. Calleman maintains that the Mayan calendar is a cosmic calendar rather than a solar calendar. These cosmic waves emanate from the center of our galaxy and influence us through our consciousness. They are evolutionary waves of creation, each wave triggering a quantum leap in our evolution because they affect our awareness about what is possible in our world. Anyone who is in harmony with this energy can tune into ideas/concepts that facilitate such quantum leaps in human development. Machinery and technical inventions are one example of how these cosmic waves have affected our development. There appears to be a cosmic plan that gradually allows people to develop these inventions so humanity can progress on its path towards enlightenment.

Everything required to make the world's first car had always been there, but it was not until the arrival of the energy wave containing this consciousness that Henry Ford got the idea of making the very first car. Since the Source expresses itself through us, perhaps it does so through these evolutionary waves of creation as maintained by Dr. Calleman. "These waves help to create quantum leaps in our evolution," he says. [132] In his book he also argues that Darwin was wrong. All life stems from the tree of life and different life forms are created when these energy waves arrive for certain periods of time as they have been doing ever since the Big Bang.

In April 2000 I, Camillo, attended a one-day seminar held by Dr. Calleman in Oslo, Norway about the Mayan Calendar. During the seminar I asked him if it was possible for us to do something about the puppet state that currently applies to us. He explained that it appears that the cosmos is using these energy waves to provide us with new filters— new glasses—that are enabling us to see reality through new eyes each time a wave arrives, but that we cannot see the whole picture.

He also said that our current stage of evolution has brought us into a framework of consciousness where free will plays a greater role and that we now have the opportunity to actually choose our way forward. This immediately made me think of Pinocchio—we can become alive like Pinocchio by cutting the invisible strings that control us.

Are we going to allow ourselves to be governed by our subconscious minds and the thought patterns that lie there, or are we going to choose to be conscious of what we take in as our truth? Are we ready to wake up from an existence where we operate on autopilot without thinking about who we really are and what we want? Are we ready for a shift in consciousness? It is all about what we are aware of.

According to Dr. Calleman we have the opportunity to choose our future path. He says that the shift in energy will end in 2011, not 2012. People have lived through many shifts in energy and consciousness, but this is now coming to an end. Stable energy will give us hope.

At the seminar Dr. Calleman said: "We are now in the ninth and final energy wave that will remove our glasses, our filters, and show us the real world." What we do next is up to each and every one of us. What do we want to be conscious of?

Chapter 17 - Everything is Consciousness

David Icke says that everything stems from consciousness:
"Consciousness is the basis of life, and life is principally about compassion, empathy and love. The global society has been constructed to sell us the myth that life is about the accumulation of wealth and 'things', and chasing all the illusory trinkets that confirm how 'successful' we are. It is designed to divert us from our true and infinite self." [133]

In other words we have forgotten where we come from and who we are.

In order to change he encourages everyone to do as follows:

- Stop living life like "society" has trained you.
- Stop watching TV, reading newspapers and being influenced by circumstances outside yourself.
- Stop eating processed foods that are designed to keep you vibrating at a low frequency.
- Stop drinking fluoridated water that causes calcification of the pineal gland.
- Stand in your truth.
- Live in love.

One of these items is about avoiding being influenced by anything outside yourself. People like Anthony Robbins, Bob Proctor, Wallace D. Wattles and others mentioned in this book say the same thing: Guard your mind and know that you can think independently of the circumstances surrounding you.

One of the other items on Icke's list concerns cutting out food that causes us to vibrate at a low level. At the primary level everything is vibrating, including our thoughts and feelings. The super hologram emits vibrations and our five senses convert them into electronic signals that in turn create the three-dimensional world that we consider to be real.

If we want to be alive like Pinocchio and thus avoid being at the mercy of a puppet-like state, we must access the primary level of vibrations. Icke uses a cinema film projector as an example to explain what we need to do in order to change anything on this level of vibration. The film connected to a projector located at the rear of the cinema projects the contents of the film onto the screen. There is nothing one can do to change the information being projected. It's already created. As Icke says: "It's a done deal." [62]

If we want to change the film, we would have to do it before the film is connected to the projector.

Similarly we cannot change our reality (the film) unless we enter the primary area (vibrations) that creates our reality. Our feelings are being constantly broadcast as vibrations from our bodies and they have the power to change our world. The best way of doing this is by tuning into lower brain wave levels such as the alpha level.

It is therefore important to quiet our brain activity by using methods such as meditation. In our hectic everyday lives, few are able to calm down the activity of their brains. It's a full-time job to be assimilating all the impressions that we receive from the outer world. Whatever vibrations we send out are the result of whatever is lying in our subconscious mind, which in turn is being fed with impressions from the outer world. We fail to realize that the power to change the world is inherent in each and every one of us. We have no idea that we can actually create any "film" that we want.

Icke's ideas are identical to what has previously been mentioned in this book about creating our own reality. His message is the same as that advocated by people like Robbins, Proctor, Canfield, Wattles, Hill and many others. Our world becomes what we think, what we give energy to, what we feel and what we vibrate out.

Our consciousness has chosen to be the observer in this holographic, three-dimensional world in order to evolve, staying true to the creative nature of the Source. The physical world allows for development and experience that cannot be obtained on the other side, where we are one with everything and one with the Source, where time and space do not exist.

Our three-dimensional world has been designed as a gigantic theater stage where time and space provide the very proof of the act of creation—our bodies and perception are the very expression of God, seeking to know itself. They may be illusions but they are the important aspects of our experience, for in the details we think we perceive there, we will find the way inward.

We have all chosen to become actors in the play of life. We are in charge of playing our own roles. But the very minute we are born into this play, we lose our memories and forget that it's just a play that we can shape as we wish—a virtual reality program. However, if we want to change the program, the play or the cinema film, we need to access the primary level—the vibratory level. We change our reality from there.

Feeling Leads Us

Creation of physical reality is governed by our feelings. This frequency forms the basis of the decisions we make.

By tuning into other frequencies, by vibrating at a different level, we gain access to the level from which everything is governed—the universal consciousness. It is like listening to the radio. If you want to listen to one channel, but the radio has been tuned to another, you need to radiate at the same frequency and rate that channel one is broadcasting.

Some people tune into and out of different frequencies all the time—clairvoyants, healers, mediums. Lilli does this when she contacts the energies on "the other side." She then articulates the information from these energy beings through channeling. Since they exist on frequencies outside time and space, they can provide us with information about our possible futures.

Since futures are merely mathematical potentials, they can "do the math" and tell us what potentials are more likely to manifest in the physical world if we continue to vibrate at the same rate as at present. When we change our vibrations we change our future. So many people are running on "autopilot" in respect of their vibrations, they have the impression that life is just a coincidence—that things just happen. But we are the ones making them happen.

This is why any future prophecy is just potential images of the future, based on our current vibrations. When we change our vibrations, we detach from the outside world's influence.

Icke's challenge to stop being affected by outside influences is important. He believes that we have a reduced number of DNA strands and are thus unable to tune into as many channels as was originally intended for life forms such as ours. The medium Barbara Marciniak concurs with this:

"Many thousands of years ago the human race had 12 strands of DNA, but now we only have two. Powerful forces exist that only want us to have as little access as possible to the various frequencies, and we are thus at the mercy of a world where we do not know who we are and we can easily be controlled.[42]

"There has been a deliberate manipulation of our consciousness so that the elite can control the population and steer them away from their divine nature," says Icke. [62] But an increasing number of people are waking up. A shift in consciousness is occurring. This is a time of major changes as millions of people reactivate their own 12 active DNA strands. The process has already commenced.

Ever increasing numbers of us are opening our minds and realizing that there is more to the world than meets the eye. During the last few years more people have started asking themselves the hard questions—how am I living my life, how is society organized and how am I allowing myself to be controlled by my ego and materialism. We are realizing that wealth and fame are not a recipe for success. Now we know we can find answers to the meaning of life by looking inside ourselves.

Who hasn't heard the stories about rich, famous people dying of alcohol and drug abuse? Outwardly they appear to have everything—they are rich and famous, and apparently successful, admired and looked up to. So why do they escape into a world of intoxication that results in death? Because they are empty inside. Money and fame cannot fill the emptiness, even though culture would have them believe that, to keep them in control.

In truth, we operate on three levels, with a body, mind and soul that need to be satisfied. Money provides comfort to satisfy the body, but we must not forget the mind and soul. There needs to be a balance between the three.

We need to wake up from our long sleep and see who we really are—thinking, spiritual beings, with a physical experience in charge of our own domain. It is our job to live, to be, to believe and to develop so that the human race can take the next step in its evolution and undergo a massive shift in consciousness.

Echart Tolle says, "The arising of space consciousness is the next stage in the evolution of humanity."[63]

Indigenous populations all over the world have been saying this for a long time. We are currently living during a period where everything is changing. The time is now! Much attention has been devoted to prophecies about a new age or the possible end of the world as we know it.

Is there any connection between this and who we are and what we are doing here? Yes, we believe that there is a direct connection.

Chapter 18 - Prophecies

Why are prophecies presented to us? Is it so that we can make our own decisions about them being one of many future possibilities because we create our own reality? Yes, they are, was the response we received when we asked the Council of Elders about this very subject on July 29, 2010.

If we do not make any conscious decisions about our own future, we are at the mercy of whatever our subconscious minds expect will happen in the future. The sum of human expectations will decide which future scenarios will be played out. What we are vibrating out will manifest as the future.

One key year appearing in many prophecies is 2012. We believe that 2012 will be a symbolic alarm clock for the human race. This particular year is not necessarily the year, even though several people researching this phenomenon believe that it is. We believe that 2012 represents one more step in waking us up from our collective sleep to take control of our own domain and accept who we are. We asked the Council of Elders about 2012 and its significance.

Camillo: Is 2012 a symbolic alarm clock designed to wake us up? Is this year significant in any way?

The Council of Elders via Lilli: It is significant because people are identifying with its significance. If people completely fail to identify with its significance it will pass more or less unnoticed in your consciousness. But when consciousness is roused and resonates with the significance of a cosmic alarm clock or a window opening up to new experience, then whatever existed in the original thought or concept will be created because each cycle has an energetic influence. But individuals can either feel energetic influences strongly or weakly. The Earth's own evolutionary model is much more connected to these cycles and it is undergoing its own upheavals. You could say that this is happening almost independently of mankind, although at the same time people's thoughts are inextricably linked to the Earth. They think that they live on a planet that is solid and the planet retains its solid mass because people make this happen. These things are interconnected.

Thus the Earth is also influenced by human thoughts about what the Earth is. And if five billion people think that the Earth will collapse, the Earth will concur and play along in this scenario.

It is therefore very important to think that the Earth will establish and preserve its identity and adapt itself to a cosmic idea or thought governing such processes and creating the cycles that people identify with, because originally this was also the creative thought of mankind. Once again - what is a human being - what is God? They are the same.

These cycles have magnetic attraction and repulsion that means that their dates may vary. Nevertheless the cosmic clock is precise and the identity of the Earth and its denizens follows the cosmic clock. However, it is interesting to note that free will also allows the masses to change and adapt over the course of minutes, hours, days and years. If the discrepancy between the cosmic clock and the thoughts of the masses is too great, there will be blowouts, convulsions and disasters. People interacting with the original cosmic clock through the original thought can cause the Earth to pass through its transformation in a much more gentle way.

Throughout the ages people have experienced themselves as being connected to the Creator. When the Creator connects to creation and these are both one and understand that they are one, destruction, break-down and reconstruction will occur in harmonic resonance and people will incarnate into those eras when the resonance adjusts itself from one plane to another. And if an earthquake occurs because there is complete harmonious resonance between such an event and breakdown and reconstruction, then the plan for each individual is to experience such an earthquake. If people are supposed to die in the earthquake, then this is also part of the plan and it is consequently not a disaster, but a resonance that is not understood at the time by the individuals involved or those who observe the earthquake and the so-called disaster. However, in the greater picture everything is in harmonic resonance.

Human conflicts are moving towards understanding the greater whole and accepting their role in the whole. So there is no point in storing food in huge storehouses or building houses that are earthquake-proof. Because someone living in a quake-proof house with enough food stored for the next 100 years might go on holiday to a country that is hit by an earthquake out of the blue and they would lose their body and their physical cells. Their house would remain, the food would still be stored there, but they would ascend to a new level of consciousness where they would understand what they had agreed to and they would smile at the idea of their reinforced house.

Channeled by Lilli Bendriss on 29 July 2010 - from the energy-beings the Council of Elders

The cycles referred to here are cosmic cycles that some think will end on December 21, 2012. However, Mayan High Priest Don Alejandro Cirilo Perez Oxlaj, also known as Wakatel Utiw (Wandering Wolf), is of another opinion:

"We don't know if it will be 2012, 2015 or 2020, etc. We have lost the correct end-date," he says.[65]

Possibly there is no end-date, as the Council of Elders have conveyed, i.e. people are controlling this with their expectations and thoughts about what will happen.

Worldwide, people are troubled and anxious about what 2012 might bring! This paralyzing global gloom is overwhelming the masses, simply, because, in the midst of this tremendous 2012 media blitz, there appear to be no answers. The purpose of this chapter is to shed light on the

2012 phenomenon in order to wake the world's population from their sleep to higher consciousness. Clearly, we can all attempt to get a better understanding of the 2012 phenomenon by researching the topic. Unfortunately, there are so many diverse beliefs, proposals, theories and discussions about the so-called "end of the world as we know it" event that it demands a tremendous amount of time, effort, and, energy to get even the remotest degree of clarity.

The information in this chapter is an honest and sincere effort to provide more specific insights about the various 2012 prophecies. This information is to better explain the 2012 phenomenon as well as reveal what the "prophecies" really are. Its sole purpose is to allow you to be fearless!

What will happen in 2012? People all over the planet are searching for answers to this question. Why? Because numerous books, TV documentaries, videos, movies, websites and discussions groups have escalated their focus on this topic of a worldwide change for our planet in 2012 due to the release of the epic adventure movie 2012 by Sony Pictures (release date November 13th 2009).

The 2012 phenomenon is a range of beliefs and proposals positing that cataclysmic or transformative events will occur in the year 2012. The forecast is based primarily on what is claimed to be the end-date of the Mayan Long Count calendar, which is presented as lasting 5,125 years and as terminating on December 21, 2012.

Some people think we will undergo a positive physical or spiritual transformation, and that 2012 may mark the beginning of a new era. Conversely, some believe that the 2012 date marks the beginning of an apocalypse as shown in the film 2012. It portrays an epic adventure involving a global disaster and frightening results in the form of floods and earthquakes taking place all over the world. Director Roland Emmerich is a veteran creator of disaster films such as *Independence Day* and *The Day After Tomorrow*. Emmerich was inspired by theories concerning the calendar of the old

Mayan culture that predicts the end of our civilization on December 21, 2012. In an interview about what he calls "the mother of all disaster films," he says, "The famous Mayan prophecy inspired an excellent story."

However, this prophecy is unknown to the modern Mayans living in Guatemala and Mexico. Instead they regard the industry's increasing interest in "the end of our world in 2012" with a mixture of confusion, embitterment and anger. They perceive it as a Western distortion of their traditions and beliefs.

In November 2009 Jesus Gomez, the head of the Guatemalan Confederation of Mayan Priests and Spiritual Guides, told the Sunday Telegraph that: "There is no concept of apocalypse in the Mayan culture." Jose Huchim, a Mayan archaeologist in the Yucatan, says: "If I went to Mayan-speaking communities and asked people what is going to happen in 2012, they wouldn't have any idea. That the world is going to end? They wouldn't believe you. We have real concerns these days, like rain."[66]

It is true that there is a 2012 link to the Mayan calendar. "The calendar ends in that year," explains Mark Van Stone, Mayanist, professional art historian and epigrapher or glypher—someone who can read and write Mayan hieroglyphs. For over a decade he has focused his scholarly research specifically on Mayan culture and writing. He explains, "Those of us who study the ancient and modern Mayans—anthropologists, archaeologists, art historians, linguists, historians, amateurs, collectors—have been anticipating the end of the Mayan Great Cycle for some time. Let me affirm that the year 2012 does hold particular significance in Mayan scholarship. We write it *13.0.0.0.0 4 Ajaw 3 K'ank'in*. We have known for half a century that this date probably correlates to December 21 (or December 23) in the year 2012 in the Gregorian calendar." However, he also emphasises that his research concludes that this is not the end of the world.[67]

This date and the era in which we are currently living have been given many different names: the 2012 apocalypse, the

Time of Trial on Earth, Judgement Day, the 2012 Mayan Prophecies, the Time of Great Purification, the End of this Creation, the Quickening, the 2012 Doomsday, the End of Time as We Know It, the Shift of the Ages, and many more. But no one really knows what will happen. Why do some believe that the Mayan calendar forecasts the end of civilization? Or does it?

The Mayan Calendar
The Mayan calendar is a system of different calendars and almanacs used by the Mayans in Central America. The Mayan was a Mesoamerican civilization known for having the only fully developed written language in pre-Columbian America. The Mayans were also famous for their art, architecture, mathematical and astronomical systems.

Initially established during the Pre-Classical period (approximately 2,000 BC to 250 AD), many cities achieved their highest state of development during the Classical period (250 to 900 AD), which continued through the Post-Classical period and up until the arrival of the Spaniards. At its highest stage of development this was the most populated and culturally dynamic society in the world.[68]

The Mayans had an extremely precise understanding of the cycles of our solar system. They discovered that the entire solar system moved and has its own cycle of repetitive periods that begin and end like our day and night. These discoveries led to the understanding that our solar system rotates on an ellipse that brings it closer and further away from the center of the galaxy. Just as the moon orbits the Earth and the Earth orbits the sun, so does our solar system orbit the center of our galaxy, the Milky Way.

It takes approximately 225 to 250 million years for our solar system to make one cycle on this ellipse. The Milky Way has a diameter of around 100,000 light years. Furthermore, the Earth is also slowly wobbling like a spinning top that is not upright. This is called the Precession of the Equinoxes. It takes 25,625 years for the axis to make a full 360-degree circle, and this long cycle has been given several different names, one of which is the Great Year.

The Mayans, Sumerians, Tibetans, Egyptians, Cherokees and Hopi Indians all refer to this 25,625-year cycle in their mystical belief systems and each have developed calendars based on this great cycle. The ancient Mayans understood this 25,625-year cycle to be specifically composed of five lesser cycles of 5,125 years each. In his book, *Maya Cosmogenesis 2012*, John Major Jenkins shows that the Mayan Great Cycle is the fifth and final cycle in the 25,625-year Precession of the Equinoxes. Each of these five cycles was considered its own World Age or Creation Cycle. As depicted on the familiar, circular Meso-American Sun Stone, often called the Aztec Calendar, each Creation Cycle is said to have been ruled and destroyed by one of five elements, specifically: four Jaguar, four Wind, four Rain, four Water. Our present great cycle is called the Age of the Fifth Sun. This time period is ruled by four Earth which has several meanings, including: movement, shift, evolution, earthquake, navigation and synchronicity.

Within the 5,125 year cycle lie 13 smaller cycles, known as the "13 Baktun Count," or the "Long Count." Each baktun cycle is app. 394 years long, or 144,000 days. Each baktun was its own historical epoch or Age within the Great Creation Cycle, carrying a specific destiny for the evolution of those who incarnated in each baktun. We (Earth and everyone on Earth) are currently travelling through the 13th baktun cycle—the final period of 1618-2012 AD. This cycle is known both as "the triumph of materialism" and "the transformation of matter." The Mayans predicted this final baktun would be a time of great forgetting in which we drift very far from our sense of oneness with nature and experience a collective amnesia. Like a memory virus in which we begin to believe the limited reality of appearances and grow dense to the spiritual essence which fuels this world, so humanity's sense of ego and domination has grown.[69]

The Mayan calendar is a complex system of multiple calendars used in conjunction with each other. In this system the Long Count System has received considerable attention in connection with the 2012 phenomenon.

The Long Count

The Mayan calendar uses a system called the *Long Count* that runs for just over 5,125 years. It is based upon the number of elapsed days since a mythological starting point. No one knows who exactly set this 2012 Mayan calendar turning, but its starting point is equivalent to August 11, 3114 BC in the proleptic Gregorian calendar and is set to complete on December 21, 2012. The Mayans called this cycle the Fifth Great Cycle.

The Mayans believed that the universal processes move in cycles that never change. However what is changing is the consciousness of man who passes through the cycles—always striving to be more complete. This is the same as what the Hindu scriptures are saying: Earth and mankind go through these cycles as a whole.

The Mayans said that when the sun synchronized with the central galaxy it would cause the sun to shine more intensely producing solar flares as well as changes in the magnetic field of the sun. They said that this happens every 5,125 years and as a result the sun's polarity would change and produce a great cosmic event. Whether or not it is a coincidence, the sun has actually started changing and has lost part of its magnetic field. According to an article featured in the *Daily Telegraph* in 2008 the sun has already lost 25% of its magnetic field making it more exposed to the effects of cosmic rays, which could result in more powerful solar flares reaching the Earth.[70]

The Sun newspaper also published an article on September 23, 2010 that stated British scientists have issued warnings about a powerful solar storm that will peak in 2013. A solar storm is a large explosion in the sun's atmosphere. The Earth has been hit in the past by such explosions, most recently in 2003, resulting in the destruction of three satellites, causing power cuts in three Swedish towns and affecting air traffic. A powerful solar storm in 1989 was responsible for knocking out the entire electricity system in Quebec, Canada. British scientists are saying that the solar storm predicated in 2013 only occurs once a century and is expected to be more powerful than the one that occurred in 2003. Perhaps there is a link between this and the fact that we are now moving into the final cycle in the Mayan calendar, during which the sun is being synchronised with the central galaxy, and that this will produce such a powerful solar storm.[115]

Cosmic Forces - Nine Waves of Energy

Dr. Carl Johan Calleman, regarded as being an international authority on the subject, has been studying the Mayan calendar for several decades and has written several books, including *The Mayan Calendar* and *The Transformation of Consciousness*. Dr. Calleman theorizes that the calendar is all about energy waves that affect the human race by altering our consciousness:

"The only existing inscription from ancient times that discusses the meaning of the Mayan calendar 'end date' speaks of nine 'deities' that will descend then as its crucial event. This would in modern wording mean that nine energies or nine cosmic forces would fully manifest then since the ancient Maya would look upon time periods as 'deities.' As far as we can tell these 'deities' or cosmic forces are like evolutionary wave movements, built on top of one another where we are currently riding on the eighth one getting ready to ride on the ninth." [132]

Dr. Calleman believes that behind these cosmic forces is an intelligent plan for the history of humanity that comes from a higher source and has a benevolent intention. He continues:

"These nine cosmic forces are influencing and in fact governing our collective consciousness and so we have every reason to pay attention to what is going on in this cosmic time plan."[132]

In *Tuning the Diamonds*, Susan Joy Rennison also writes about cosmic forces and energy being radiated from the center of our galaxy. These are now entering our atmosphere because the protective magnetic fields surrounding the Earth and the sun have been reduced and may be significantly affecting our consciousness.

Investigators of the 2012 phenomenon such as David Wilcock are saying that these cosmic waves are helping to change and activate parts of our DNA that are in turn transforming our consciousness.

Maharishi Mahesh Yogi from India (January 12, 1918 - February 5, 2008) was one of the world's foremost teachers of meditation. He thought that the collective consciousness was influenced by individual consciousness. If these cosmic waves influence individual consciousness then they will also influence the collective consciousness as maintained by Dr. Calleman.

While some people believe that 2012 will be all about changes in our consciousness, others believe that we will be hit by global disasters. One of these is Patrick Geryl with his pole shift theory.

Polar Reversal

The author Patrick Geryl has conducted comprehensive research on old star codes and the results have been published in his book entitled *The Orion Prophecy*. He also writes about solar flares and their effects on Earth. He believes that the poles will reverse in 2012. He says:

"The Earth will soon be subjected to an immense disaster. The cause: upheavals in the sun's magnetic fields will generate gigantic solar flares that will affect the polarity of the entire Earth. The result: our magnetic field will reverse all at once, with catastrophic consequences for humanity. Massive earthquakes will demolish all buildings on the planet, and instigate colossal tsunamis and intense volcanic activity. In fact, the Earth's crust will shift, sweeping continents thousands of miles away from their present positions." [134]

The pole shift theory says that this shift in the Earth's magnetic field will completely reverse in one go and hence there will be devastating earthquakes and tidal waves which will destroy our civilization.

According to Geryl these predictions stem from the Maya and Egyptians. They are descendants of the legendary Atlantis. The Atlanteans had highly evolved astronomical knowledge and were able to exactly predict the previous worldwide flood in 9792 BC. They built tens of thousands of boats and escaped to South America and Egypt.

Patrick Geryl launched this somber message after having cracked several ancient star codes that are over 10,000 years old and are of crucial importance to civilization as we approach the year 2012. In that year Venus, Orion and several other stars will take the same "code–positions" as in 9792 BC, the year of the previous cataclysm. [134]

This polar reversal hypothesis alleges that either the rotation axis of the planet has not always been in its current position or that the axis will not remain where it is. In other words, its physical poles have shifted or will shift.

One of the most well known spokesmen for this theory was an American academic Charles Hutchins Hapgood (1904-1982). He was one of the best-known advocates of the pole shift theory. In his book, *The Earth's Shifting Crust* (1958) and in two subsequent books entitled, *Maps of the Ancient Sea Kings* (1966) and *The Path of the Pole*, Hapgood proposed the radical theory that the Earth's axis has shifted numerous times during geological history. He speculated that the ice mass at one or both poles over-accumulates and destabilizes the Earth's rotational balance, causing slippage of all or much of Earth's outer crust around the Earth's core, which retains its axial orientation. Hapgood wrote to the Canadian librarian Rand Flem-Ath encouraging him in his pursuit of scientific evidence to back Hapgood's claims and in his expansion of the hypothesis. Flem-Ath engaged in extended correspondence with Hapgood, and greatly expanded on Hapgood's work by developing his own theories in the 1995 book, *When the Sky Fell*, co-written with his wife, Rose.[72]

Flem-Ath was inspired by the theory that at various stages in prehistory the Earth's crust shifted dramatically causing violent earthquakes, tidal waves and devastating climatic changes. The authors examine the clues as to the location of Atlantis entrusted to Plato by Egyptian priests; the extraordinary similarities between myths from around the world; and ancient and amazingly accurate maps of South America and ice-free Antarctica that date long before the first European explorers ever reached those shores. They conclude that a civilization of highly intelligent seafarers did exist some 12,000 years ago, but was destroyed by a geological disaster leaving only a few survivors to safeguard its relics and legends for posterity.

Could such a shift in polar ice occur? Is it real? Are the origins of this theory based on the sun's generation of solar flares and the loss of its magnetic field as a result of the sun synchronizing with the central galaxy as claimed by the Mayans?

The Mayans say that this occurs every 25,625 years and that this great cycle is divided into five smaller sub-cycles each lasting 5,125 years. We are now at the end of one such sub-cycle that commenced in 3,114 BC and will end in 2012.

So is it a coincidence that the fourth stage of the Divya-Yuga cycle of the Hindu scriptures, called the Kali Yuga cycle, commenced on February 18, 3102 BC, just 12 years before the beginning of the Mayan's fifth great cycle?

The Mayan and Hindu Calendars

The last Divya Yuga cycle, Kali Yuga, started at around the same time (3,102 BC) as the beginning of the Mayan's fifth cycle (3,114 BC). The starting point for these two systems are just 12 years apart and they originated on opposite sides of the globe. Is this a coincidence? Let's take a closer look at this last Divya Yuga cycle often referred to as Kali Yuga in the Hindu scriptures.

The Hindu scriptures talk about the four stages that the world goes through as part of the Divya Yuga cycle. In Hindu philosophy Yugas refer to the name of an "epoch" or "era" within a cycle of four ages. According to Hindu cosmology, the world is created, destroyed and recreated every 4,320,000 years. Each Yuga from within the four Yugas is an age with distinctive features. The four Yugas make up a cycle called Divya Yuga, which lasts for 4,320,000 years. The four stages go from divine to darkness and back to divine again: from the first golden age of Satya Yuga, where everything is pure and the world lives in harmony and peace, to the final fourth dark stage called Kali Yuga—a time of wickedness and greed. Just like four seasons (summer, autumn, winter, spring) exist within a year, so too the four Yugas exist within the Divya Yuga. They engage themselves into stages of gradual changes.

Earth and mankind go through these cycles as a whole. A complete Divya Yuga cycle from the high Golden Age with peace, harmony, stability and prosperity to the last fourth Dark Age and back again. This cycle is believed to be induced by the solar system's rotation and revolution around a central sun. The four stages are as follows:

1. Satya Yuga: The Era of Truth when mankind is governed by gods: The Golden Age. The Hindu texts state that this age lasts 1,728,000 years and is an age of extreme splendour when the beings on our planet appear to live much longer than they do now. In this age there are no wars, famines, strife or evil. The average lifespan in the Satya Yuga cycle is 100,000 years.

2. Treta Yuga: This age is also called the Silver Age and its time span of existence is 1,296,000 human years. In this age the beings on Earth begin to deteriorate. Corruption and evil are introduced into the planetary sphere. The average life span in Treta Yuga is 10,000 years.

3. Dvapara Yuga: This third stage is also called the Bronze
    Age. This is the beginning of the "fall" of humanity.
    Corruption and evil begin to spread. It is the start of
    disharmony. This age lasts 864,000 years and average
    life expectancy is a mere 1,000 years.

4. Kali Yuga: This stage is also called the Iron Age and is
    the fourth and final stage in the Divya Yuga cycle. This
    is the age we are living in right now. In this dark stage
    evil and corruption are the driving forces. Man kills
    man—greed, wars, famine and disease spread across
    the planet and moral decent and spiritual bleakness
    rule. The Kali Yuga is traditionally thought to last
    432,000 years and life expectancy is just 100 years.[114]

According to Hindu scriptures we are now in the final
stage—Kali Yuga—that started just 12 years before the
Mayan Long Count Calendar. Even though there is a
link between the starts of these two cycles there is no link
relating to when they end. The Kali Yuga is thought to
last 432,000 years and cannot therefore coincide with the
ending of the fifth great Mayan cycle in 2012. Could there
be something to indicate that the Kali Yuga actually ends
in 2012?

Jay Weidner, author, filmmaker and hermetic scholar
thinks that there is. He spent almost nineteen years
researching the Great Cross of Hendaye and the French
alchemist Fulcanelli. His research can be found in the
two books he co-authored: *A Monument to the End of Time:
Alchemy, Fulcanelli* and *The Great Cross and Mysteries of the
Great Cross of Hendaye: Alchemy at the End of Time.*

From his research Weidner concludes that the Great
Cross of Hendaye appears to be describing not only the end
of the four great ages of the Hindu Yuga system, but also
the four ages of alchemical chronological time keeping.

The Great Cross of Hendaye is a stone cross located in
the town square of Hendaye, in the Pyrénées-Atlantiques,
in south-western France. The cross is carved with

alchemical symbols that occultists find to contain encrypted information on a future global catastrophe.

According to Weidner the Iron Age, or the Kali Yuga, will be coming to an end with the galactic alignment at the winter solstice on December 21, 2012.[73]

The Hopi Prophecy and 2012

The Hopi Indians are Native Americans living in the south-western United States. According to Hopi beliefs, the times we are currently living in are the fourth creation of life; the preceding three ending in destruction. Each time conflict came about as men forgot or denied the plan of the Creator. According to the Hopi, the Fourth World will also end soon, and the Fifth World will begin. The Signs over many years have been fulfilled, and so few are left.

The First Sign: We were told of the coming of the white-skinned men, like Pahana, but not living like Pahana—men who took the land that was not theirs and who struck their enemies with thunder (guns).

The Second Sign: Our lands will see the coming of spinning wheels filled with voices (covered wagons).

The Third Sign: A strange beast like a buffalo, but with great long horns, will overrun the land in large numbers (longhorn cattle).

The Fourth Sign: The land will be crossed by snakes of iron (railroad tracks).

The Fifth Sign: The land shall be criss-crossed by a giant spider's web (power and telephone lines).

The Sixth Sign: The land shall be criss-crossed with rivers of stone that make pictures in the sun (concrete roads and their mirage-producing effects).

The Seventh Sign: You will hear of the sea turning black, and many living things dying because of it (oil spills).

The Eighth Sign: You will see many youth who wear their hair long like our people come and join the tribal nations, to learn our ways and wisdom (hippies).

The Ninth and Last Sign: You will hear of a dwelling-place in the heavens, above the Earth, that shall fall with a great crash. It will appear as a blue star. Very soon after this, the ceremonies of the Hopi people will cease. [135]

The Hopi Indians are saying that we have forgotten where we come from and who we are. The signs are messages explaining that the fourth world is in the process of coming to an end because we do not respect all life. We are not in harmony with Mother Earth.

We all know that the Hopis, the Mayans and others have made prophecies but the fact that computer programs are doing the same is news for many people. The Web Bot program is one such example.

The Web Bot Project and 2012

Cliff High is a former Microsoft programmer who has created a special program which goes by the name of Web Bot. It supposedly predicts future events by tracking keywords entered on the Internet. Cliff High subsequently engaged the help of George Ure to work on the program.

Web Bot gathers and analyzes information based on keywords and in order to provide the essence of the emotional content it holds. Created in 1997 originally to predict stock market trends, High and Ure, who call themselves "The Time Monks," keep the technology and algorithms largely secret and sell the predictions via their website.

Even though it was originally designed to make predictions about the stock market, the people behind the program soon noticed a strange thing. In 2001, the Web Bot operators realized that stock market predictions were not the only matters being accurately predicted by the program. One of these took place in June 2001. At that time, the program predicted that a life-altering event would take place within the next 60-90 days—an occurrence of such magnitude that its effects would be felt worldwide. The program based its prediction on its filtered web chatter content. Regrettably, the program's prediction proved accurate and the Twin Towers fell on September 11, 2001. Web Bot also predicted other events:

- The Space Shuttle Columbia tragedy when the Bot predicted a maritime disaster.
- The New York blackout in 2003.
- The gun shot that wounded Vice President Dick Cheney.
- The anthrax attack in Washington DC in 2001.
- The massive US east coast power cut in 2003.
- Water rising that led to the tsunami in December 2004 in Thailand.
- Hurricane Katherina in 2005.
- The crash of the US dollar at the end of 2007.

Like the Hindu scriptures, the Hopi, the Mayans and others, the Web Bot program also has predictions for 2012. The program predicts pandemics, economic collapse, the breakdown of health care, unknown energies arriving from space and possible reversal of the Earth's magnetic poles.

It sounds incredible that a software program can predict the future. It works like science fiction, but apparently the emotional content of this program seems to pick up and predict future events. So how does it work?

Much like Google or other search engines this program also uses a system of spiders, agents and crawlers to search for information on the Internet looking for particular kinds of words. It targets discussion groups, translation sites and sites where ordinary people post large volumes of text.[74]

The Web Bot program keeps coming up with new, rather dark predictions based on the information it finds on the Internet. Regrettably most of Web Bot's predictions appear to be accurate. But how can a computer program predict future events?

According to the people behind the technology, Cliff High and George Ure, Web Bot obtains information from our subconscious minds that are linked to a greater consciousness. They call it a preconscious area. They do not use the name universal consciousness or global consciousness, but if the program obtains information from the unified field where all information is stored and time does not exist, this would explain how it is possible to predict the future. Every night we "tune into" this field via our subconscious minds. Time and space do not exist there and we can thus tap into information about potential futures. When we wake up we do not remember anything, but the information lies in our subconscious and surfaces when we start writing on various online forums and chat pages. This is what Web Bot picks up and uses to make its predictions and provides a possible explanation about how the program works.

Another "program" which has also made predictions about the future and the outcome of 2012 is Time Wave Zero by Terrence Kemp McKenna.

Time Wave Zero and 2012
Terence Kemp McKenna (November 16, 1946 - April 3, 2000) was a writer, public speaker and philosopher. He developed a program in the mid-1970s and called it *Time Wave Zero*. Time Wave Zero is a numerological formula that purports to show different events in time, defined as an increase in the universe's interconnectedness. McKenna conceived the idea of this program over the course of several years in the early-mid 1970s while taking hallucinogenic mushrooms and DMT, a psychoactive substance that can cause hallucinations. According to McKenna the universe will increase its ability to make connections. Everything will speed up and we will move from space-time to time-space. The universe will reach a singularity in 2012 at which point anything and everything imaginable will occur instantaneously. Time will cease to exist.

This Time Wave Zero program was based on his extensive research into the *I Ching—the Book of Changes*, also called Zhouyi—one of the oldest classical Chinese texts. Such texts may refer to texts that existed before

1912, when the last imperial Chinese dynasty, the Qing Dynasty, fell. These can include historical, literary and philosophical works, but also works on agriculture, medicine, mathematics, astronomy, divination, art criticism and all sorts of miscellaneous writings.[75]

The I Ching consists of 64 hexagrams and each hexagram is a figure composed of six stacked horizontal lines where each line is either a Yang line (an unbroken or solid line) or a Yin line (a broken or open line with a gap in the center).

After undertaking intense research on the I Ching and its hexagrams, McKenna began to see a pattern emerging. He could see the possibility for expressing the hexagrams and their 64 combinations as a ratio of change in each hexagram.

From that pattern he then produced a time-line graph and called it the Time Wave Zero theory. This time line ends on December 21, 2012, when he concluded that we would no longer have linear time. We will progress from space-time to time-space, and we will see that we are all connected. We will see that we are one entity.

What Do All These Prophecies Mean?
What will happen on December 21, 2012? Will the world end? Will we all die? Or will we survive, but with a whole new level of consciousness—an entirely new way of life without the material goods many of us possess now? Or will nothing happen and it will be "business as usual," just like we experienced in the year 2000?

Many predications were made concerning the start of the new millennium, but none turned out to be true. Dr. Robert Sitler, Director of Latin American Studies at Stetson University in DeLand, Florida has visited and studied the Maya for over 30 years and has direct knowledge of their culture and their outlook on 2012. In his article 2012 and

the Maya World that features in the book, *The Mystery of 2012*, he said: "December 21, 2012 will likely be a 'non-event' similar to the widely anticipated Y2K phenomenon."
136

Others, such as Mayan researcher John Major Jenkins, refer to the symbolism connected to the date December 21, 2012. Once every 25,652 years the Earth falls into line with the Sun and the center of our galaxy at the winter solstice. According to Jenkins crossing the galactic plane is not something that can be achieved during the course of one day, but rather a 36-year period between 1980 and 2016. The winter solstice on December 21, 2012 lies within this window. Jenkins believes that the Mayans therefore ended their calendar within this window since it symbolized the end and the beginning of a cycle. But what does this mean for those of us who are living now? Most of us will be here when December 21, 2012 arrives, but what will happen?

No one knows, but one theory is that absolutely nothing will happen, as claimed by Robert Sitler. Another, the polar shift theory, claims that Earth's core will shift over the course of just a few days and alter the location of the North and South Poles resulting in a global catastrophe involving massive earthquakes and tsunamis. A third theory is that 2012 marks a shift in consciousness because the energy waves emanating from the galactic center will affect our DNA and thus alter our consciousness. This view was also that of the "Sleeping Prophet" Edgar Cayce.

Edgar Cayce and 2012

Edgar Cayce (March 18, 1877 - January 3, 1945), often referred to as the "Sleeping Prophet," was an American who claimed to be psychic with the ability to channel answers to questions about many different topics. He addressed everything from health to Atlantis while he was in a self-induced trance. For more than 40 years Cayce gave readings to thousands of people. In an unconscious trance state he diagnosed illnesses, revealed past lives and made prophecies about the future. John Van Auken has written about Edgar Cayce and his views about the New Age in an article entitled *December 21, 2012 - Mayan Year of Destiny.* When Cayce was asked about what the New Age would mean for humanity, he replied:

"The full consciousness of the ability to communicate with the Creative Forces and be aware of the relationships to the Creative Forces and the uses of same in material environs. This awareness during the era or age in the Age of Atlantis and Lemuria or Mu brought what? Destruction to man, and his beginning of the needs of the journey up through that of selfishness."

In his article Van Auken goes on to say: "Cayce is informing us that in a previous time cycle, humanity had a level of consciousness and relationship with the Creative Forces that allowed us to live at higher levels of material, mental and spiritual activity on the Earth and beyond. Unfortunately, we misused this consciousness and the power that came with the close relationship to the Forces. This misuse brought on the destruction of our great cultures and a long, karmic soul journey through the pain and confusion that resulted from our selfishness and self-centered focus on our will without regard for the will of the Creator and others.

"Now, as the cycles come around again, we are nearing a time when the level of consciousness and relationship with the Creative Forces will allow us once again to regain these powers."[76]

"What happens in January 2013 is up to us. It is dependent on how many of us manage to increase our vibrations and consciousness in order to contribute towards a completely new age—an age of enlightenment," says Van Auken.

Chapter 19 - A New Age

Cayce and Van Auken say that we are living in an age in which a window of opportunity has opened—an opportunity to leave behind humanity's current stage of evolution and move on to the next. Adrian Cooper, says the same in his book, *Our Ultimate Reality:*

"We now have the opportunity to evolve from Homo Sapiens to become Homo Spiritus or Homo Luminous—enlightened beings."

Hypnotherapist and remote viewing expert Gerald O'Donnell also says that the age we are living in is special and that we are facing a shift in consciousness. In the article *Gerald O'Donnell's Thoughts On The Coming 2012 Shift* featured on FinerMinds.com he says: "We are entering a new period for mankind: a period of bestowal of the gifts of the harvest of what has been planted by our acts and thought patterns for aeons until this very point in time/space, a period of reflection and analysis, a moment of introspection and sublimation of our, for now, finite human Self, that will call us to rise a bit above the immediate perspective we are used to and our old ingrained familiar thought programs.

"When this moment reaches the shores of our consciousness we will have no other choice than to perceive that our world is but one unit, one planet, where ALL separations are just illusions planted and ferociously guarded by fear-based interests born into and conditioned by a consciousness of great lack."

He continues: "The moment of this great shift is getting very close in our perception of time/space. We are heading towards it in a rapid manner: it is situated around the 2012 time frame. All is accelerating as we are nearing it. This is the time of the final clash between separation and unity, gifted to us, so that we never again repeat history and go back to these unworkable patterns. What really counts is for us to decide, in common accord, to enter a bountiful oriented consciousness that knows that all that is needed is already present."

He goes on to say: "What is needed is to dream and act for the good of all humanity and be willing to gift unconditionally in the name of unconditional Love your presents, and presence, to all, without expecting anything in return, as a mother or a father would want to gift to their child."[77]

Our reason for existing as human beings is primarily to become as separate as possible from each other—and then finally to find our way back to *the unity*—from which we all derive. Many people talking about "the end of the world as we know it" are echoing exactly what O'Donnel is saying. A shift in consciousness is upon us and is changing how we view the world and each other. We are once again remembering and understanding that we are all ONE.

Many people have opinions, viewpoints and prophecies about our current age and what is brewing, but no one truly knows what will happen. These are all just assumptions. Perhaps nothing will happen or perhaps we are entering a new age as forecasted by the Mayans, the Hopi Indians and McKenna. Are we on the threshold of yet another golden age—an era of peace and goodwill? Will harmony, peace and spiritual awakening be dominant? If a new golden age awaits us, will we be lifted up to a new dimension? And will we place all hate, jealousy, greed and corruption behind us? Will we realize that we are all connected and part of a universal whole?

Dolores Cannon is a past-life regressionist, hypnotherapist and author of several spiritual books. She has been talking about a transition to a new dimension—a fifth dimension. From our third dimension we move via time, which is the fourth dimension (also called the Rainbow Bridge) to the fifth dimension where we will become one with everything and everyone. We will be able to practice telepathy, telekinesis, levitation and many other things that are currently regarded as being impossible.

"We are surrounded by dimensions," says Cannon, "but we cannot see them because they are vibrating at different frequencies that we are unable to perceive."

She also has an explanation as to why the Mayans and some Indian tribes suddenly disappeared. No one knows what happened to them, but according to Cannon they knew how to change frequency and tune into a different dimension. They knew how a whole civilization could make the transition to another dimension. Furthermore, they understood that the next dimensional shift will apply to the whole planet, hence they stopped their calendar in 2012.

"We are living in an age where this has started to happen. Our three-dimensional world is one of challenges and fear, while the fifth dimensional world is one of love and peace. It started in 2003, and we are right in the middle of it now," she says.

She also refers to the medium Annie Kirkwood and her vision of Earth cloning itself and becoming two planets: the old three-dimensional Earth and the new fifth dimensional Earth. Not everyone will migrate to the new fifth dimensional Earth because they cannot change their vibrations fast enough. If they are still struggling with negativity they will be left behind on the old Earth. "They will be left behind with what they created. They will continue working on their karma there," Cannon explains.

People who understand what is happening will have the opportunity to migrate to the new fifth dimensional Earth. It is time to make a choice. Thought = manifestation. Anyone who is locked into negativity and the wheels of the karmic cycle will not migrate. She continues:

"The new shift will come—a new dimension. When this happens there will be a separation of the old world from the new. This has never happened before in the history of the universe—an entire planet will shift to another dimension. This is the greatest show in the universe. All extraterrestrial beings are watching this to see if we can pull it off. We will feel it in our bodies—things are changing. When the planet changes frequency we will have to do the same. We are going through this with Mother Earth, and therefore we also have to change our vibrations."[78]

The possibility of a great show taking place is supported by George Green in *The Handbook for the New Paradigm*:

"Observers of this drama that is being played out on planet Earth are looking at you with wisdom and know that the outcome will be positive, but with thoughts for how many people will be left behind in order to be led through the process leading to the next opportunity. It will be a great relief for them when this experience on Mother Earth has been completed. Exactly how this will occur has become very interesting, because you yourselves have created your own magnificent and spectacular play."[27]

Dolores Cannon says that Mother Earth has already started changing frequency and moving over into a new dimension. If we can verify that the Earth is in the process of changing its frequency, would this indicate that Cannon might possibly be right? But how can the frequency of the Earth be measured?

One of the greatest inventors of the last century was Nicola Tesla. His research included the remote transference of power and energy over long distances. He succeeded in generating strong electrical currents that resulted in the creation of artificial lightening and also produced radio waves. Because of their extremely low frequency these waves can penetrate into the Earth without any resistance. Tesla thus discovered the Earth's resonance frequency.

Unfortunately Tesla was a man before his time and his discoveries were not taken seriously. It was not until 1952 that we became aware of what Tesla had discovered, but it was the German physicist Professor Winfried Otto Schumann who was granted the honor of discovering the Earth's frequency. He predicted that there are electromagnetic waves in the atmosphere, in the cavity formed by the Earth's surface and ionosphere. His discovery became known as *the Schumann Resonance*.[79]

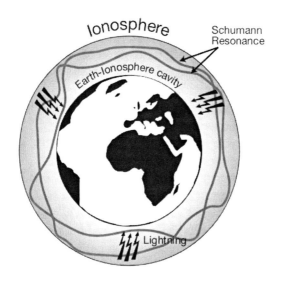

In *Tuning the Diamonds*, Susan Joy Rennison talks about how the intensity of the whole spectrum of the Schumann Resonance frequencies has become *much stronger*. Furthermore, the book *Seth Speaks* says that each atom has consciousness and that Mother Earth is thus no exception. Is it then possible that Mother Earth is in the process of changing her frequency and thus preparing for a shift in consciousness? Is Dolores Cannon right? Will we be able to migrate to a fifth dimensional Earth? Others are talking about an entirely different change than a transition to a fifth dimensional Earth.

One of these is Jay Weidner, who believes that we will go back to basics. Weidner talks about how we will spend 80% of our time on growing food and learning to live in tune with nature again. According to Weidner we will see an even greater downturn in the economy during the forthcoming years. [73]

The good news is, we will no longer be slaves of an economic structure where society is run by corrupt politicians and rich, greedy people with an agenda aimed at becoming even richer and more powerful. The masses will be liberated and we will experience a new level of consciousness.

There are many different views about what the future will bring, but no one can say what will happen with any degree of certainty.

Is there something we can do to ensure a harmonious and peaceful outcome for 2012?

Pacal Votan, a 7th century Mayan prophet, left behind the following message for future generations:

"If humanity wishes to save itself from biospheric destruction it must return to living in natural time."

What does this message mean? He foretold of our accelerated technological society and the resulting damage of our collective divergence from natural law in exchange for materialist values. His prophetic call is alerting present-day humanity that our biological process is transforming, approaching the culmination of a 26,000-year evolutionary program. Bringing the return of universal telepathy, heightened sense capacity and self-reflective consciousness, this is the return to the sacred domain of our inner technology. This grand cycle of evolution will culminate at the winter solstice on December 21, 2012 AD. [80]

Our individual efforts will enable us to avoid heading towards the major catastrophe that our planet would have to suffer in order to start a new age, the sixth cycle of the Sun. The Mayan civilization occurred during the fifth cycle of the Sun, and prior to that four other major civilizations were destroyed by large natural disasters. They thought that each cycle represented just one stage of humanity's collective consciousness. The forthcoming changes will enable us to make a quantum leap in the development of our consciousness and thus create a new civilization that will allow all people to experience harmony and compassion. The answer to the question about whether or not we can help to bring about the future that we seek is YES. We can help to achieve whatever outcome we desire. But how?

In order to answer that, let us look at the possibilities relating to the existence of a universal consciousness—a universal mind. How could the Mayans, the Hopi Indians, Edgar Cayce, Terence McKenna and his Time Wave Zero software, Cliff High and his Web Bot software and many others see into the future and predict more or less the same results?

Some of the people researching this material are astounded and suspect that these various people, from different times and cultures, appear to have been able to tune into a sort of common universal mind and that all these prophecies represent the collective unconscious part of the universe and its inhabitants. But how can computer software or some people tune into the collective unconscious part of the universe? The previously mentioned unified field provides one likely explanation.

The Unified Field: The Universal Fabric That Connects Us All

What scientists once thought was empty space between stars and planets actually consist of small energy bundles called quarks and leptons surfing on an ocean of pure consciousness. Scientists are realizing that space is not empty—something does exist at sub-atomic level. Many researchers, such as the previously mentioned Dr. Hammeroff, Dr. Wolf, Dr. Hagelin and others have said that there is a intelligent information field that serves as the basis for everything that exists—a unified field that connects us all. Professor Hagelin and several others believe that we can benefit from this by gathering all the information we need from this field of universal consciousness. But how do we do this?

One way is through meditation. A technique called *Transcendental Meditation* introduced by the guru Maharishi Mahesh Yogi has shown remarkable results in reaching this level of universal consciousness. Yogi says that anyone can attain this level of universal consciousness.

This field from which energy arises appears to be an ocean of pure consciousness. Everything in the physical world is made out of atoms. Atoms are pure energy and energy is made out of consciousness. Consciousness is what the universe is made of. Matter and energy are just two of the forms adopted by consciousness.

It could be possible that the Web Bot program obtains information from this field through our communications. The software collects, analyzes and displays the information that we all pick up from this field with our subconscious minds. We pick up this information during our waking states, our dream state and states of meditation. We then convey this information in our communications on the Internet with each other without really being consciously aware that we are reflecting information from this field—the unified field.

If such a unified field of consciousness exists, this would explain a lot. Such a field of information would explain why the Mayans, the Hopi Indians, Edgar Cayce, Terence McKenna, Cliff High and others could be so precise when making their predictions. This unified field contains *all knowledge*—all that has ever been and all that will ever be. There are no space or time constraints in this field. The answers to everything we ever wanted to know are contained within this field.

We are all particles of this incredible universal consciousness—this thinking, powerful, vibrating universe. We are thinking beings, living in a thinking universe. Anyone tapping into this field through meditation and the subconscious mind will be able to retrieve any information they desire.

Napoleon Hill talked about this in his book, *Think & Grow Rich*. Both Wallace D. Wattles and Charles F. Haanel talked about it in their books, *The Science of Getting Rich* and *The Master Key System*. The unified field holds all the answers. There is only *now*. Our past, present and future are all happening *now* in the unified field. Hence the future is already present.

Edgar Cayce, the people behind the Mayan Calendar, the Hopi Indians, the Web Bot project and others have all been tapping into the unified field. It's what we do when we use transcendental meditation—we obtain access to the unified field where everything exists independently of time.

The Mayans were preoccupied with time and were keen stargazers, they were known for having developed a precise understanding of our solar system and its cycles. They had to develop an understanding of what they observed in the skies before creating their calendar. It is quite possible that they obtained their amazing understanding from the unified field—the field of all knowledge.

The Mayan religion displays characteristic Mesoamerican mythology, with strong emphasis on individuals being communicators between the physical and spiritual worlds. Did they use meditation for making spiritual contact, or was there something else involved? According to Adrian Cooper their shamanic culture often made use of substances that could "expand the mind." These substances (entheogens) were used for entering altered states of consciousness and obtaining access to the inner areas of life. Although many entheogens are hallucinatory substances, there are apparently some types that can induce genuine inner experiences. By virtue of their shamanic arts, the Mayan shamen would undoubtedly have been able to gain access to the Source of collective knowledge and events in the universe in all areas of life and reality.[81]

One ongoing scientific project that is examining subtle correlations that may reflect the presence of consciousness is the *Global Consciousness Project*. The people behind this project say that there appears to be a global consciousness of which we are all part.[82]

Tom Atlee, who is involved in the Global Consciousness Project, has written an article called: *Something bigger than life is trying to work through us.* The article is saying that our collective consciousness is creating the world that we experience:

"Crises are doorways that look like hurricanes. Hidden by our institutionalized not-see-ism, the crises that are coming are being co-created moment-to-moment by our collective consciousness, our technologies, our social systems, simply by doing what they were designed to do. These co-created crises are magnificent in their complexity, their challenge, and their perfect fit for our evolutionary awakening, which is underway even as you read this. They call us to look in the mirror of evolution and see ourselves clearly, to look at how we have set up our world. They call us to step out of the box—for the box is burning!—and to transform ourselves and our world by wise choice, creating the path as we walk it." [137]

People find this hard to believe because we cannot see the effects of what we are thinking. But we are thinking beings, and our thoughts are powerful cosmic waves that penetrate all time and space. We are all part of this thinking universe. It's time to wake up. This is our wake-up call. We must once again remember who we are—co-creators of this universe. We all participate in this creation and we are all interconnected—Mother Earth, plants, animals and humans.

However the human race regard themselves as being superior to the animal and plant kingdoms due to their superior intelligence and consciousness. But what if both animals and plants perceive our thoughts and our energy on a level that we are not even aware exists?

Plants Respond To Thoughts
Cleve Backster has been researching bio-communication (primary perception) for 40 years. His research shows that plants respond to our thoughts. He used to work for the CIA on interrogation tactics and as the Director of the Keeler Polygraph Institute was an expert on lie detectors. Back in 1966 he carried out tests to see if plants reacted to the polygraph machine. To his great surprise he discovered that a polygraph machine attached to a plant leaf registered a change in electrical resistance when the plant was harmed or even threatened with harm. Even the thought of harming a plant was enough to elicit a response from Backster's

monitoring equipment. This marked the beginning of his amazing biocommunication research revealing that plants actually react to our thoughts.

We wanted to ask the Council of Elders about Backster's research.

Camillo: I have read about Cleve Backster's extremely important research on bio-communications and how plants react to our thoughts. What can the Council tell us about this?

The Council of Elders via Lilli: An interesting film has been produced which many people have seen—*Avatar*—where someone was surrounded by a dark, scary jungle teeming with aggressive, dangerous animals. However, when this person's sight was opened the darkness changed to become living consciousnesses that were in harmony with each other. Being able to see the unique life in each individual plant resulted in a natural display of care and communication with plants that existed to provide human food so that they could be co-creators, co-exist with humans and willingly give their petals in service to each other for medicinal purposes without breaking the divine laws.

This is evolution. When our collective awareness reaches a critical point, there is a moment, as in the film, where night becomes day and we become surrounded by a natural understanding of all life. Tribal and indigenous people have a far better understanding because they live in tune with nature. For their survival as individuals and as people they need to look after what is growing and what the animals provide them. However, for many people this is groundbreaking research.

In some tribes the shaman created medicines that were so complex with exactly the right quantities of each ingredient, that the Western scientists who analyzed such medicines were totally unable to understand how an ignorant native could have made them. When asked how he could know that a particular quantity of plant material was necessary, the medicine man replied laconically: "Because the plant told me." This is what will happen to humans—the plants will talk to them and there will be mutual respect—quite naturally.

Channeled by Lilli Bendriss on July 29, 2010 - from the energy-beings the Council of Elders

This explanation indicates that all life is part of a universal consciousness and that cells are linked to a non-local spaceless-timeless continuum often referred to as the *Absolute*, EVERYTHING, the Source, the Power, the unified field, the universal field, the divine operation, the universal mind, the universal consciousness, the one mind, the higher intelligence, and God, just to mention a few.

Does the possibility of such a field/mind/power existing sound like science fiction? Not if you have an open mind. When you start studying this material, talking to like-minded people and critically thinking about it, you will realize that everything is consciousness. We are all part of it. Everything is energy—everything is vibrating.

New fields have been discovered during the last 20 years through the application of quantum mechanics and physics. Science and theology are now approaching each other. Science reveals that everything is vibrating energy that has its own frequency. This is the energy present everywhere on the surface of a universal consciousness.

At the same time theology is saying that God is everywhere—in everything and everyone. It would therefore appear that we are all part of an amazing knowledge/information field. We are spiritual beings having a physical experience, and when we understand who we are we can move on to the next phase in an amazing shift in consciousness that is already in motion.

Chapter 20 - A Fantastic Opportunity

A thought does not just exist inside our heads. It is broadcast to the universe as an electromagnetic entity. We become what we are thinking about. We become whatever we choose to give energy to, whatever we visualise and envisage within. Our thoughts really do mean something.

"Everything we are is the product of our thoughts."
– Buddha (563 – 483 BC)

This message has been reiterated by many throughout the centuries, and was also a large part of the film, *The Secret*. Millions of people around the world started to understand the power inherent in their own thoughts. What we think, say or feel creates ripples in the ocean of energy in which we exist. These ripples affect other people, our planet and even the rest of the cosmos. We should therefore pay attention to what we think, say and feel.

We all have the ability to tap into the unified field via our subconscious. Following 40 years of research José Silva was able to show that it is possible to consciously program the subconscious mind when engaging with the lower brain wave frequencies, e.g. the alpha level.

There are fantastic opportunities available to us since we are all part of this universal field of consciousness. It provides us with the opportunity to decide how we want our future to be. Together we can reach agreement about particular ways in which we want our future to develop because it can be exactly how we want it to be. We create the "film" and can decide what we want the film projector to show. Everything is about creating from the inside out. Whatever we create in our minds manifests in the outside world. Whatever we give energy to, whatever we pay attention to, whatever we think, say and feel, create vibrations and a creative process that is incredibly powerful.

On Earth linear time enables us to enjoy the process that elapses from concept to reality through our physical experience.

"We are here on Earth in this linear time system to experience all phases of the manifestation process."
- Michelle Belanger

We have the power to create, but fear prevents us from using it. We are frightened by doomsday prophecies about the world as we know it coming to an end. However, we believe that these prophecies have been given to us so that we can make up our own minds about them. The outcome cannot be taken for granted because it is conditional on what we expect to happen. We have the power to change the results that have been forecast in these prophecies that serve as small nudges designed to wake us up. It is as though the Source is talking to us and saying:

"If you continue thinking like that, the film/play will continue to be played out in the same vein and the prophecy will be fulfilled." In order to change the outcome we have to change what we think, what we give energy to, what we create in our own minds. No one knows what the future holds, no matter how "convincing" these prophecies may seem.

Everything is in constant movement. Everything is constantly changing. We are the creators of the film/play and can decide which direction it will take. However, we need to be aware that we have the power to change it with our feelings/vibrations. Several scientific studies have been conducted showing the power inherent in human intention. When many people with a common intent gather to meditate together (send out vibrations) they are able to change the "film" that we are living in.

In 1960 Maharishi Mahesh Yogi forecasted that if 1% of a given part of the population practiced Transcendental Meditation this would create measurable improvements in the quality of life of the whole population. This became known as the *Maharishi Effect,* and it is based on how individual consciousness affects collective consciousness.

The long-term positive benefits of this unique effect have been confirmed by a number of scientific studies conducted over the last 25 years. Professor John Hagelin has been instrumental in many of these studies showing how our thoughts can have a great impact on the world. The research in which he has been involved has backed up the predictions of Maharishi Mahesh Yogi.[83]

Also in the book, *Transition Now, Redefining Duality, 2012 and Beyond* by Martine Vallée, we find the following information regarding collective consciousness, "No more than half of 1 % among you is needed to create a movement which will lead to world peace." [116]

"A man is but the product of his thoughts—what he thinks, he becomes."
- Mahatma Gandhi

"Change your thoughts and you change your world."
- Norma Vincent Peale

"You are today where your thoughts have brought you. You will be tomorrow where your thoughts take you."
- James Allan

"Each emotion and thought has its own electromagnetic reality, completely unique. Each of you acts as a transformer, unconsciously, automatically transforming highly sophisticated electromagnetic units into physical objects."
- Seth Speaks

The world as we know it is a reflection of our inner world. In *Seth Speaks* we learn that the intensity of our feelings and thoughts decides both the strength and permanence of whatever physical object we create. This is why all religions and indigenous populations all over the world say: "Go within."

We are made of the same ingredients as a chair, a stone, a bird or a planet. Our world is created by consciousness uniting in a gigantic joint venture. We create on both an individual level and a global/collective level. By mobilizing our thoughts/feelings/vibrations to use this creative power, we can create our own world and thus decide our future. We have the ability to think independently of the circumstances surrounding us. We are not at the mercy of outside forces, even though many believe that we are. Many people just sit and wait for life to happen. This is unnecessary because we are the creators of events—either consciously or unconsciously. All power is inside each and every one of us.

During the last 48 years, Joseph Robert Jochmans has been a keen investigator of the mysteries of the past. He has been "hunting" for the hidden wisdom of lost civilizations and the revelations contained in ancient prophecies from all corners of the world. He says:

"The Hopi and Mayan elders do not prophecy that everything will come to an end. Rather, this is a time of transition from one world age into another. The message they give concerns our making a choice of how we enter the future ahead. Our moving through with either resistance or acceptance will determine whether the transition will happen with cataclysmic changes or gradual peace and tranquillity. The same theme can be found reflected in the prophecies of many other Native American visionaries from Black Elk to Sun Bear."
- **Joseph Robert Jochmans** [138]

Global changes will continue to occur during the forthcoming period. This process could either be an easy, tranquil process, or one involving unrest and disaster. Human energy and thoughts will be the deciding factors. Your energy, your thoughts, your feelings and your consciousness will help to decide the future.

Increasing numbers of people are gradually starting to undergo an awakening, recognizing that we are part of something bigger. Our frequencies are starting to increase and everything is vibrating at a higher rate. Earth and humanity are being exposed to cosmic rays that are increasing our consciousness.

As previously mentioned, it is not just the Earth that is experiencing global warming. All the planets in our solar system are experiencing the same thing, as shown in Wilcock and Hoagland's 2004 report entitled, *Interplanetary "Day After Tomorrow?" An Enterprise Mission Hyperdimensional Report*.[44]

"The increase in frequency has started," says Dolores Cannon. David Icke believes that this will continue during the forthcoming years and that we can either opt to resist or participate. Like a river growing in force, we are standing in the middle and can either stop fighting against it and allow ourselves to flow onwards with the current by opening our minds, or we can resist with all our might while the river becomes increasingly more powerful.

It is important to increase people's awareness about the power that we all possess—the power to think and create our own outer world. The masses need to alter their thoughts, but far too many people are hurting other people both physically and mentally by sending negative thoughts. Every time you have a negative thought about someone else you are actually transmitting a wave of negative energy. This is hard to understand because it is not something that we can see. We have grown up learning to only trust what our five senses tell us. We do not believe that our thoughts actually mean something. We say: "It is just something I'm thinking and it's inside my head." But your thoughts create vibrations that are broadcast to the cosmos. Our bodies exist in a universal consciousness. Not the other way round.

Far too many people are ignorant about the power they bear inside themselves—the power to think independently of circumstances. People simply react to the outside world. They do not stop to think. We believe we are thinking, but this is a mental activity. We react, but we have to *respond*. Stop and think. We must not allow the outside world to dictate our future. We must not allow apocalyptic films, books or prophecies to upset us and create fear. When you worry about something, you are actually helping to create the very situation that you are worried about. You should know that you have the power to create the reality you want with your thoughts.

"You are not the victim of your circumstances, but the *master* of them."
- **Legson Keyira**

We must dream, visualize and expect the future we want and it *will* happen. We have to start changing the way we look at ourselves, and our relationship to our fellow beings, nature, animals and plants—everything that is part of our lives. If we start thinking more life for everyone and less for no one, we will be broadcasting such a strong collective wave of positive thoughts to the cosmos that the world will become a harmonious place. We must be in tune with nature and Mother Earth—we must respect and look after our planet that gives us life.

During a channeling session conducted by Lilli in 1993, the Council had the following to say about Mother Earth:

"People will see the power of nature and they will see the range of nature as if she is saying: "You have to balance yourselves or I will attack you. What you do comes back to you. I return it to you. You think you have so much control, that you can do whatever you want without consequences, but it is not so. I will return to you what you have sent to me."

"This is what people must become aware of. They cannot go on misusing and abusing everything around them. They must become aware that they must begin to cooperate with nature. They must work towards balance. This is the point."

Channeled by Lilli Bendriss on July 31, 1993 – from the energy-beings called the Council of Elders

People have exploited nature and caused great harm to their fellow beings. Man is killing man—greed, war, famine and disease are spreading across the whole planet. We have brought this on ourselves as a result of our collective thoughts.

There is an old saying that reads as follows:
Watch your thoughts, for they become words.
Watch your words, for they become actions.
Watch your actions, for they become habits.
Watch your habits, for they become your character.
Watch your character, for it becomes your destiny.

In 2008 Jay Weidner made the following statement at a conference held in the USA:

"The film *The Secret* only shows the surface of the secret. The secret behind *The Secret* is that we can all use our consciousness to change and reorganize the universe. This is the secret behind all secrets. We can collectively decide what sort of world we want." [73]

We can decide the future we want, but to do this we have to change the way we think and we have to do it now. We must start looking inwards rather than searching for answers outside ourselves. The inner world creates the outer world. We are undergoing a process of transformation from one world age to another, right now, at this very moment. These changes are ongoing and they will continue.

Part 3

Chapter 21 - Where Do We Come From?

"Where do I actually come from?" People have been asking this question for as long as there have been people on the planet. The answer defines what it means to be a human being. Various theories exist about our origins, and obviously this affects our attitude to life. Our origins are decisive for our understanding of who we actually are and what we are doing here. They are also the subject of considerable debate between those who look at our origins from a scientific point of view and those who adopt a religious stance.

Do we believe that our universe has been created by pure chance and that Darwin's Theory of Evolution is correct, or do we believe that there is a Creator behind everything that exists? Is life a coincidence, or not? Our beliefs will also determine our views about where we come from.

Charles Darwin was known as the most important scientist to demonstrate the evolution of species. He rejected all suggestions that evolution had been brought about by any sort of idea or opinion, and his theory thus denied that there could be any divine influence involved.

This resulted in heated debates breaking out between Darwinists and Christians—debates that have continued ever since Darwin's time. Darwin's Theory of Evolution shows that life develops slowly in stages and involves natural selection:

"Natural selection acts only by taking advantage of slight successive variations. It can never take a great and sudden leap, but must advance by short and slow steps."[89]

According to Darwinism, the diversity of life did not suddenly occurred, but has slowly emerged over a long period of time. The development of man today has been a long evolutionary process governed by coincidences, as opposed to involving divine guidance or an intelligent Creator.

Today we know that everything is composed of atoms. Every stone, every tree, every human being is made of atoms. When everything in the universe is broken down, we find that we are all made of the same "material."

The great diversity that exists in the universe, from tiny beetles to massive planets, results from the various combinations of atoms from which such things are made. This is rather like Lego blocks, because it is possible to build absolutely anything using just one set of Lego blocks, e.g. cars, houses, castles and much more. We decide what we want to make. We are aware of what we are creating when we use building materials like Lego blocks. There are no coincidences involved in what we are building. On the other hand, the Theory of Evolution says that there is no conscious Creator behind the origins of life.

This implies there is no "Lego builder" (you) assembling the blocks needed for the life you are currently living on Earth. Life on Earth occurred by accident. But what about the building blocks which constitute the origins of all life? Where do the atoms come from? Did they come from the Big Bang, and what came before the Big Bang?

Scientists are able to show what happened just one millisecond after the Big Bang occurred, but science does not know what proceeded the Big Bang. How did the Big Bang occur?

In the book, *Transition Now, Redefining Duality, 2012 and Beyond* the author Martine Vallée has included information from people channeling different energies. One of them is Lee Carroll who has been channeling Kryon for many years. In the book Carroll channels information about The Big Bang. He says: "The Big Bang never occurred. The thought of a Big Bang is a three-dimensional explanation for an interdimensional property. Universes are being created all the time through interdimensional changes—when one dimension literally collides with another. These are great quantum events. This is the moment all the properties arise which you call Big Bang." [139]

Caroll is talking about many universes and hence many Big Bangs. Thomas Mellen-Benedict does the same. In his near death experience he explained that he saw millions of Big Bangs. He says: "Do you know what is on the other side of a Black Hole? We are; our galaxy; which has been reprocessed from another Universe." [21]

The Council has told us the same thing: "Mini black holes are a transformation from one state to another." So is the Big Bang the start of a new state that has emerged from the other side of a black hole? Is it the Cosmos breathing in and out? Is the inhalation the same as when everything is pulled into a black hole and the subsequent exhalation the start of another Big Bang? In Darwin's day the Big Bang, the birth of the universe and the fact that everything in the universe is made of atoms and sub-atomic particles were unknown concepts. The Big Bang is regarded as being the birth of the universe, and most scientists agree that this occurred around 13.7 billion years ago.

The term Big Bang was originally coined by the British astronomer Fred Hoyle (1915-2001) on BBC radio's *Third Program* broadcast on March 28, 1949. Ironically enough, Hoyle did not believe in the Bag Bang theory. He thought that such a theory meant that the universe had a beginning and that this posed a philosophical dilemma, since many people thought that a beginning involved a cause, and thus also a Creator.[90]

Consequently Darwinists do not believe that we came here in order to accomplish a life task or that there is anything waiting for us after death. They believe that when we die we are gone forever and life ceases to exist for all eternity. We are erased by time and life, and evolution continues with its natural, accidental selection without us. Our origins are a cosmic accident.

Dr. Calleman does not agree with this and refers to the fact that Darwin himself said the following:

"Natural selection acts only by taking advantage of slight successive variations. It can never take a great and sudden leap."

Calleman refers to fossil discoveries that show that evolution must have occurred by making quantum leaps, since new species have suddenly emerged. He goes on to say that based on the development of different classes of organisms it would appear that many different species with new biological properties not apparent in earlier species have suddenly emerged during specific periods of time. He believes that the sudden emergence of such new species cannot be attributed to Darwin's Theory of Evolution, but rather to the Cosmic Tree of Life, with energy waves containing DNA information hitting the Earth at regular intervals and contributing to quantum leaps being made in the development of life. [140]

David Wilcock shares this view. "Cosmic energy cycles occur which contain DNA information and affect life here on Earth," he says. Wilcock refers to the work of Dave Raup and Jack Sepkoskis who studied fossils and came to the conclusion that the mass extinction of species appears to occur in regular cycles lasting 26 million years. They also discovered another 62-million-year cycle that appears to do the same.

Wilcock says these cosmic energies consist of different frequencies of microwave energy and move away from the center of the galaxy at regular intervals. These fields appear to contain energy from the galaxy that is reprogramming all DNA and all life on Earth. This is also causing the planets in our solar system to become warmer.[44]

"This is due to the fact that these energy waves are coming from the center of the galaxy and entering the heliosphere," says Wilcock.

These energy waves are "shooting" particles into our solar system, causing the planets to become warmer, lighter and more magnetic.

He goes on to say that this energy contains DNA information in the form of waves that are transforming every single life form on the planet and causing them to move on to their next stage of evolution. According to Wilcock the evolution of man and the changes taking place in our DNA are occurring rapidly. He refers to anthropologist John Hawks at the University of Wisconsin who has studied the evolution of man.

Hawks's research shows that during the last 5,000 years human DNA has evolved 100 times faster than at any time in the history of man. We are genetically more different from people living 5,000 years ago than they were from the Neanderthals.[91]

During a channeling session that Lilli conducted with me, Camillo, in 2009, we were told that our cells would change as maintained by Wilcock and Dr. Calleman:

"The light from the North shall set you free—that sentence has been spoken through many years now and that is correct. The illumination of the light particles radiating in from the gamma is now forcing cells to open. Mind and body are becoming one. Cellular systems are corresponding. It is equally important to keep the body fit so that it can rejuvenate through the understanding of metamorphosis and the food that the new body requires. This food may be taken and ingested each day and should be as poison-free as possible and full of nutrients that contain the suns rays in abundance.

"Chlorophyll and oxygen are needed to clear the blood stream, because communication is provided by higher frequency identities through the finer veins alongside the spine and clogged blood prevents this information from reaching the mind/brain. Physical bodies are currently undergoing great adjustments and this may cause aches and pains and yet it is a wake-up call to keep your temple glowing."

Channeled by Lilli Bendriss on September 13, 2009 - from the energy-beings the Council of Elders

Dr. Calleman and Wilcock agree that our evolution is being guided by cosmic waves containing DNA information and that this is not an accidental process as suggested by Darwin. We wondered what the Council of Elders could tell us about Darwin's Theory of Evolution.

Camillo: The Council has previously told us that our DNA is being affected by cosmic waves coming from the center of our galaxy, as suggested by the work of Wilcock and Dr. Calleman, and that this is powering our evolution. If this is correct, does it mean that Darwin's Theory of Evolution is wrong? What does the Council have to say about this?

The Council of Elders via Lilli: Darwin was wandering along the edge of the cliff all the time. He followed a line that appeared to be obvious to him because of what he saw in the physical rather than the non-physical world, i.e. what he saw was not based on consciousness and the waves behind it. If Darwin had lived today and had access to scientific research and the progress that has been made, his theory would have been very different. He was a man of his time and was subject to the point at which evolution had progressed during his days. His theory was formulated on the basis of this time perspective.
Channeled by Lilli Bendriss, on August 11, 2010 - from the energy-beings the Council of Elders

The radiant beauty of our natural surroundings provides us with evidence of the vast number of life forms that interact with the dance of life. It can be hard to understand that all living things have come about as a result of chance as claimed by people like Darwin.

Just by walking in the countryside we are able to experience the huge diversity of life that exists, from tiny ants to magnificent Norwegian fir trees swaying majestically in the wind. All such life is growing and living because of the amazing, complicated mechanisms found in all life forms. All such life consists of cells.

The term "cell" has been derived from the Latin word "cellula" meaning *small compartment*. This compartment contains many elements and tasks that are constantly being performed. Cells come in many different shapes and sizes. In multi-cell organisms like us, different types of cells perform many different functions. For example, the cells in the eye are able to detect light, while muscle cells are able to contract and nerve cells can transmit and receive electrical impulses. Each individual cell is partly self-sustaining and self-maintaining. They absorb nutrients that they convert into energy, can perform specialist tasks and reproduce if required. Each cell contains instructions on how to perform these tasks.

To enable the functioning of nature in all its glory, this amazingly complicated interplay of cellular tasks has to take place without a hitch. If any of the cellular tasks performed in the human body malfunction we become ill. If a spanner is thrown in the works, the body has a fantastic ability to recover so that it can once again function properly.

Anyone who has witnessed the teeming life that exists in the human body cannot fail to be hugely impressed by the fantastic way in which everything is connected. Life in the human body is like a clock that keeps accurate time, where all the parts work together in order to display the time in a perfect manner. The possibility that life and its constantly functioning advanced mechanisms might be an accident is something that is hard for many people to understand.

It is even more amazing when one starts looking at *fractals* and the *Golden Ratio*.

Chapter 22 - Fractals and The Golden Ratio

"Mathematics is the language with which God has written the Universe."
- **Galileo Galilei (1564 - 1642)**

In his book entitled, *Fractal Time*, Gregg Braden shows that everything, from the biology of DNA and the laws of physics to the history of our planet and the evolution of the universe (our world of matter), follows very precise rules that allow things to "be" as they are.[92]

He says that nature offers us two powerful keys that make it possible to predict repeating patterns in the cycles of time. These keys are *fractals* and the *Golden Ratio.*

The first person to use the word "fractal" in 1975 was a Professor of Mathematics at Yale University, Benoit Mandelbrot. The word comes from the Latin "fractus" which means "broken." Fractal figures are geometric objects that are as uneven and irregular as circles are smooth and well-formed. Some fractals can be divided up into bits—others are identical to the original figure. Fractals are said to be "self-similar" because each part is like the whole.

Mandelbrot developed a method that would allow us to see the underlying structure of the world. This structure is composed of patterns within patterns within patterns, and so on. He called his new way of seeing things *fractal geometry.*

Gregg Braden explains that nature does not use perfect lines and curves to build mountains, clouds and trees. Rather it uses irregular fragments that, when taken as a whole, *become* the mountains, clouds and trees. The key in a fractal is that each fragment, no matter how small, looks like the larger that it is part of. These small patterns repeat themselves and together they constitute a larger pattern that is the same as the smaller ones. Examples of fractals found in nature include Romanesco broccoli. From the individual flowers to the entire stalk, the same patterns repeat on varying scales to create the whole broccoli.

Fractals can be found everywhere in nature, in snowflakes, in shells, in lightening, in a neuron that is "firing up," in peacocks, pineapples, crystals, trees and leaves, rivers and fjords, starfish, etc.

This is a repeating pattern that creates a whole of the same pattern. Are such repeating patterns the result of chance as suggested by Darwin? Or are they a sign that there is an intelligence behind everything—a "designer" with a sort of "program" that has "programmed" such a "pattern system?" Gregg Braden believes that it is possible to think of nature as being a program that runs the universe.

Another natural phenomenon that indicates that there may be a grand design behind the universe is the *Golden Ratio*.

The *Golden Ratio* describes the special relationship found in nature between two parts of a whole.

Imagine a line that is one unit long. Then divide the line in two unequal parts so that the longest part divided by the smallest part is also equal to the total line divided by the longest part.

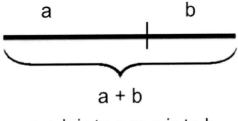

a + b is to a as a is to b

This gives you the *Golden Ratio* that is equivalent to 1.61803399. The Greek letter *phi* is often used for expressing the *Golden Ratio*. The Italian mathematician Leonardo Fibonacci discovered an infinite series of numbers that relate to the *Golden Ratio*. Here are the first few numbers in the Fibonacci series:

0, 1, 1, 2, 3, 5, 8, 13, 21, 34, 55, 89, 144, and so on.

The Fibonacci number sequence (its modern name) is a series of numbers wherein each number equals the sum of the two preceding numbers.

For example, 3 is the sum of 1 + 2.

5 is the sum of 2 + 3;

8 is the sum of 3 + 5, and so on.

Fibonacci numbers have an interesting feature. When you divide one number in the series by the number before it, you obtain numbers very close to one another.

144/89 = 1.617

89/55 = 1.618

55/34 = 1.618

The results are not exactly the same, as shown in the above examples, but after the thirteenth number in the series, 1.618 is obtained each time.

0, 1, 1, 2, 3, 5, 8, 13, 21, 34, 55, 89, 144, 233, 377, 610, 987, 1597, 2584, 4181, 6765 . . .

6765/4181 = 1.618

4181/2584 = 1.618

2584/1597 = 1.618

1597/987 = 1.618

987/610 = 1.618

The Golden Ratio occurs everywhere in nature, including human beings.

Here are a few examples relating to an average human body:

- When the distance between the navel and the foot is taken as one unit, the height of a human being is equivalent to 1.618.
- When the distance between the wrist and the elbow is taken as one unit, the distance from the finger tips to the elbow is equivalent to 1.618.
- When the length of the head is taken as one unit, the distance from the shoulders to the top of the head is equivalent to 1.618.

- When the distance from the shoulders to the head is taken as one unit, the distance from the navel to the top of the head is equivalent to 1.618.
- When the distance from the knee to the foot is taken as one unit, the distance from the navel to the knee is equivalent to 1.618.
- The total width of the two front teeth in the upper jaw divided by their height is equivalent to 1.618.
- The length of the face divided by its width is equivalent to 1.618.
- The distance from the lips to where the eyebrows meet, divided by the length of the nose is equivalent to 1.618.
- The length of the mouth divided by the width of the nose is equivalent to 1.618.
- The distance between the pupils divided by the distance between the eyebrows is equivalent to 1.618.

This ratio has also been found in our lungs and our DNA. The length of the curves in each of the DNA strands divided by their width is also equivalent to 1.618. In his book entitled, *The Purposeful Universe,* Dr. Carl Johan Calleman states: "The double helix structure of the DNA is clearly designed based on *phi* and the Fibonacci numbers that *phi* is related to. The width of one round of the DNA double helix is 21 *ångstrøm* and the height is 34." (One ångstrøm—"Å"—is a unit used for measuring distance. One ångstrøm is equivalent to 10^{10} meters.)

34 follows 21 in the Fibonacci sequence—thus these DNA measurements also comply with the *Golden Ratio.* Calleman also says the following: "The Fibonacci correlations support the argument that the DNA, the amazing double helix, is not something that emerged by accident from random chemical reactions in the early history of the Earth.[93]

He argues instead that all life originates from the Cosmic Tree of Life:

"It seems likely that all life, everywhere in the universe, has a common origin in DNA generated in the image of the Cosmic Tree of Life," he says. It is not the result of a series of accidental reactions that evolved step by step until the long helices were complete. Instead Dr. Calleman believes that our DNA has received its information as a whole by resonating with the Tree of Life and has therefore been created as an image of this as a whole.

The *Golden Ratio* has been called the fingerprint of God. It is found everywhere in nature. Is this a total coincidence, or has it been designed by a universal intelligence?

Those who swear by Darwin's Theory of Evolution say that life consists of coincidences and that it is all about the *survival of the fittest*—an expression coined by Darwin as a suitable synonym for natural selection.

Although many people supported Darwin's theory, there are now more people who believe in a higher power, and thus a Creator, than those who do not. A survey conducted by Harris Poll in December 2008 shows that more Americans believe in God than in Darwin's Theory of Evolution. [94]

Both *fractals* and the *Golden Ratio* indicate that there is an intelligent design behind the creation of our universe.

Chapter 23 - Belief in a Higher Power

There are many more religious adherents who believe in a higher power than those who do not. If we look at the three largest religions in the world, 33% of the global population are Christians, 21% are Muslims and approximately 14% are Hindus. Approximately 16% have no religion, including agnostics, freethinkers and humanists. The remainder are Buddhists and adherents of traditional Chinese religions and other faiths.[95]

This means that the majority of the world's population believes in some form of higher power—a Creator. Thus the majority believes that life is not an accident as suggested by Darwinists.

Even though the world's religions are different, they agree on this particular point, i.e. that life did not occur by chance. They believe that there is some form of higher power behind creation and that we emerge from this higher power. But what is it? Is it an external entity outside ourselves, or is it part of us? Are we reflections of this Creator?

Some branches of science say that everything is energy and that this energy surfs on a wave of consciousness, an information field or universal consciousness. David Bohm, Michael Talbot, Gregg Braden, David Icke and many others believe that we live in a holographic universe and that we are therefore tiny reflections of the whole. The same patterns are reproduced in all levels of the cosmos, from the largest scale (macrocosm or universe-level) all the way down to the smallest scale (microcosm or sub sub-atomic level).

Is the Whole Universe a Hologram?

In 1982 a group of scientists lead by the physicist Alain Aspect at the University of Paris conducted an experiment that has been highly significant in respect of how many scientists view the world today. Aspect and his team discovered that under certain circumstances subatomic particles such as electrons are able to instantaneously communicate with each other regardless of the distance separating them. Whether they are ten feet or ten billion miles apart, somehow each particle always seems to know what the others are doing. The problem with this feat is that it violates Einstein's long-held tenet that no communication can travel faster than the speed of light. Since travelling faster than the speed of light is tantamount to breaking the time barrier, this daunting prospect has caused some physicists to try to come up with elaborate ways to explain away Aspect's findings.

One of these was the British physicist David Bohm (1917-1994) who was a pupil of Einstein. He challenged the conventional understanding of quantum theory and in turn led scientists to re-examine and question the nature of their theories and scientific methodology. Bohm believes Aspect's findings imply that objective reality does not exist, that despite its apparent solidity the universe is at heart a phantasm, a gigantic and splendidly detailed hologram.

What is a Hologram?

Michael Talbot (1953–1992), the American author of a number of books dealing with parallels between the mysticism of antiquity and quantum mechanics, believed that our physical universe is a gigantic hologram. Talbot regarded ESP, telepathy and other paranormal phenomena as being real and a product of this holographic model of reality. In an article written about the universe as a hologram, he describes a hologram as follows:

"A hologram is a three-dimensional photograph made with the aid of a laser. To make a hologram, the object to be photographed is first bathed in the light of a laser beam. Then a second laser beam is bounced off the reflected light of the first and the resulting interference pattern (the area where the two laser beams co-mingle) is captured on film.

When the film is developed, it looks like a meaningless swirl of light and dark lines. But when the developed film is illuminated by another laser beam, a three-dimensional image of the original object appears.

"The three-dimensionality of such images is not the only remarkable characteristic of holograms. If a hologram of a rose is cut in half and then illuminated by a laser, each half will still be found to contain the entire image of the rose. Indeed, even if the halves are divided again, each snippet of film will always contain a smaller but intact version of the original image. Unlike normal photographs, every part of a hologram contains all the information possessed by the whole.

"The 'whole in every part' nature of a hologram provides us with an entirely new way of understanding organization and order. For most of its history, Western science has labored under the bias that the best way to understand a physical phenomenon, whether a frog or an atom, is to dissect it and study its respective parts. A hologram teaches us that some things in the universe may not lend themselves to this approach. If we try to take apart something constructed holographically, we will not get the pieces of which it is made, we will only get smaller wholes."[96]

In this article Talbot explores the idea that a superhologram is the matrix that has given birth to everything in our universe and contains every subatomic particle that has ever been or will be—every configuration of matter and energy that is possible, from snowflakes to quasars, from blue whales to gamma rays. It must be seen as a sort of cosmic storehouse of "All That Is."

Talbot bases his article on none other than David Bohm's holographic model. Bohm believed that the findings of Aspect and his team could be explained by using a holographic model. Bohm believed the reason subatomic particles are able to remain in contact with one another regardless of the distance separating them is not because they are sending some sort of mysterious signal back and forth, but because their separateness is an illusion. He argues that at some deeper level of reality such particles are not individual entities, but are actually extensions of the same fundamental something. Bohm admitted that we have no way of knowing what else might be concealed in such a hologram, but that we have no reason to assume that they do not contain anything else. "Perhaps the superholographic level of reality is a 'mere stage' beyond which lies 'an infinity of further development,'" he said.

Bohm's knowledge about physics and cosmology was exhaustive and way ahead of his time, so consequently few people were able to appreciate it. Physicists regarded his theories as being mysterious, and few mystics were able to follow his scientific arguments. However, today there are many people talking about the possibility that we exist in a holographic universe, just like Bohm suggested.

If this is correct then our memories are not limited to our physical brains. If we are part of a hologram, our memories would be located elsewhere than in the brain.

In the 2008 film entitled, *The Living Matrix,* we learn that no one has succeeded in locating the memory in the brain. The film talks about the research conducted on this subject by Karl Pribrams, who for many years tried to find the physical area of the brain containing the memory. Accompanied by Karl Lashley he conducted terrible experiments on rats in order to find the location of the memory. They removed parts of the rats' brains to see if the rats could still perform certain tasks that they had been taught. Regardless of how much brain was removed, the rats still continued to perform the set tasks. They concluded that memory is non-local, i.e. that it is not located in any particular part of the brain.

This agrees with Bohm's concept of a holographic universe. In a holographic "something," every piece of the "something" mirrors the whole "something." A hologram is simply a pattern that is whole and complete onto itself, and at the same time, is part of an even greater pattern. This pattern may be non-physical energy, or it could be physical matter.

"For each of you is a holographic fragment of the Source."
- **George Green** in *The Handbook for The New Paradigm.*

We are many individualized expressions of a unity consciousness. According to theology, God permeates everything and is all-knowing. A hologram can explain how this is actually possible. If you make a slight change to one part of the pattern in a hologram it will be reflected in the rest of the hologram. A change on a microcosmic level (sub-subatomic level) will be reflected all the way up to the macrocosmic level (universe-level). Everything is connected.

We were keen to obtain a statement from the Council of Elders about this subject and so we asked them the following question:

Camillo: Do we live in an illusion, in a holographic universe that has been designed so that we can experience and develop?

The Council of Elders via Lilli: That is correct. Once again there is a downwardly-transformed truth that comes from outside what people are able to understand. For the holographic universe is like your understanding of the first dimension. The holographic universe develops at the same rate as the expansion of dimensional belonging. The truth about the hologram appears different in the fifth dimension or on the fifth plane—different to the first plane.

It is like when people observed the outside of the body hundreds of years ago without knowing what was inside it. They could dissect the body and look at the organs, but when X-rays were discovered it was possible to see through the body and realize that it had a bone structure. Gradually more advanced equipment was invented which provided more information and could see through the bone structure, not just the form of the bones, but it was possible to go in and read the cells. In this way the world's understanding of the body became much more complementary.

This also applies to understanding the hologram. It is now showing itself in its simplest form. Gradually as things develop in the human condition you will see that there is an even deeper understanding—intricate models—because the equipment that is able to measure and understand it was invented or activated by the human brain in cooperation with scientific instruments. The purpose is to break down everything into its component parts and see the smallest part that is in turn a black hole and the entrance to something new again.

But at the moment this is far too complex and will not be sent through as information at humanity's current stage of experience.

Channeled by Lilli Bendriss on July 29, 2010 - from the energy-beings the Council of Elders

This indicates that we are like drops in a large universal ocean where each drop reflects the whole ocean? Is the Source in everything and everyone? In every single cell—in each atom?

According to theology *GOD is inside everything and everyone.* Thanks to quantum physics and the Zero Point Field theory, science is saying that *ENERGY is in everything and everyone* and that this energy surfs on a wave of consciousness—a wave of information. Does this indicate that we are not living in a universe that has been created by chance?

The father of our space program, Dr. Wernher von Braun, believed that our universe did not come about by chance. The following is an excerpt from a letter Dr. Von Braun wrote to the California State Board of Education in 1972:

"To be forced to believe only one conclusion—that everything in the universe happened by chance—would violate the very objectivity of science itself. Certainly there are those who argue that the universe evolved out of a random process, but what random process could produce the brain of a man or the system of the human eye? Some people say that science has been unable to prove the existence of a Designer. They challenge science to prove the existence of God. But, must we really light a candle to see the sun?"[141]

"The cosmos is inside us," said Carl Edward Sagan (1934 – 1996), an American astronomer, astrophysicist, author and cosmologist who achieved fame as the presenter of the TV series *Cosmos: A Personal Voyage* in 1980. This program was broadcast in over 60 different countries and viewed by more than 500 million people.[97]

Carl Sagan thought that the cosmos was also inside us because we are all made of star dust. When everything in the universe is broken down, we are all made of the same "stuff." The beauty of a living thing is not the atoms that go into it, but the way the atoms are put together.

"We are all connected; to each other biologically, to the Earth chemically, to the rest of the universe atomically."
- Neil Degrasse Tyson, American astrophysicist

All the diversity in the universe is the cosmos expressing itself in order to learn about itself, as pointed out by Carl Sagan in *Cosmos*.

"We are a way for the Cosmos to know itself."
- Carl Sagan

So how likely is it that our fantastic universe was created by chance? Do you believe that a program that is more complicated than the most complicated program running on a supercomputer can be designed by chance through evolution, regardless of how much time, how many mutations and how much natural selection is taken into account?

Our DNA works like a complicated computer program. It is a carrier of genetic information in the form of "building blocks" called "bases" which can be abbreviated as A, T, C or G, according to their chemical designations: adenine, thymine, cytosine and guanine. These letters are used as abbreviations for sequences of DNA fragments, e.g. CCAAGTAC. These sequences are coded for genetic information.

According to molecular biologist Michael Denton, a teaspoon of DNA could contain all the information needed to build the proteins for every species of organism that has ever lived on Earth, and still there would be room enough to store all the information in every book ever written.[98]

So are these amazing DNA molecules excellent examples of intelligent design or is DNA and thus all living things the result of chance? The adherents of Darwinism have had to combat many obstacles ever since the discovery of DNA in 1953 by James Watson and Francis Crick. Anyone who seriously investigates the miracle of the DNA molecule will become aware of its complexity. The DNA molecule is like an incredible micro-digital, error-correcting, self duplicating, information storage and retrieval system that has the potential to develop any organism from raw biological material.

"The coding regions of DNA have exactly the same relevant properties as a computer code or language."
- Dr. Stephen Meyer, Director of the Discovery Institute's Center for Science and Culture [142]

Dr. Stephen Meyer has written a book entitled, *Signature in the Cell* in which he argues in favor of a sort of intelligence being behind the design of the complex DNA molecule. One human cell contains approximately three billion units of DNA that constitute the chromosomes. These three billion DNA units create the molecular machinery in the cell that enables the cell to work. The operations that take place in the cell are complex, much more advanced than the most advanced car factory where car components are assembled. If just one thing goes wrong the cell will break down. [99]

Scientists now know that our cells contain complicated units, but in Darwin's time they thought that the basis of life, the cell, was a simple gel-like substance that was not hard to explain. In his book, *The Case for a Creator,* Lee Strobel discusses the cell with Professor of Biochemistry Michael Behe at Lehigh University in Pennsylvania. Behe says:

"Most scientists speculated that the deeper they delved into the cell, the more simplicity they would find. But the opposite happened." [143]

"Cells have always been underestimated," says Bruce Alberts, the President of the National Academy of Sciences. "We have always underestimated cells...the entire cell can be viewed as a factory that contains an elaborate network of interlocking assembly lines, each of which is composed of a set of large protein machines." [144]

The cells are small factories with a vast number of pieces of machinery. One example is the bacterial flagellum. Howard Berg, Professor of Molecular and Cellular Biology and Physics at Harvard University in Cambridge, Massachusetts, has called this cell "the most efficient machine in the universe." He thinks that the bacterial flagellum is a marvel of nano-engineering. A total of 40 different protein parts are required in order to make one "flagellum machine" and if any of these parts are missing it will not work. According to Professor Behe, these parts cannot have been developed over time since they all need to be present at the same time in order for the machinery to work, and this therefore contradicts Darwin's Theory of Evolution. [145]

"It is design—not an accidental arrangement of parts."
-Professor Michael Behe

Since the discovery of the bacterial flagellum in 1973, biologists have tried to understand how a machine with such an incredibly complex design could have been created by chance, without a plan, as suggested by Darwin about all life.[100]

Darwin himself wrote the following in *The Origin of Species*:

"Natural selection acts only by taking advantage of slight successive variations. It can never take a great and sudden leap, but must advance by short and slow steps."

He continued: "If it could be demonstrated that any complex organ existed which could not possibly have been formed by numerous, successive, slight modifications, my theory would absolutely break down. But I can find out no such case."[101]

Professor Behe says that the bacterial flagellum is one such case that causes Darwin's theory to collapse. He elaborates on this in his book entitled, *Darwin's Black Box: The Biochemical Challenge to Evolution*, in which he presents the concept of "irreducible complexity" i.e. that if just one part is missing in such an advanced system as that found in the bacterial flagellum, the system would not have been able to have developed in line with Darwin's theories. The presence of all the parts in many biochemical systems indicates therefore that they must be the result of intelligent design rather than evolutionary processes. Behe says, "Such complexity at molecular level cannot be explained by the Theory of Evolution."

Not everyone agrees with Professor Behe about this issue, and the possibility of the bacterial flagellum being an irreducible system has been the subject of much debate. On the other hand it is important to consider that even tiny changes in the laws of nature would have meant that life would most likely never have occurred. As the previously mentioned cosmologist Paul Davies says:

"If even slight changes were made to the existing laws of nature this would have a tremendous impact on all life in the universe."

So is a cellular machine like the bacterial flagellum something that could have developed over time, or was it designed by an intelligence? Is our DNA the result of chance as claimed by Darwin and his supporters, or are Professor Behe, Dr. Meyer and many others right in claiming that it is the result of intelligent design?

In *Seth Speaks*, Seth has the following to say about Darwin and his Theory of Evolution:

"He spent his last years proving it, and yet it has no real validity. It has validity within very limited perspectives only; for consciousness does, indeed, evolve form. Form does not evolve consciousness. All consciousness does, indeed, exist at once, and therefore it did not evolve in those terms. It is according to when you come into the picture, and what you choose to observe, and what part of the play you decide to observe.

It is more the other way round, in that evolved consciousness forms itself into many different patterns and rains down on reality. Consciousness did not come from atoms and molecules scattered by chance through the universe, or scattered by chance through many universes. Consciousness did not arrive because inert matter suddenly soared into activity and song. The consciousness existed first, and evolved the form into which it then began to manifest itself."[102]

If we are part of this consciousness we must also come from the same consciousness, or what some people call God. In the Hindu religion God is referred to as *Brahman*.

Adrian Cooper discusses religions such as Hinduism and Buddhism in his book, *Our Ultimate Reality*. With regard to Hinduism and Brahman he says:

"Brahman or universal consciousness is regarded as being the ultimate reality. Brahman is infinite, exists beyond the limited perception of the five physical senses and is incomprehensible." [146]

Previously mentioned Ashayana Deane says that we are conscious energy from the universal consciousness— from the Source:

"We are created in the image of Source, meaning that we are Co-Creators with Source in that we create with our thoughts and are created of the energy of Source. Everything in all of creation is the Energy of Source stepped down into smaller units of conscious energy and therefore, everything in all of creation is Source that has stepped down Its energy to experience. The process of Source stepping down Its energy is called the *Stair Step Creation Process.*" [37]

So are we an expression of a universal consciousness and is that where we come from? Are we all consciousness? Have our bodies and our three-dimensional world simply been designed so that we will have a place to discover ourselves as co-creators, create what we want, and then enjoy the manifestation process? Are we here to learn, develop and gain experience from this process of creation?

If the Source is consciousness and we are part of this consciousness, where is the "place" from which we come? Are we just a thought? How can we experience matter and move around in a three-dimensional world?

Chapter 24 - Space-Time versus Time-Space

In order to understand alternative realities and thus possibly where we come from, it is important to explain the difference between the concepts of *space-time* and *time-space*.

The physical reality has three dimensions of space: length, width and height, plus one dimension of time.

Albert Einstein was responsible for introducing the fourth dimension in physics—what he called space-time. In 1905 he published his *Theory of Relativity* in which he linked space and time. He said that space and time were not actually separate and he placed them together in one dynamic unit. Einstein regarded this as a fabric woven together from space and time to form a sort of "carpet." He then introduced gravitation and its effect on this space-time "carpet."

According to Einstein the planets in the universe are sunk into this space-time "carpet"—they do not just float around in the empty space in the universe. This space-time "carpet" is curved in the presence of matter. It can respond dynamically by either contracting or expanding.

Try envisioning a large stone sinking into a trampoline. The fabric of the trampoline represents space-time that is woven together from space and time. The stone represents a planet. All the planets are thus sinking into this space-time "carpet." The astrophysicist Neil deGrasse Tysen explains this in the following way:

"Gravitation is not actually a force—it is a substance. It is forms of space and time. We (Earth) move via the curves of these forms. In doing this, something that would otherwise have been a straight line is converted into what we call *paths* through the cosmos."[103]

Sir Isaac Newton discovered gravity in 1665. He understood that the force that causes an apple to fall to the Earth was the same force that causes the moon to orbit the Earth. With his theory of gravitation, Newton united the celestial and earthly kingdoms. He created an entirely new way of looking at nature. The realization that both the orbits of heavenly bodies, like the moon, and events on Earth, like an apple falling, were governed by the same force was quite amazing. It served to unite various views about how nature operates. Newton revolutionized our ideas about the universe. His work was nothing less than sensational.

The formula that Newton used to describe his law of gravitation still applies today. Newton's formulas are so precise that they were used to plot the course of the rocket that took man to the moon. However, despite this precision and the fact that Newton was able to calculate the various orbits of the planets and moons, he was unable to explain exactly *how* gravitation worked.

This is where Einstein's Theory of Relativity comes in. Einstein's theory showed that planets move in orbits determined by space-time geometry. Space and time are not separate, but a dynamic unit woven together like a "carpet" on which the planets and stars move.

Following Einstein's discoveries, the concept of space-time has therefore been used for explaining the reality in which we live. It consists of three dimensions of space (height, width and length), and we are able to move around in it. Here on Earth we can move around in a three-dimensional world, and the Earth moves around our solar system in the same three-dimensional world. In this space-time-reality, time is one-dimensional and it is locked. You cannot move around in time. You cannot go to the past or the future.

In his lectures David Wilcock explains that the opposite of space-time is time-space. He refers to Dewey Larson's work on this subject: *The Reciprocal System of Theory.*

Dewey B. Larson (1898-1990) was an American engineer and the originator of *The Reciprocal System of Theory*, a comprehensive theoretical framework capable of explaining all physical phenomena from subatomic particles to galactic clusters.

"In this general physical theory space and time are simply the two reciprocal aspects of the sole constituent of the universe—motion," says Larson.[104]

The thesis of *The Reciprocal System* is that the universe is not a universe of matter, but a universe of motion, one in which the basic reality is motion, and all entities—photons, particles, atoms, fields, forces, and all forms of energy— are merely manifestations of motion. Space and time are the two reciprocal aspects of this motion, and cannot exist independently.

We observe space as being three-dimensional, but space does not exist without time, therefore time must be three-dimensional as well. This discovery opened the door to the world of quantum physics, where experiments showed that particles such as electronics (electrons = matter) behaved like waves. They appeared to float around instead of behaving like fixed matter, shifting between these two states. Dewey B. Larson is the man who realized that time must also be three-dimensional.

In the time-space reality there are three dimensions of time (past, present and future for us) and one dimension of space (for us). We can move around in these three dimensions of time. This is what we experience when we dream. We can suddenly be in what we regard as being the past and then the next second we find ourselves in the present. Everything is happening now. Time is not linear. It only appears to be linear to us because we are in the space-time reality. In time-space, time is not linear. Everything actually happens now—the past, present and future are connected. In this time-space reality it is possible to see forwards and backwards in time.

Anyone who tunes into this reality will therefore be able to obtain information about what, in our reality, we call the future. Prophets, fortune tellers, clairvoyants, the Mayans and other indigenous peoples have been able to tune into the time-space reality by meditating or taking substances that stimulate the pineal gland. They have thus been able to provide us with an insight into what could happen in the future.

People who have had near-death experiences say that they become one with everything and everyone. They are consciousness. They are thoughts. Do we come from a time-space reality where we exist before we come to this three-dimensional world—into a space-time reality?

According to Michelle Belanger we do. As previously mentioned she remembers all her previous lives on Earth. When we die we do not go anywhere:

"You don't really go anywhere—you are in between spaces and you are one with everything."

This agrees with what PMH Atwater discovered when she was engaged in her mammoth task involving people who have had near-death experiences. The 3,000 people she interviewed said that they could hear all thoughts and that they became one with everything and everyone. We are consciousness.

Are we part of a holographic universe as suggested by Talbot, Bohm and Braden? Is our body inside consciousness rather than the other way round? Is this life—an illusion created by consciousness so that we will have a place where we can experience and create ourselves anew?

Scientists are showing us that what we perceive with our five senses are simply electrical impulses. So is our world an illusion? Are we living inside a hologram where our memories are not in the same place as our physical brains? Are they instead distributed in space and stored there in a holographic manner as concluded by the previously mentioned scientist Karl Pribram in his experiments?[105]

Could we all derive from a universal, intelligent consciousness that then enters a virtual reality so that it can experience and develop itself? Have we voluntarily agreed to come here in order to participate in creating experiences for this consciousness?

If there is an intelligent consciousness behind the design of all life, including humanity and our DNA, then this designer would also possess the powers to change our DNA. Many people believe that such DNA changes are exactly what is happening in our current age. Dr. Calleman, Wilcock and Rennison think that cosmic waves of energy are arriving in cycles and that one such wave is currently here. They believe that this wave is facilitating changes in our DNA so that we can continue to develop. Several esoteric masters and spiritual teachers are saying that we are a life form with a consciousness that can communicate at certain frequencies and that these frequencies are determined by our DNA. If our DNA changes, this would enable us to communicate on more frequencies and we would thus also experience expansion of our consciousness. This means that we are moving into a new phase of human development.

Part 4 _____

Chapter 25 - Where Are We Going?

We will all die at some stage—both people and all other living organisms. But what happens when we die? Where do we end up? Do we go to heaven—a paradise—or do we end up in hell? Perhaps we don't end up anywhere at all. Everything is just over, suddenly and abruptly and we simply cease to exist. Or perhaps we are reborn as another form of life or in another human body, either here on Earth or elsewhere in the universe. Or would death involve several of these alternatives?

Our beliefs about what will happen when we die are related to what we believe about the origins of life. Is life just a cosmic accident that evolved as claimed by Darwin in his Theory of Evolution, or is there a Higher Intelligence behind all life? For anyone sharing Darwin's view, life after death would not be an option. If we were created by chance we would also be gone forever when we die. We would be erased by time and would never again experience life. The "I am" would be gone for all eternity. This is a scary thought and it probably is the reason why many people are afraid to die. No longer existing would be like turning off the light—suddenly everything would go black, we would be gone and we would be nothing. We would be gone from the Earth, the universe and this world forever.

However, if we believe that an intelligent creator designed everything, then likely death would just be a transformation to another realm. There would be life after this life. The various religions have different ideas about what happens when we die.

Christians believe that we only have one life. When we die our souls are immediately separated from our bodies and we go to heaven or hell, while our bodies remain on Earth to decay. "Earth to earth, ashes to ashes, dust to dust." Christianity promises that as long as we believe, we will have everlasting life. The Bible states:

"For God so loved the world, that he gave his only begotten Son, that whosoever believeth in him should not perish, but have everlasting life."
- **John 3:16**

According to Christianity we all have an immortal soul. If we believe in Jesus as our savior, as someone who took our sins upon himself when he died on the cross, then we will go to heaven. On the other hand, if we do not believe in him, do we end up in hell?

Muslims also believe in life after death—when we die, we will be presented to Allah on the Day of Judgement, and all our good deeds and sins will be reviewed before judgement is pronounced. We are either rewarded by going to paradise or we go to hell.

The world's two main religions do not believe that we are reborn. They do not believe in reincarnation. Despite the fact that most Christian and Islamic sects do not believe that individuals reincarnate, there are a few groups belonging to these faiths that endorse reincarnation, but the current view is that reincarnation is not part of these religions.[106]

Hindus and Buddhists on the other hand believe in reincarnation and karma.

"Hinduism therefore views the world as an ever changing and fluid manifestation of the powerful magic of Brahman, where nothing ever stands still and everything is in a constant state of motion."
- **Adrian Cooper** [146]

Hinduism also talks about karma as representing the ultimate power of creation, the Source of all life. Karma is also appropriate on a more personal level where the accumulation of good and evil, or positive and negative deeds in one life carry over into many different lives. We are only released from the cycle of karma when we understand our complete unity with all aspects of the Source and live in complete harmony with *all that is* without creating any negative waves. When we die, the soul, Atman, continues to live on in the karmic cycle right up until we are released from rebirth and death.

Buddhists also believe in reincarnation, but in order to achieve a state of Nirvana (obtain an end to suffering) one has to pass through what Buddhism calls the eight-fold path that is part of the four noble truths:

The first noble truth teaches that to most people life is suffering, including pain, disease, loneliness, fear, frustration, disappointment, anger and ultimately death.

The second noble truth teaches that people will suffer if they expect others to conform to their expectations. This noble truth also teaches that wanting deprives people of contentment and happiness due to always striving for more and more material gain and possessions over others. A lifetime of craving and wanting, especially the craving to continue to exist in the current physical body, creates a powerful energy in which people become trapped and ultimately the result after passing is to be reborn once again in order to learn the lessons failed to be learned in the previous life.

The third noble truth states that suffering can be overcome and happiness attained. This noble truth teaches that if all useless craving and desires are set aside, and each day is lived one at a time not dwelling on the past or an imagined future, then you will be set free and attain happiness and contentment. This is a condition known as *Nirvana.*

The fourth noble truth states that the eight-fold path leads to the end of suffering. In order to attain Nirvana one has to live life in accordance with the eight-fold path, as follows:

1. Perfected vision: the vision of the true nature of reality.
2. Perfected emotion or aspiration: acting from love or compassion.
3. Perfected or whole speech: clear, truthful, uplifting and non-harmful communication.
4. Integral action: an ethical foundation for life based upon the principle of non-exploitation of self or others.
5. Proper livelihood: based on correct action and ethical principles of non-exploitation.
6. Complete or full effort, energy or vitality: consciously directing life energy to the transformative path of creative and healing action.
7. Complete or thorough awareness: levels of awareness and mindfulness of everything, oneself, feelings, thought, people and reality.
8. Full, integral holistic "oneness" with the Source or the All: this includes concentration, meditation and single pointedness of mind, and the progressive establishment of the whole being into the many levels of conscious awareness.[107]

Buddhism believes that if we are still consumed by anger, hate, desire and ignorance then we will be bound by the karmic cycles and continue to be born again and again.

Buddhism and Hinduism have different concepts of the soul. Instead of eternal souls, Buddha said that individuals consist of a "bundle" of habits, memories, sensations, desires, and so forth, which together delude one into thinking that he or she consists of a stable, lasting self. Despite its transitory nature, this false self hangs together as a unit, and even reincarnates in body after body.

In Buddhism, as well as in Hinduism, life in a corporeal body is viewed negatively as the source of all suffering. Hence, the goal is to obtain release from the karmic cycle and reincarnation by attaining full enlightenment.

In other words Hinduism and Buddhism have different views than Christianity and Islam about life after death.

To put it in a nutshell, the world's major religions say that we either go to heaven or hell, or that we are reborn repeatedly until we break out of the karmic cycle.

Is it possible for both views to be correct? What do people say that have paid a "quick visit" to the other side?

Chapter 26 – Near-Death Experiences (NDE)

A great number of people have experienced dying (declared clinically dead) and then returned to life again. They have had a near-death experience (NDE). NDEs involve a common pattern of events that are experienced by many people when they have been close to dying. Although near-death experiences vary from one person to another, they often contain a number of common characteristics:

- A feeling of leaving the body. Sometimes being able to see one's own physical body while floating above it.
- A feeling of being pulled into a tunnel or darkness.
- A bright light. Sometimes at the end of the tunnel.
- A feeling of overwhelming peace, well-being or absolute, unconditional love.
- A feeling of having access to unlimited knowledge.
- A life review—feedback about important events during the life that has just been lived.
- A preview of future events.
- Meeting loved ones who have already passed away, or other beings that can be identified as religious figures.

Those involved all say the same—they are taken into the light, that they experience love, that they meet people they have known, that they possess all knowledge and that they are subjected to a review of the life they lived on Earth. However, no one is judged for their deeds. You are your own judge, and after undergoing your own review you realize that the best way of learning from your own negative actions is to experience them for yourself.

"You can only learn after you have worn the sandals of another."
-Renate Dollinger

Alberto Villoldo, the author of *Courageous Dreaming*, explains in the film *Infinity* that he died for the first time when he was six years old. He was able to see his own body lying on the bed. He shares with us what he experienced after his death:

"When you die, you undergo a life review. Everything you have done in your life that is emotionally charged, either positive or negative, is reviewed. Every single person who you said nasty things to or treated badly. Every single person who you helped or loved, but not just in this life, but in all the lives you have ever lived. Everything is reviewed, including everything you have been. In this way you obtain the opportunity to look at the karma you acquired during these lives. You are your own judge, prosecutor, defense counsel and jury—you are everything. If you are able to find forgiveness your life review will pass quickly. Ideally this is something that you ought to do before you die."[108]

Dannion Brinkley, author of *Saved by the Light*, died in 1975 at the age of 25. He was declared dead for 25 minutes. This was the first of three near-death experiences that he had. He has no doubt there is life after death. He says:

"There is no judgement and no punishment. I was the only judge presiding over my day in court! I was given the opportunity to know, first hand, both the happiness and the sorrow I had created through my actions."

Dr. Michael Newton says the same thing in his book, *Journey of Souls*. We all undergo a review before returning to another life, unless we have achieved full enlightenment. All the clients he refers to in his book say the same thing: upon death their souls left their bodies and they were able to see their lifeless bodies lying below as they floated above them. They were met by their guides and then by loved ones who had previously left this life. They could remember every single second, every single moment, and they were one with everything and everyone. Everything was thought—consciousness. They experienced a review of the life they had just left.

These situations experienced by a number of people indicate that we go somewhere where we review our lives and return to a new life if we have failed to understand our complete unity with all aspects of the Source. The aim is to live in total harmony with everything that *is* and to never again create any further negative waves. These experiences suggest to us that reincarnation is real—it is part of the cycle of life. Everything moves in cycles, including us.

People who have had such experiences talk about the light. They say that they are one with all that is and all that has ever been. They do not talk about a *place* as we might understand in our three-dimensional world. Is this what is waiting for us when we eventually die? Do we all go to the same "empty space?" And where does it exist? Is it on another frequency or in another dimension?

Dimensions, Frequencies, Density Levels
We know that we live in a three-dimensional world of height, width and length. It is a world in which we can move. But where do we end up when we die if life exists after death? We have mentioned Ashayana Deane and her comprehensive model of 15-dimensional physics, and Ra from *The Law of One* who talks about eight levels of density and an infinite number of dimensions within these.

During a channeling session conducted by Lilli many years ago the Council of Elders were asked about the concept of dimensions and they answered:

"Imagine that you are holding a hank of wool and you are going to twine it into a ball. You twine it layer upon layer, crossing over and under, until finally you are holding a thick ball of wool in your hand. From your perspective the outer layer of wool is closest to you, but if you had been observing it from the middle then the inner layer would have been closest. Your understanding of closeness or distance is based on the point from which you observe the ball of wool. How could you then say what was best or highest? The ball is made from the same wool.

"Let's pretend it is tweed wool with a different structure and as you wind the wool different patterns will cross each other. If you undo the wool and rewind it you will also create new patterns. This is how dimensions are arranged. Not symmetrically, with one lower or higher than the other, but crossing each other and changing.

"Let's also pretend that the tweed wool is transparent and that you hold the ball out at arm's length. You would then be able to see the whole thing, from the inside to the outside. Nothing would be concealed from you, because, as it says in the Bible, God so loved the world that he created it in his image. He has a complete overview, because he created the wool, he had the thought about making the ball, and he regarded the master-work he created from both the inside and outside, and his essence flowed through the wool."

Channeled by Lilli Bendriss - from the energy-beings the Council of Elders

Everything is woven into everything else. Everything is connected. But do we end up somewhere special in the "ball of wool" when we die? If we are the Source and the Source is us, then we are everything. And we can be everywhere. However, the soul is evolving at the same time in order to experience, and consequently it would be natural for the soul to "end up" somewhere in the world of dimensions/consciousness.

Ashayana Deane talks about five levels of density, each of which contains three dimensions. Our reality is found on the lowest density level - level one - which has dimensions one, two and three. This level is called Incarnated, and the next level - level two - which has dimensions four, five and six, is called Soul.

So when we die and leave this three-dimensional world do we go to level two?

Sal Rachele is a teacher, author, healer and clairvoyant. He graduated from Silva Mind Control in 1976 and was the founder and director of Alpha-Theta Seminars in the late 1970s. He studied rebirthing (conscious breathing), meditation and the healing arts during the 80s and 90s. He does not talk about density levels, but he does speak of higher dimensions. He says that the transition from a three-dimensional existence to higher dimensions occurs in two steps. He explains what happens in one of his articles:

"Ascension occurs in two stages:

1. Transition from a three-dimensional dense body to a lighter fourth-dimensional body.
2. Transition from the fourth-dimensional body to a fifth-dimensional light body.

"There are actually two kinds of ascension: *spiritual* ascension and *physical* ascension.

"*Spiritual* ascension involves the liberation of the soul through dropping the physical body. Any soul who has progressed sufficiently in awareness and understanding can go through spiritual ascension. The simplified equivalent to this is 'going to Heaven after you die.'

"*Physical* ascension has, in the past, been reserved for a select few souls who have mastered the physical, emotional, mental and spiritual facets of life and are able to take their bodies with them into the higher realms.

"At the present time, a major change in the Divine Plan has been implemented, which allows for a large number of souls to go through physical ascension without having mastered every detail of physical life. This Divine Dispensation normally only occurs at the end of a Great Cycle (every 26,000 years)."[109]

The cycle that he is referring to here is what John Major Jenkins, Gregg Braden and many others call *The Precession of the Equinoxes*, associated with the 2012 phenomena.

Esoteric and spiritual teachers are talking about the higher dimensions as being a plane with a higher frequency. Everything vibrates at a different frequency on the higher planes, and consequently we are unable to see these dimensions in our three-dimensional world.

In *Seth Speaks*, Seth explains that these levels are levels of consciousness and that we go to a higher level when we have developed our consciousness to a certain stage. Also there is not just one dimension in which non-physical consciousness resides any more than there is only one country on our planet or one planet within our solar system:

"My environment, now, is not the one in which you will find yourself immediately after death. You must die many times before you enter this particular place of existence. You must understand that no objective reality exists but that which is created by consciousness. Consciousness always creates form, and not the other way around.

"So my environment is a reality of existence created by myself and others like me, and it represents the manifestation of our development." [147]

Adrian Cooper says exactly the same. He does not talk about dimensions since dimensions are a scientific concept created by people on the basis of their perception of the five physical senses. He says that we go to different astral planes that reflect the vibrational frequency operating when we die.

"Like all other planes, astral planes are also density levels of the Source," he says.

The astral planes have many "denizens," many beings and intelligences that have never incarnated on Earth. It is their job to help humanity to develop here on Earth. Cooper goes on to say:

"There are many levels of vibration and comparative density of the astral worlds, all of which exhibit their own unique energy. A human being, indeed any being will after physical death automatically transition to the most appropriate astral world, most closely matching his or her own particular vibration, ego, temperament, character, and most importantly the beliefs and attitudes of the person at the time of physical 'death.'

"If a person is open-minded and fully understands the true process of death, they will effortlessly transition to the light, peace and harmony of the mid-astral worlds.

However, there are no actual definitive borders or boundaries between the various astral planes. The entire universe is a continuum consisting of conscious, intelligent, vibrating energy, from the very highest level of the Source down to the very lowest level of the physical world of matter."[110]

Ra also expresses the same in *The Law of One*:

"Entities inhabit the various planes due to their vibration/nature. The astral planes vary from thought-forms in the lower extremities to enlightened beings who become dedicated to teaching/learning in the higher astral planes."[111]

We believe a shift in vibrations is occurring in the age in which we are currently living. People are operating on a special frequency now, but they are gaining the opportunity to access higher frequencies and thus also a higher level of consciousness. When we die, we move from one density level, one dimension, one frequency, to another.

We are being presented with a unique opportunity to experience a shift in consciousness. This is an age in which we ourselves have chosen to participate. We decided to reincarnate during this very age in order to participate in the shift in consciousness and thus experience a quantum leap in our evolution, both as souls and as part of the human race.

We asked the Council of Elders about their views on the shift in consciousness.

Camillo: Are we right in thinking that we are now on the threshold of the next shift in human evolution and that we will progress from being Homo Sapiens to Homo Luminous—Enlightened Beings?

The Council of Elders via Lilli: "In the original master plan this was plotted in as an idea—a thought with a very high likelihood of success. Although it might seem impossible to achieve within the allotted time, a huge landslide is starting to occur high up, and as it races down the mountainside it is gaining greater momentum, become broader and sweeping everything with it on its way.

"This age is characterized by the fact that this landslide has already begun. On its way down the mountainside, although the topography of the mountainside is causing it to not just roar down, but to adopt certain forms off its steep downhill path—its taking turns to the left and right, pausing momentarily and then gaining momentum again. One quarter of the slope down has already been completed. Its current momentum involves massive expansion, and during the next two years an opening will be created, opening out towards a new thousand-year period where the expression *Adam* will become *Amadeus*—with HU MAN representing the merger of man and angel, in which angel is man and man is angel—HU MAN - AN GEL. These two will now become the future and be characteristic of the biological third dimensional form, including its fourth and fifth dimensional forms in a physical expression.

"The density that binds atoms and light intensely together will undergo a change in its structure. A less dense, lighter structure will form the new physical system, the temple, a house in which the soul will take up residence and from which the navigator will be able to undertake new excursions. A vast amount will occur in the mental part of the human brain, because concepts will need to be understood and related to via logic, while the right, vibrating side of the brain will rebuild the dominoes in a new design."

Camillo: Thank you very much. Is there a connection between this and Dolores Cannon's statements about Earth splitting in two and creating a fifth-dimensional Earth, i.e. that Earth is in the process of undergoing something similar to a cell division?

The Council of Elders via Lilli: This is a very interesting observation made by someone who was tasked with making just such an observation and sharing it with the masses. Because obviously Earth also has a need to take on its light form, let go of its old karma and allow its light form to be its essential empirical model. The Earth will still recognize its present form with great love and will relate to itself within the grid that is being established.

The new Earth will be experienced by those souls who manifest their divine right to experience that existence. They will have the opportunity to allow their frequencies to vary and thus co-exist simultaneously during a period of transition both on the new Earth of less substance and greater light experience, and as human beings on the old Earth. There will be two coinciding existences. When you hear that mankind co-exists everywhere because everything is the now, this is relevant and can be absorbed by mankind's higher or expanded understanding.

So what is the difference between dying—moving on to an astral world with a higher frequency—or moving on to an Earth that has been created in a new field of light? When you move on to the new Earth—in the light field— you can travel back and forth, as there is a bridge and you will be conscious of the fact that your cells will have divided into a physical and a light body that is not dead—it will just be a different process. This is more like individuals understanding that they are individuals on one plane of development—living as physical beings—and being able to move and understand that there is more than one of them.

Channeled by Lilli Bendriss on 29 July 2010 - from the energy-beings the Council of Elders

Many people in spiritual circles share this view about Earth and all life on Earth moving over into a new phase, although not everyone will be able to make the transition. Why? Because we must be *conscious* of the shift that is occurring.

A window of opportunity has now opened, much like many people believe occurred during the days of Atlantis. According to the sleeping prophet Edgar Cayce, the inhabitants of Atlantis possessed a deep understanding of the forces operating in the universe and the fact that they could use them to create their own reality. However, they abused their power over nature. Because they chose an egotistical and materialistic path, thus causing a setback in human evolution, Atlantis disappeared in a major catastrophe.[112]

"This misuse brought on the destruction of our great cultures and a long, karmic soul journey through the pain and confusion that resulted from our selfishness and self-centered focus on our will without regard for the will of the Creator and others."
- **Edgar Cayce** [71]

In 1990 Lilli channeled information about Atlantis from the energy being Wounded Eagle which also talk about our long karmic soul journey:

"Atlantis disappeared and the human race had to commence its long journey towards the next window of opportunity that would open up to allow this quantum leap in its evolution. The time has come. That opportunity has arrived. Our long, karmic soul journey is over. The shift in consciousness is occurring now.

"I have a rendezvous with knowledge, abused in the olden days. I see Atlantis, where you were given skills by the divine. Your knowledge is now buried in the depths of the ocean. Atlantis will once again resurface in your minds and your memories about who and what you were during those days will be reactivated. You are riding a wave of hope designed to create rather than destroy this time round. You will then keep the promise you made to yourselves on your long journey - you will then have found peace."
Channeled by Lilli Bendriss in 1990 - from the energy-being Wounded Eagle

Chapter 27 - Human Development and The Shift in Consciousness

Once again we are given the opportunity to embark on the next step of our evolution in consciousness. We have all been through a long, karmic soul journey since the days of Atlantis. We are living in an age where a conscious awakening is occurring in every single person. We are starting to remember who we really are and why we chose to be part of this great shift. More and more people understand that we ourselves create the reality that we see around us. We are the ones we have been waiting for.

In 1996 Lilli channeled some interesting information from The Council of Elders about this special time we live in and the power we have to change the world:

"A time of understanding is about to occur. It is a time when humans ask what it will be like living in the next century? So many prophecies have been given, most of them a tale of doomsday, the ending of your world as you know it. Is this to become your reality? Are you helpless victims, or do you have a saying in the building and shaping of your life and surroundings?

"Slowly, there is a stirring in the consciousness of man, like ripples on the water, creating movements. Do you see the little boy laughing as he throws stones in the pond, breaking the spell of his mirrored image? By his actions, he changed the visible picture of the water. You are now at the exact same point. Your arm is ready to throw the stones to change what is seemingly the surface of an element. The act of transformation is yours to behold.

"As you stay there on the brink of the water, deep in reflections, knowing that as you change the waters surface, you distort your own image. Do you also realize that everything is movement, the swaying of a pendulum—after the ripple, comes stillness, after distortion comes clarity, and if time did not exist, maybe would you see another person in the mirror?

"The pond represents the spinning of illusions in which you have been spellbound, caught, bewitched. You may now break that spell and dive into the depth of the pond.

"Maybe somebody told you as a child that the big monster slept down there, and even with all your intelligence stating that this is nonsense, there is still this unreasonable fear springing out from your subconscious.

"All that you are today is influenced by your childhood, your earlier existences, from time primordial. All your fears, suspicions, insecurity exist because somebody convinced you that this is so. The biggest fear is that you will loose yourself. So you build material wealth as protection from all possible dangers, because you are made to believe that you are a victim of powers outside you—that what is happening around you dictates who are you.

"As the ripples of the water came about from an outsider's action, it does not change the element the waters consist of. You may empty the pond and still the molecules will just move elsewhere, to challenge a new experience.

"It is correct that you are about to experience the end of a world as you have come to understand it. What has been the knowledge of a few elect ones is about to be the knowledge of all that care to listen. And when a critical mass of knowledgeable people is obtained it will be manifested and transferred through the morphogenic field and so become the knowledge of all humans. What is this knowledge?

"Simply that you may never die as you understand death. You may only transform into other experiences of yourself. You are not separate, ever, but a holistic spark of divine creation in all forms and shapes. Speculating if you became man through a Darwinian evolution or was cloned by extraterrestrial colonization is not the issue in this quest. You are that you are. I am that I am.

"You are all, and in all, God exists and so you are God in Man. Man is God unto himself and creation is a mantle by which you are carried fourth. With angelic wings you explore the universes unlimited, with eyes of hope you seize your power. With love manifest you reach out toward yourself and embrace those that come in your way to teach you love`s lessons.

"The law of causality is just: you at one time or another will receive what you throughout the millennium have given out. There is no heaven and hell awaiting you. Heaven and hell are limitations of thoughts. Liberation of hell and heaven make you responsible for what shade of existence you choose to walk through. You are both, since you exist in the all, and only you can create your reality on Earth, outside Earth, in worlds innumerable. It is time now to fly on your wings of truth, and we will meet you there in the shadows between the winds."
Channeled by Lilli Bendriss in 1996 - from the energy-being The Council of Elders

Yes, we are co-creators of this universe, but what will we choose—what will the road forward be like? One possible route runs towards a shift in consciousness representing a new age and a new Earth—one step forward in human evolution. Another route is our current one—a route where we miss out on this opportunity because we do not believe in it. We live, we die, but what happens then? Where will we end up if we do not participate in a shift in consciousness that is taking place on our new Earth?

We as souls have cycles like everything else in the universe. If we do not seize the opportunity to undergo a shift in consciousness, we will live until we die and then move on to a level on the astral plane that resonates with our vibrations and feelings, still a part of the karmic cycle and from there, we will continue our evolution accordingly.

Taking a quantum leap towards a shift in consciousness would break the karmic cycle and we could embark on the next step in the evolution of man.

If we decide to participate in the shift in consciousness we will first of all need to dispose of feelings such as fear, worry and guilt. These feelings hold us down on a low vibrational/frequency level and they will prevent us from expanding our consciousness.

Fear is our worst enemy.

"Fear defeats more people than any other one thing in the world."
- **Ralph W. Emerson**

Fear holds us back, but by redefining who we are and what we are doing here we will allow the good that exists in each and every one of us to flourish.

"There is something good in every single human being. You just have to look for it".
- **Bob Proctor**

Dolores Cannon and David Wilcock say that we have to forgive in order to be ready for the shift in consciousness. Forgiveness disposes of negative karma—forgiving yourself of guilt and forgiving those who have hurt you. Understand that we are all *one*, and that everything actually relates to the greatest feeling of all—love.

By transcending fear, worry and guilt we expand our consciousness and boost our frequency. We will then be ready for the shift. By expanding our consciousness we also contribute towards lifting the collective consciousness. This is important, because what we expect to happen *will* happen.

"Only one factor can be regarded as being definite. Whatever the collective consciousness of humanity and all life on Earth expects to happen over the next few years and beyond will happen. We are facing the ultimate proof that we really do create our own reality at all levels."
- **Adrian Cooper** [87]

The coming changes will allow us to unite and to undergo a quantum leap in our evolution as human beings. We have the opportunity to progress from being Homo Sapiens to Homo Luminous—Enlightened Beings. We are in the process of changing and participating in a more spiritual development as explained by Susan Joy Rennison in *Tuning the Diamonds*:

"According to our scientists, we are technically facing the sixth mass extinction of species living on planet Earth. The last time that happened was 65 million years ago with the disappearance of the dinosaurs. I believe that we are experiencing energy driven evolution and for humans that means that our DNA is dramatically changing. The next rung of the evolutionary ladder means the development of spiritual qualities, basically greater degrees of harmony and balance within us, in our relationships and in our relationship with planet Earth."[85]

By consciously choosing to take the next step in our evolution through a shift in consciousness we will create a new world characterized by harmony and compassion for all people and all life. But we need to be ready for this shift, as also pointed out by Dr. Carl Johan Calleman:

"In order for a consciousness shift to manifest, human beings must be in resonance with it and at some point at least subconsciously have made a choice to align with it. Hence, a large-scale consciousness shift is not something that can happen against the will of human beings. It can only happen through human beings that choose to serve as co-creators."[86]

This means that we must first of all understand that we are co-creators—that we are all involved in creating the world in which we live.

We must wake up from our collective loss of memory and realize our unity with nature and all life.

We must tone down our dominant ego and pay more attention to the spiritual essence that lies within each and every one of us.

Only then will we realize that we are connected and a part of an incredible, powerful universal consciousness capable of changing the world exactly in accordance with our desires.

We can only tune into a shift in consciousness by understanding that we are all like *a finger on a hand*, as expressed by the Mayan Elder Don Alejandro Cirilo Perez Oxlaj. We are part of the Source—part of universal consciousness. The human race can now experience a quantum leap in its evolution.

This is what the 2012 phenomenon is all about—*this* is what this age of awakening is all about.

If we do not understand this then the evolution of mankind is in danger of stagnating. We cannot allow ourselves to adopt a passive attitude simply because we do not believe that we have the power to do anything. We cannot believe that life is accidental, that it just happens to us, that some people have luck while others have bad luck—that that is just how things are. We cannot just lean back and say, "This does not concern me."

Such an attitude will put human evolution on hold, and as souls we would then have to take the long route, passing through many successive lives until the next window of opportunity opens. A new, long karmic soul journey would thus await us.

On the other hand, if we choose to take advantage of the present opportunity, this could be compared to standing in a long queue as it crawls slowly along. We could jump out of the queue and advance. This is a divine dispensation that has now been given us. We can make a quantum leap and raise humanity up to the next level of evolution without having to take the long route via reincarnation in life after life.

However, in order for humanity to experience this lift, this shift in consciousness, many individuals need to expand their consciousness.

The Indian meditation guru Maharishi Mahesh Yogi taught the West: *Individual consciousness affects the collective consciousness.*

If enough people do this, we can be pioneers for the human race as it undergoes this giant shift in consciousness and embarks on the next step in its evolution: progressing from being Homo Sapiens to Homo Luminous—*Enlightened Beings!*

Which will YOU choose?

References

1. http://www.telegraph.co.uk/science/science-news/3347592/Looking-for-the-biggest-answers.html

2. *The Science of Getting Rich Program,* http://www.one-mind-one-energy.com/SGRFreePackage.html

3. *You Were Born Rich,* Bob Proctor, Life Success Productions, 1997, p. 109

4. *The Symbiotic Universe: Life and mind in the cosmos,* George Greenstein, Morrow 1998, p. 27

5. http://en.wikiquote.org/wiki/Freeman_Dyson

6. http://en.wikiquote.org/wiki/Max_Planck

7. *Video:* http://www.youtube.com/watch?v=cEyqT2_ricA

8.http://www.seminarsondvd.com/ProductPages/LiveFullDieEmptyLesBrown.aspx

9. *The Master Key System,* Charles F. Haanel, 1912

10. *The Strangest Secret,* Earl Nightingale, 1957

11. *The Science of Getting Rich,* Wallace D. Wattles, 1910

12. *The Devine Matrix,* Gregg Braden, © 2007, Hay House Inc. Carlsbad, p. 39

13. *A Course in Miracles,* Helen Schuman and William Thetford, Foundation for Inner Peace, 1975

14. *The Complete Conversations with God – An Uncommon Dialogue,* Neale Donald Walsh, © 2005, Hampton Roads Publishing Company Inc. and G.P. Putnam's Sons, p. 29

15. *The Psychic Energy Codex - Awakening Your Subtle Senses,* Michelle Belanger, © 2007, Red Wheel/Weiser, LLC, p. 1

16. *The Prosperity Program,* Burt Goldman, http://www.one-mind-one-energy.com/multiverse.html

17. *Think & Grow Rich,* Napoloen Hill, 1937, p. 79 - http://www.one-mind-one-energy.com/ebooks.html

18. *A Happy Pocket Full of Money*, David Cameron, © 2008, Xlibris Corporation

19. *Seth Speaks: the Eternal Validity of the Soul,* Jane Roberts and Robert F. Butts (1972), reprinted (1994), Amber-Allen Publishing, p. 41. Reprinted with the permission from New World Library—www.NewWorldLibrary.com

20. *The Living Matrix—The Movie,* © 2009, The Living Matrix, LTD and Becker Massey, LLC

21. http://www.mellen-thomas.com/stories.htm

22. *What The Bleep Do We Know!?,* © 2004 Lord of the Wind Films, LLC

23. *The Answer,* John Assaraf and Murray Smith, © 2008, Ria Ventures, LLC, and Murrey Smith, Simon & Schuster Uk Ltd., p. 16

24. *Power of the Soul,* John Holland, © 2007, Hay House Inc. Carlsbad, p. 186

25. http://members.optusnet.com.au/~acceptance/YourPurposeWeb/MultidimensionalConsciousness.htm

26. *Light Emerging,* Barbara Ann Brennan, © 1993, Bantam Book – a division of Bantam Doubleday Dell Publishing Group, Inc., p. 8

27. *Handbook for the New Paradigm* by George Green – Bridger House Publisher, Inc. *http://www.nohoax.com/?p=58*

28. *Ra – The Law of One, THE RA MATERIAL – Book II*, Carla Rueckert, Don Elkins and Jim McCarty, 1981 – 1984. p. 61. Reprinted with the permission from L/L Research – www. llresearch.org

29. http://www.theorionproject.org/en/quantumvacuum.html

30. http://en.wikipedia.org/wiki/Reincarnation_research

31. http://home.sandiego.edu/~baber/logic/gallup.html

32. http://www.harrisinteractive.com/Insights/HarrisVault848 2aspx?PID=982

33. http://www.medicine.virginia.edu/clinical/departments/ psychiatry/sections/cspp/dops

34. *Old Souls - Scientific Search for Proof of Past Lives*, Tom Shroder, © 1999, Simon & Schuster Paperbacks

35. http://www.medicine.virginia.edu/clinical/departments/ psychiatry/sections/cspp/dops/case_types-page#CORT

36. *The Law of One: Volume II, THE RA MATERIAL,* Carla Rueckert, Don Elkins and Jim McCarty, 1981 – 1984, p. 124. Reprinted with the permission from L/L Research – www. llresearch.org

37. Article: Azurite Press- Ashayana & Azurtanya Deane http://www.azuritepress.co.za/time_matrix.html

38. http://www.keylonticdictionary.org/

39. http://www.ornl.gov/sci/techresources/Human_Genome/ home.shtml

40. http://en.wikipedia.org/wiki/Junk_DNA and http://www. fractal.org/Life-Science-Technology/Peter-Gariaev.htm

41. http://www.rexresearch.com/gajarev/gajarev.htm

42. *Bringers of the Dawn: Teachings from the Pleiadians,* Barbara Marciniak, © 1992, Bear & Company, p. 8

43. http://www.whalesinspace.com/2009/10/russian-dna-discoveries-proof-of-12-strand-dna-activation-theory/

44. http://www.enterprisemission.com/_articles/05-14-2004_Interplanetary_Part_1/Interplanetary_1.htm

45. *Tuning the Diamonds – Electromagnetism & Spiritual Evolution,* Susan Joy Rennison, © 2006, JoyFire Publishing, p. 3-4

46. Video: http://www.youtube.com/watch?v=iOh4W44ZcNM

47. *The Complete Conversations with God – An Uncommon Dialogue,* Neale Donald Walsh, © 2005, Hampton Roads Publishing Company Inc. and G.P. Putnam's Sons, p. 16

48. *A New Earth – Create a Better Life*, Eckhart Tolle, © 2005, Penguin Books, p. 257

49. *A New Earth – Create a Better Life*, Eckhart Tolle, © 2005, Penguin Books, p. 218

50. http://thomastroward.wwwhubs.com/

51. http://www.one-mind-one-energy.com/Divine.html

52. http://www.krystallkulen.no/?text=53

53. *Our Ultimate Reality, Life, the Universe and Destiny of Mankind,* Adrian P. Cooper, © 2007, Mind Power Corporations, pp. 127-128

54. Video: http://www.youtube.com/watch?v=kEtHT02limQ

55. *The Law of One: Volume II, THE RA MATERIAL,* Carla Rueckert, Don Elkins and Jim McCarty, 1981 – 1984, p. 48. Reprinted with the permission from L/L Research – www.llresearch.org

56. *http://www.dannion.com* and *Infinity – The Ultimate Trip,* Jay Weidner, © 2009, Sacred Mysteries Productions

57. http://www.near-death.com/experiences/research24.html

58. *The Complete Conversations with God – An Uncommon Dialogue,* Neale Donald Walsh, © 2005, Hampton Roads Publishing Company Inc. and G.P. Putnam's Sons, p. 13

59. Article: William A. Tiller Foundation, © 2011, http://tillerfoundation.com/model.php

60. http://www.theintentionexperiment.com

61. *Psycho-Cybernetics: A New Way to Get More Living out of Life* by Maxwell Maltz, 1960

62. http://www.consciousmedianetwork.com/interviews/dicke6.htm

63. *A New Earth – Create a Better Life,* Eckhart Tolle, © 2005, Penguin Books p. 227

64. *The Law of One: Volume III, THE RA MATERIAL,* Carla Rueckert, Don Elkins and Jim McCarty, 1981 – 1984, p. 97 Reprinted with the permission from L/L Research – www.llresearch.org

65. http://www.shiftoftheages.com/wandering_wolfs_message

66.http://www.telegraph.co.uk/news/worldnews/northamerica/usa/6519923/Ignore-the-movie-2012-will-not-be-the-end-of-world-say-Mayans.html

67. http://www.famsi.org/

68.Wikipedia, http://en.wikipedia.org/wiki/Maya_civilization

69. http://www.13moon.com/prophecypage.htm

70. http://www.telegraph.co.uk/news/worldnews/
northamerica/usa/3222476/Suns-protective-bubble-is-
shrinking.html

71. Article - *December 21, 2012: The Mayan Year of Destiny*, John
Van Auken – http://www.edgarcayce.org/2012/

72. Wikipedia: http://en.wikipedia.org/wiki/Charles_
Hapgood

73. A 12-part video series featuring Jay Weidner at the 2012
Conference in San Francisco, 2009, http://www.youtube.com/
watch?v=XvG13K37Ic8&p=5F67194E98CF43FE

74. Video: http://www.youtube.com/watch?v=wJLZU_b4iao
and http://www.urbansurvival.com/simplebots.htm

75. http://en.wikipedia.org/wiki/I_Ching

76. http://www.edgarcayce.org/are/blogaspx?id=3030&blogid
=445

77. Article: http://www.finerminds.com/metaphysical/
gerald-odonnell-thanksgiving-2012-shift/ - Reprinted with the
permission of MindValley and www.FinerMinds.com

78.Video: http://www.youtube.com/watch?v=riQdyr1hkuI

79. http://en.wikipedia.org/wiki/Nikola_Tesla

80. http://www.13moon.com/prophecypage.htm

81. *Our Ultimate Reality, Life, the Universe and Destiny of Mankind*,
Adrian P. Cooper, © 2007, Mind Power Corporations, p. 555

82. http://globalconsciousnessproject.org/

83. http://www.mum.edu/m_effect/

84. *A New Earth – Create a Better Life*, Eckhart Tolle, © 2005,
Penguin Books pp. 12 -13

85. Article: http://www.susanrennison.com
NoMysteryEMChaos.html

86. Article: http://www.calleman.com/content/articles/ninth_
wave.htm

87. *Our Ultimate Reality, Life, the Universe and Destiny of Mankind,*
Adrian P. Cooper, © 2007, Mind Power Corporations, p. 550

88. *Conversations with God - Volume I,* Neale Donald Walsh, p.
40

89. *On the Origin of Species.* London, John Murray, p. 194,
Chapter VI by Charles Darwin, 1859

90. http://en.wikipedia.org/wiki/Fred_Hoyle

91. Video: http://www.youtube.com/
watch?v=rzF9SiYCgK0&NR=1

92. *Fractal Time – The Secret of 2012 and a New World Age,* Gregg
Braden, © 2009, Hay House Inc. Carlsbad, pp. 82-83

93. *The Purposeful Universe – How Quantum Theory and Mayan
Cosmology Explain the Origin and Evolution of Life,* Carl Johan
Calleman, © 2009, Bear & Company, pp. 216-217

94. http://www.harrisinteractive.com/Insights/
HarrisVault8482.aspx?PID=982

95. http://www.adherents.com/Religions_By_Adherents.html

96. http://twm.co.nz/hologram.html

97. http://en.wikipedia.org/wiki/Carl_Sagan%27s_Cosmos

98. *Evolution: A Theory in Crisis,* Michael Denton © 1986, Adler
& Adler, p. 318

99. Video: http://www.youtube.com/watch?v=q1iCjKWzeEE

100. http://executableoutlines.com/cc/cc_03.htm

101. *On the Origin of Species.* London, John Murray, p. 189, Chapter VI by Charles Darwin, 1859

102. *Seth Speaks: the Eternal Validity of the Soul,* Jane Roberts and Robert F. Butts (1972), reprinted (1994), Amber-Allen Publishing, p. 309. Reprinted with the permission from New World Library – www.NewWorldLibrary.com

103. Video: http://www.youtube.com watch?v=AAqSCuHA0j8

104. Video: http://www.youtube.com watch?v=1TNj9UrZLzA

105. *Tuning the Diamonds – Electromagnetism & Spiritual Evolution,* Susan Joy Rennison, © 2006, JoyFire Publishing p. 145

106. http://en.wikipedia.org/wiki/Reincarnation

107. *Our Ultimate Reality, Life, the Universe and Destiny of Mankind,* Adrian P. Cooper, © 2007, Mind Power Corporations pp. 37-38

108. *Infinity – The Ultimate Trip* (the film), Jay Weidner, © 2009 Sacred Mysteries Productions

109. http://www.salrachele.com/webarticles/ascension.htm

110. *Our Ultimate Reality, Life, the Universe and Destiny of Mankind,* Adrian P. Cooper, © 2007, Mind Power Corporations, pp. 211-213

111. *The Law of One: Volume I, THE RA MATERIAL,* Carla Rueckert, Don Elkins and Jim McCarty, 1981 – 1984, p. 175. Reprinted with the permission from L/L Research – www.llresearch.org

112. Video: http://www.youtube.com/ watch?v=hVCAca2r1LM

113. *The Law of One: Volume I, THE RA MATERIAL,* Carla Rueckert, Don Elkins and Jim McCarty, 1981 – 1984, p. 122. Reprinted with the permission from L/L Research – www. llresearch.org

114. http://www.indianetzone.com/40/four_yugas.htm

115. http://www.thesun.co.uk/sol/homepage/news/3145874/ Solar-flare-to-paralyse-Earth-in-2013.html, and http://www. vg.no/nyheter/innenriks/artikkel.php?artid=561263, and http://www.vg.no/nyheter/utenriks/artikkel. php?artid=10027420

116. *Transition Now, Redefining Duality, 2012 and Beyond,* Martine Vallée, © 2009. Norwegian copy Cappelen Damm 2011 – p. 82

117. *Supernatural – Meetings With the Ancient Teachers of Mankind,* Graham Hancock, © 2005, p. 587

118. *upernatural – Meetings With the Ancient Teachers of Mankind,* Graham Hancock, © 2005, pp. 589-591

119. http://www.theresonanceproject.org/

120. Article: "Har vi levd før?" featured in the Magazine *Ildsjelen* no. 4 – 2004 http://www.ildsjelen.no/2009/05/ reinkarnasjon

121. *The Art of Happiness,* Howard C. Cutler, © 2008, Norwegian copy, Arnberg

122. *The Science of Getting Rich,* Wallace D. Wattles, 1910, p. 21, http://www.one-mind-one-energy.com/ebooks.html

123. *The Science of Getting Rich,* Wallace D. Wattles, 1910, p. 13, http://www.one-mind-one-energy.com/ebooks.html

124. http://inthefootstepsofthebuddha.com/your-religion-is-not-important/

125. *Our Ultimate Reality, Life, The Universe and Destiny of Mankind*, Adrian P. Cooper, © 2007, Mind Power Corporations, p. 550

126. Article: Bruce H. Lipton, PhD http://www.brucelipton. com/articles/interview-with-bruce-in-planeta-magazine-part-2/

127. *Think & Grow Rich,* Napoloen Hill, 1937, p. 66 http:// www.one-mind-one-energy.com/ebooks.html

128. *The Answer,* John Assaraf and Murray Smith, © 2008, Ria Ventures, LLC, and Murrey Smith, Simon & Schuster Uk Ltd, p. 50

129. *The Complete Conversations with God – An Uncommon Dialogue,* Neale Donald Walsh, © 2005, Hampton Roads Publishing Company Inc. and G.P.Putnam's Sons, p.12

130. Video: http://www.youtube.com/watch?v=qFb2rvmrahc

131. Video: http://www.youtube.com/watch?v=UyyjU8fzEYU

132. Article: http://www.calleman.com/content/articles/999_ and_the_mayan_calendar.htm

133. David Icke Newsletter – May 13th 2007

134. Article: http://www.howtosurvive2012.com/htm_night/ home.htm and *The Orion Prophecy: Will the World Be Destroyed in 2012,* Patrick Gerly. Adventures Unlimited Press 2002

135. Article: http://www.twohawks.com/hopi/hopififthworld. shtml

136. http://books.google.no/books?id=V2VuYC2HhSsC&lpg= PP1&dq=The%20Mystery%20of%202012%3A%20Predictions %2C%20Prophecies%20%26%20Possibilities&pg=PA93#v=on epage&q&f=false

137. Article by Tom Atlee: *Something Bigger than Life is Trying to Work Through Us*, August 2009 http://co-intelligence.org/ SomethingBigger.html

References

138. Article by Joseph Robert Jochmans, *What have the Hopis, Mayans, and other native American peoples foreseen about the destruction of the world in the year 2000?* http://www.atlantisrising.com/backissues/issue2/ar2topten.html

139. *Transition Now, Redefining Duality, 2012 and Beyond*, Martine Vallée, © 2009. Norwegian copy Cappelen Damm 2011 – pp. 88-89

140. *The Purposeful Universe – How Quantum Theory and Mayan Cosmology Explain the Origin and Evolution of Life*, Carl Johan Calleman, © 2009, Bear & Company, pp. 77-80

141. Article: http://www.konig.org/wc179.htm

142. *The Case For A Creator*, Lee Strobel, © 2004, Zondervan, p. 155

143. *The Case For A Creator*, Lee Strobel, © 2004, Zondervan, p. 128

144. Alberts, Bruce. 1998. *The Cell as a Collection of Protein Machines: Preparing the NextGeneration of Molecular Biologists.* Cell. vol. 92 (February 6, 1998), pp. 291-294

145. Video: Questioning evolution theory: http://www.youtube.com/watch?v=q1iCjKWzeEE

146. *Our Ultimate Reality, Life, the Universe and Destiny of Mankind*, Adrian P. Cooper, © 2007, Mind Power Corporations, pp. 25-26

147. *Seth Speaks: the Eternal Validity of the Soul*, Jane Roberts and Robert F. Butts (1972), reprinted (1994), Amber-Allen Publishing, p. 16. Reprinted with the permission from New World Library – www.NewWorldLibrary.com

148. http://www.whalesinspace.com/2009/10/russian-dna-discoveries-proof-of-12-strand-dna-activation-theory

149 *Gene Keys – Unlocking the Higher Purpose Hidden in Your DNA*, Richard Rudd, © 2009, Gene Keys Publishing, pp. xx

Index

Symbols

2012 viii, ix, 30, 34, 44, 192, 199, 201, 202, 203, 204, 205, 206,
208, 209, 210, 212-219, 221, 223, 226, 237, 244, 285,
296, 303-305, 307-309

A

astral plane viii, ix, 30, 34, 44, 125, 157, 183, 192, 199, 201–
206, 208–210, 212–219, 221, 223, 226, 237, 244, 285,
293, 296, 303–305, 307–309
Atlantis 104, 209-210, 218-219, 289-291
atom 39, 41, 65, 73, 74, 80, 81, 101, 151, 152, 225, 259, 262
awakening vii-viii, ix, 32, 56, 145, 222, 230, 239, 291, 296

B

Big Bang 74, 80, 85-86, 190, 191, 244, 245
brain waves 67-68

C

consciousness viii, ix, 14, 20-21, 23, 29, 32-33, 38-39, 45, 53-
56, 60, 66, 72-78, 81-84, 86, 91-92, 96, 100, 102-104, 108,
121, 130, 140-142, 144-145, 147, 151, 158, 162, 166-167,
169-173, 177, 179, 183-187, 190-193, 195-197, 199, 201-
202, 206-208, 216-219, 221-222, 225-230, 232-233, 235,
237-240, 242, 248, 257, 261-262, 267-268, 272-273, 282,
284-287, 290-291, 293-297
cosmic forces 207-208
Creator 84, 98, 109-110, 119, 155, 162-163, 200, 213, 219, 243-
245, 255, 257, 265, 290, 309

D

Darwin 27, 147, 191, 243, 245, 246, 248, 252, 255, 265-267,
275, 305-306
dimensions vii, 47, 69-70, 87, 97, 102, 116-118, 123, 130, 138,
142, 149, 188, 223, 269, 270-271, 283-286
DNA 3, 33, 38, 68-69, 105, 125, 127-130, 137-142, 188, 196,
208, 218, 246-248, 251, 254-255, 263-264, 267, 273, 295,
301

I

I Ching 216-217
illusion 65, 92, 96, 103, 116, 121, 146, 148, 165, 187-189, 260-261, 272
indigenous people 231
inner world 18, 43-45, 55-57, 67, 103, 149, 169, 238, 242

K

Kali Yuga 210-213
karma 44, 95, 107, 149, 155, 156, 158, 161-167, 185, 223, 276-277, 282, 289, 294

L

Language of Light 131–136
law of vibration 68-69

M

manifestation 50, 90, 118, 149, 166, 185, 223, 236, 268, 276, 286
matter 22, 39, 41, 54, 59, 65-66, 73, 77-81, 84, 112, 118, 145, 154, 162, 169, 189, 205, 236, 251, 259, 260, 267-269, 271, 287
Mayan Calendar 191, 204, 207, 228
meditation viii, 18, 25, 46, 60, 68, 186, 194, 208, 227-229, 278, 285, 297
memory 107, 115, 117, 130, 142, 205, 260, 295

N

near-death experience 73-75, 79-80, 84, 86, 281

P

pole shift 208-209
prophecies 197, 199, 202, 214, 218, 222, 227, 236, 238, 240, 291

Q

quantum physics 55, 73, 75, 77, 111, 262, 271

W

Web Bot Project 214

Z

Zero Point Field 23, 77-78, 147, 262

Lightning Source UK Ltd.
Milton Keynes UK
UKOW051444260313

208207UK00001B/19/P